# GOD WILLING, DAUGHTER

*Stories of Faith, Healing, and Legacy*

A Powerful Collection of Women's God Stories & Generational Wisdom

Edited by: Eliza M. Garza

Foreword by: Leticia Chàvez - Contreras

Mija Media House

# GOD WILLING, DAUGHTER

An Anthology of Women's God Stories and Generational Wisdom

Copyright © 2025 by Eliza M. Garza

All rights reserved. No portion of this book may be reproduced, stored in a retrieval system, or transmitted in any form or by any means—electronic, mechanical, photocopying, recording, scanning, or otherwise—without prior written permission of the publisher, except in the case of brief quotations embodied in critical reviews or articles.

**ISBN:** 979-8-9870469-5-1

Printed in the United States of America

Unless otherwise noted, all Scripture quotations are taken from the New International Version® (NIV®). Copyright © 1973, 1978, 1984, 2011 by Biblica, Inc.™

Scripture quotations marked ESV are from The Holy Bible, English Standard Version® (ESV®). Copyright © 2001 by Crossway, a publishing ministry of Good News Publishers. Used by permission. All rights reserved.

Scripture quotations marked NKJV are taken from the New King James Version®. Copyright © 1982 by Thomas Nelson. Used by permission. All rights reserved.

Scripture quotations marked KJV are from the Holy Bible, King James Version. Public Domain.

# Disclaimer

This anthology contains the personal stories, reflections, and opinions of individual contributors. These narratives are presented as personal testimonies and are not intended to represent universal experiences or professional advice. The editor and publisher make no representations or warranties with respect to the accuracy, applicability, fitness, or completeness of the content.

The publisher and contributors specifically disclaim any responsibility for liability, loss, or risk—personal or otherwise—that may be incurred as a direct or indirect consequence of the use or application of any content in this book. This book is not intended to serve as medical, psychological, legal, financial, or professional counseling advice. Readers should seek qualified professional guidance for their own circumstances.

Some names, places, and identifying details have been changed or omitted to protect the privacy of individuals. Any resemblance to actual persons, living or deceased, events, or locales, outside of those explicitly identified, is entirely coincidental.

By reading this book, the reader acknowledges that the content is offered as personal narrative and inspiration only, and agrees that neither the editor, publisher, nor contributors shall be held liable for any interpretation, application, or outcome related to the material herein. *Music credits: All rights to songs referenced in this book belong to their respective copyright owners. Song titles are suggested solely for inspirational listening and are not reproduced here*

# Dedication

To my step-father, Roberto Hilario Contreras, I believe with all my heart you were an angel in disguise on this earth. Thank you for showing me the ways of Christ and planting the Word of God deep within my soul. Because of the gift of faith you shared, our family was forever changed, and I now carry the hope of Christ, knowing I will see you again one day. I didn't tell you nearly enough while you were here, but I love you. I love you more now than ever.

You led by example in everything you did, loving my mom so beautifully and embracing us as your own. The life, love, and legacy you left with us will never be forgotten.

# To the Women Whose Shoulders I Stand On

For my mother and grandmothers,
the women who came before me.

Your backs became my launch pad.
Your ceilings became my ground floor,
the place where my story could rise higher than yours was ever allowed to go.

Your tears are the soil of my firm foundation.
Your faith is my inheritance and has transferred into my soul.
Your sacrifices have lifted me,
placing me in the position to live a life beyond your dreams.

I walk in your hopes.
I breathe your prayers.
I wear your love.
I am clothed in your wisdom.

This book is our harvest; the fruit of your selfless love and relentless faith, and it will echo your names for generations to come.

Leticia Chàvez – Contreras *(Mama Bear)*
Maria Elida Rodriguez – Chàvez *(Grandma Lela)*

Maria Guadalupe Rodriguez *(Grandma Lupita)*
With all my love and admiration, Eliza Michelle Garza

# Foreword

*by Leticia Chavez - Contreras*

When my daughter Eliza asked me to write this foreword, I paused, not out of hesitation, but because I felt the weight of what this moment means. I'm not a professional writer, but I am something far greater in her life. I am her mother, her intercessor, and the first to believe (aside from her father, of course) in the dreams God placed in her heart.

I have watched my daughter blossom into an amazing young woman devoted to seeking God and walking according to His will. She has grown from a little girl with big ideas into a woman who moves boldly in her purpose. I feel honored and blessed knowing God truly set her apart for a time such as this. I am so grateful that He is faithful and true to His promises, for I have seen firsthand that when we seek Him with all our heart, He orders our steps.

But what many won't see behind the pages of this book are the prayers whispered in secret, the tears cried in surrender, and the nights I spent on my knees asking God to guide her steps, protect her heart, and bring her visions to life.

This book you're holding isn't just a project; it's a promise fulfilled. It's the fruit of faith, perseverance, and divine timing. I've seen Eliza face many challenges that could have easily made her give up, but instead, they made her stronger. And every time she felt weak, I reminded her, "Mijita, trust God. He knows the plans He has for you." I knew my prayers were watering seeds that, one day, would blossom into something beautiful, like this.

I see my daughter as a *Proverbs 31* woman, clothed in strength and dignity. To me, that means she walks with a quiet confidence that comes not from the world, but from God. She is strong because she has endured trials and still chosen faith. She carries dignity because she knows her worth is rooted in Christ, not in circumstances. Her life reflects wisdom, resilience, and grace, and I believe that is why God continues to open doors for her and use her to bless others. My prayer has always been that when my daughter speaks, it is God's good work that people hear and see. Now, seeing her use her gifts to uplift others, my prayer is that her words will touch hearts, ignite hope, and bring glory to God in ways beyond our imagination.

I have always wanted to stand on a mountaintop and let the world know of God's favor upon her, how He has greatly used her for His glory. Her books, her words, her message, every one of them carries purpose. God has shaped her journey down to the smallest detail, and each step has sparked joy not only in her life, but in mine. And I can say with certainty that I believe in her with every fiber of my being.

As a mother, there is no greater joy than seeing your child walk in what God has called them to do. I have prayed for her happiness, her strength, her hope, her dreams, and the path God would carve out for her in this world. I have prayed that He would continue to order every step, keeping her aligned with His perfect plan.

I believe with all my heart that these words will touch you in ways only God can orchestrate. Whether you're looking for hope, healing, guidance, or confirmation, I pray you find it within these pages.

This book you hold is more than pages and ink; it is the manifestation of God's faithfulness, the fruit of years of fervent prayer, and the living proof that when a life is surrendered to Him, He will use it to transform others. I pray that as you read these words, you will feel the presence of God. May it stir something inside you—a dream, a prayer, a calling—that reminds you God has not forgotten you.

I have always asked God that whoever crosses my daughter's path would not only bless her life but also be blessed by her. I believe with all my heart that every single one of the authors in this anthology was divinely appointed for such a time as this. Their presence in these pages is not by chance but by God's perfect design. I know that their words will not just inspire but also awaken hearts, and I stand in awe of how God has chosen this circle of women to walk alongside my daughter in this sacred assignment.

Before you begin, let me leave you with this blessing:

May every word you read remind you that God is faithful. May it stir up dreams you thought were forgotten. And may you know that just like these authors, you too have a great purpose.

Heavenly Father, I thank You for every reader who holds this book in their hands. May Your Spirit breathe life into every word. May those who feel weary be strengthened, those who feel forgotten be reminded of Your unfailing love, and those who have stopped dreaming begin to dream again. Let these stories be seeds of hope that take root and bear fruit in due season. I bless my daughter, her work, every contributor, reader, and all the hearts this book will touch, in the name of Jesus. Amen.

To God be all the glory for allowing me to witness this moment. May this be more than a book for you; may this be your divine appointment.

*"The LORD has done great things for us, and we are filled with joy."*

**– Psalm 126:3**

With all my love, admiration, and unending prayers,

**Leticia Chàvez – Contreras**

*Proud Mother & Prayer Warrior*

# Editor's Note

This book was not part of my original plan; it was part of God's. As a children's book author, I had my lineup of titles ready to release, but the Lord redirected my steps and placed in my heart a new assignment: to create an anthology. I knew I wanted to remain rooted in what I value most: faith, family, and honoring God, and those values echo through every page of this work.

What stirred me most was the power of testimony. I believe that when we share our stories, whether through wisdom passed down, lived experiences, generational lessons, or hard-fought victories, we give strength to one another. Scripture reminds us that God is no respecter of persons. What He has done for one, He can and will do for another. That truth is at the core of this book.

I did not seek seasoned writers. I sought hearts willing to be honest. The world has enough filters. I wanted stories that were raw, real, gritty, and unpolished because that is where God's glory shines brightest. Too often we try to confine Him to neat boxes, but His love reaches far beyond the walls of a church. He leaves the ninety-nine for the one *(Luke 15:4)*. He pursues the black sheep *(Matthew 18:12-14)*. He cares about the smallest detail *(Matthew 10:29-31)* and the greatest mountain *(Mark 11:23)* in each of our lives. Nothing is too big *(Jeremiah 32:27)* or too small *(1 Peter 5:7)* for Him.

That is why I did not seek experienced writers for this project, so please don't expect this book to be a perfect literary work. It was never meant to be. This is not about polished prose or flawless grammar. It is about bare hearts on paper. It is about honesty, vulnerability, and voices that dare to speak their truth even when it trembles. What you hold in your hands is not literature for critique, but testimonies for encounter, evidence that God moves in the real, the raw, and the flawed.

This anthology shows that we are overcomers. That pain, when surrendered to the Holy Spirit, can be transformed into purpose and power. That even in suffering, resurrection is promised. As Paul wrote, if we share in Christ's sufferings, we also share in His glory *(Romans 8:17)*.

My prayer is that if you find yourself in the valley of suffering, this book will be a guide and a light for you. May these testimonies remind you that you are not alone, that God has not forgotten you, and that you have everything it takes to rise again. Dust yourself off. Lift your head. Call out to Him.

You are not too far gone, too broken, or beyond redemption. You have not done something so bad that God's forgiveness can't cover. There is not one sin the blood of Jesus cannot wash away *(1 John 1:7, Isaiah 1:18)*. You don't have to earn your way back, good-deed your way back, hustle harder, or prove yourself worthy of His love. His grace and mercy are not wages—they are a gift *(Ephesians 2:8-9, Romans 5:8)*. All you need to do is accept it, and let His love do what only He can do.

Because He is with you. Always. *(Matthew 28:20)*

— **Eliza M. Garza, Curator**

# Table of Contents

| | |
|---|---|
| Dedication | i |
| To the Women Whose Shoulders I Stand On | ii |
| Foreword | iv |
| Editor's Note | vii |
| A Soundtrack to the Stories | xi |
| Introduction | 1 |
| Section One  The Valley | 3 |
|     Pero Dios by Perla Tamez - Casasnovas | 4 |
|     The Gilded Cage by Anonymous Contributor | 15 |
|     The Soul Touch Queen: A Journey of Awakening by Dr. Esther Akindayomi | 28 |
|     When Breath Returned by Dr. Nina Golde | 44 |
|     From Poles to Purpose by Tracey Castillo | 58 |
|     Two Carrots & An Apple by Magdalena Aguinaga | 85 |
| Section Two  The Altar | 103 |
|     Erica's Road to Surrender & Mercy by Erica Hernandez Castillo | 104 |
|     From Doing to Being: My Journey to Surrender by Giselle Dominique Mascarenhas – Villareal | 122 |
|     Broken but Restored by Cynthia L. Hernandez, M.Ed. | 142 |
|     When the Tomb Becomes Your Womb by Eliza M. Garza | 156 |
|     The Surrender That Built Me by Naomi M. Perales | 183 |
| Section Three  The Rising | 204 |

| | |
|---|---|
| The Extraordinary in the Ordinary: A Tribute to the Women Who Raised Me in Faith by Dr. Rutchie Contreras, PT, DPT | 205 |
| Signs From Heaven: From the Father Above and the Father I Loved by Carolina Chams | 216 |
| The Beauty of God's Grace by Jaimie Luna | 225 |
| Legacy in My Blood by Chelsea Victoria Gonzalez | 243 |
| Jesus and Ganas by Dr. Esmeralda Adame | 249 |
| Section Four  The Crown | 263 |
| From Knowing About God to Knowing God by Marie Salazar Garcia | 264 |
| The Woman Who Danced Beside Me by Maribel De La Fuente | 280 |
| Saved by Grace by Geraldine Valdez | 291 |
| Chains Broken: The Power of Forgiveness by Carmen Sauceda | 308 |
| **Epilogue** | **329** |
| **Final Declaration Prayer** | **331** |
| **Acknowledgments** | **332** |
| **About the Curator  Eliza M. Garza** | **334** |

# A Soundtrack to the Stories

*Songs for your soul, prayers for your heart.*

Music has a way of meeting us where words leave off. Each song listed here was chosen to complement the spirit of every chapter, to help you linger a little longer with the message, the memory, or the miracle.

You're invited to play these songs as you read, or after each chapter, during your time of journaling and reflection. Let the lyrics wash over you, stir your spirit, and remind you that God speaks not only through words, but through melody too.

**Songs by Chapter**

**Foreword:** On the Nature of Daylight—Max Richter

1. **Pero Dios by Perla Tamez-Casasnovas**: Goodness of God—CeCe Winans
2. **The Gilded Cage by Anonymous Contributor**: Made A Way—Travis Greene
3. **The Soul Touch Queen by Dr. Esther Akindayomi**: Waymaker—Michael W. Smith
4. **When Breath Returned by Dr. Nina Golde**: Breathe—Michael W. Smith
5. **From Poles to Purpose by Tracey Castillo**: You Say—Lauren Daigle
6. **Two Carrots & An Apple by Magdalena Aguinaga**: Honey in The Rock—Brooke Ligertwood & Brandon Lake
7. **Erica's Road to Surrender & Mercy by Erica Hernandez Castillo**: I Surrender—Hillsong Worship & Matt Crocker
8. **From Doing to Being by Giselle Dominique Mascarenhas-Villareal**: The Glory—Kim Walker Smith

9. **Broken but Restored by Cynthia L. Hernandez, M.Ed.**: Oceans (Where Feet May Fail)—Hillsong UNITED
10. **When the Tomb Becomes Your Womb by Eliza M. Garza**: Make Room—Community Music and The Church Will Sing
11. **The Surrender That Built Me by Naomi M. Perales**: Spirit Lead Me—Influence Music & Michael Ketterer
12. **The Extraordinary in the Ordinary by Dr. Rutchie Contreras**: The Blessing—Kari Jobe & Cody Carnes
13. **Signs From Heaven by Carolina Chams**: Gratitude—Brandon Lake
14. **The Beauty of God's Grace by Jaimie Luna**: That's Who I Praise—Brandon Lake
15. **Legacy in My Blood by Chelsea Gonzalez**: Firm Foundation—Cody Carnes
16. **Jesus and Ganas by Dr. Esmeralda Adame**: Run to the Father—Cody Carnes
17. **From Knowing About God to Knowing God by Marie Salazar Garcia**: That's My King—CeCe Winans
18. **The Woman Who Danced Beside Me by Maribel De La Fuente**: Promises—Maverick City Music, Naomi Raine, and Joe L. Barnes
19. **Saved by Grace by Geraldine Valdez**: Surrounded—Michael W. Smith
20. **Chains Broken by Carmen Sauceda:** Graves Into Gardens—Elevation Worship

**Epilogue**—Agnus Dei—Passion & Kristian Stanfill

**Final Declaration Prayer** - In Jesus Name—Katy Nichols

# ⚠ Sensitive Content Notice

This anthology contains honest and vulnerable stories of women who have walked through difficult life experiences. Some chapters include references to trauma, abuse, grief, loss, and other sensitive topics.

These stories are shared as testimonies of healing and hope, pointing to God's redeeming power. However, we recognize that certain content may be triggering or painful for some readers. Please use wisdom as you engage with these stories, and allow yourself space to pause, reflect, or seek support as needed.

If you find yourself struggling while reading, we encourage you to reach out to a trusted friend, mentor, pastor, or professional counselor for support. You are not alone.

For immediate help in the United States, please contact:

- **National Suicide Prevention Lifeline**: 988
- **National Domestic Violence Hotline**: 1-800-799-SAFE (7233)
- **Substance Abuse and Mental Health Services Administration (SAMHSA) Helpline**: 1-800-662-HELP (4357)

# Introduction

*"They overcame him by the blood of the Lamb and by the word of their testimony."*
**— Revelation 12:11**

There are moments in life when the ground beneath us gives way. When dreams collapse, relationships fracture, or the weight of grief presses so heavily that breathing feels like work. In those moments, we whisper, "God, if You are real, if You are near, show me."

This book was born out of those whispers.

*God Willing, Daughter* is more than a collection of stories. It is a living testimony of women who walked through valleys of darkness and found light. Women who surrendered what they could not carry and discovered a God who carried them instead. Women who rose from ashes, not untouched but undeniably transformed. Women who now wear crowns of grace, not because of perfection, but because of perseverance.

The voices in these pages are diverse—mothers, daughters, leaders, dreamers—but their heartbeat is the same. Every story is a thread stitched into the living fabric of God's faithfulness, carried from generation to generation. Together, they remind us that even when life feels uncertain, God's promises remain unshakable.

As you turn these pages, I invite you to see yourself within them. Maybe you are in your valley, wondering if morning will ever come. Maybe you're at the altar, wrestling with surrender. Maybe you're rising, shaky but determined, or perhaps you're tasting the sweetness of legacy. Wherever you are, may these testimonies whisper to your heart: You are not alone. You are loved. And your story is still being written.

What you're about to encounter is the living Word in action.

This is our offering to you, dear reader. A book that doesn't just tell you about hope, it breathes it. May it stir courage where there was fear, healing where there was pain, and faith where there was unbelief.

Because God is willing, mija. The crown is already set aside for you. All of heaven is simply waiting for you to say yes, rise, and claim it.

# Section One

# The Valley

*"Even though I walk through the valley of the shadow of death, I will fear no evil, for You are with me."*
— **Psalm 23:4**

Every story begins in a valley. Sometimes it's a place we stumble into by accident, and other times it feels like life itself pushes us down into its shadows. The valley is lonely. It's raw. It strips away everything we thought made us strong.

Yet, the valley is also holy ground. It's where we come face to face with our humanity and God's faithfulness. In these pages, you will meet women who wrestled with identity, who walked through grief, and carried pain in silence. Their honesty may stir the ache of your own valleys. But listen closely, between the lines, you will hear the whisper of God: "I was with you even here."

The valley is not the end. It is the place where brokenness cracks open the soil, and unseen seeds begin to take root. As you read, may you find courage in their valleys, and remember that your own shadows can still give way to light.

# Chapter 1
# Pero Dios

*by Perla Tamez-Casasnovas*

*"You intended to harm me, but God intended it for good to accomplish what is now being done, the saving of many lives."*
— **Genesis 50:20 (NIV)**

**From Rituals of Power to the Presence of Peace**

I used to think I had everything. Power. Influence. Rituals that made me feel like I could control the chaos of life. I surrounded myself with mentors who gave me books, mantras, and ceremonies that promised protection. To the outside world, I looked strong, unstoppable, young woman with confidence, success, and a "spiritual" covering.

On the outside, my "power" looked like luxury handbags, perfectly tailored suits, and the newest car parked outside my office. I was the one people came to for advice. I held myself like a woman who had it all figured out.

But behind the veil of smoke and ceremony, I was hollow. I didn't even know what I was practicing; I just knew I needed something, anything, to believe in. Something to shield me from the pain of my past and the chaos of my present.

When I lost my fiancé, it felt like my world crumbled overnight. We had everything prepared—venue planned, honeymoon paid, music selected, the ring chosen and sitting in its box—and then it was over. He was an educated professional, now behind bars. I was an educated woman, alone. And the whispers of those I'd once fought with, family who were waiting for my downfall, grew louder. I didn't know if I'd ever recover.

## When Everything Changed

I was twenty years old when my fiancé was taken from me in a legal situation that shattered my world. One day, I was planning a wedding, the next day, I was grieving like a widow with no closure.

The pain was unbearable. The nights were long and suffocating. I kept asking, "Why me? Why him?" And the lie I began to believe was that I wasn't safe unless I aligned myself with a higher power, any power, that could protect me from ever losing that much again.

Older women twice my age welcomed me into their circle. They told me this path would keep me safe—that if I gave enough, sacrificed enough, devoted myself enough, I could guard the people I loved. And I believed them.

My life became a cycle of rituals: candles lit at midnight, offerings placed on altars, whispered chants to unseen forces. My mornings started with prayers to saints, my nights ended with incense and cards laid out on a table. On the outside, I was a thriving businesswoman. On the inside, I was a desperate little girl trying to feel safe.

One ritual I'll never forget involved the killing of a male chicken. They would cut into its throat. I was told to put it in my mouth, to suck and lick it, even for just a few seconds. I was disgusted, but I did it anyway. That's how badly I wanted protection.

I could feel the feathers brush up against my mouth, and the world narrowed to one terrible, urgent instruction.

The air smelled of smoke. For a heartbeat, my mouth filled with the warm, metallic tang of fear and the ritual's demand.

Afterward, there was silence that felt heavier than the ceremony. People nodded like something sacred had been sealed, and I tucked the shame into the same pocket where I had tucked my courage. I told myself strange stories to make sense of it. If I complied, then maybe the danger would pass. If I gave them this proof, then maybe I would be protected. Hope, in that moment, looked a lot like surrender. It taught me there are rites of passage that are not holy, only harmful, and that being "saved" by fear is a false kind of salvation.

Looking back, I can name what it cost me: a piece of trust, a chunk of dignity, an invisible debt of guilt I had to repay with years of quiet rebuilding. I gave sixteen years of my life to that path.

Then came the night of the robbery—a gun to my face, my spiritual armor shattered. All those spirits I had sacrificed to were silent. Nothing could protect me from the fear that wrapped around my chest every time I closed my eyes.

I thought I was going to die and that my family would die with me. I saw my life flash before my eyes as the robber pointed the gun at my head. He tried ripping off my gold bracelets with one hand while holding the gun in the other. I was face down with my head on the floor. The gun kept hitting my forehead like it was dancing on my skin. I begged God, *Please make this go away. Please let them leave my house.* I was praying for my life with every breath. Somewhere between the gun's thud against my skin and my prayers, the robbers left.

Still, I went back to my rituals for two and a half more years, convinced I had done something wrong the first time. That maybe this time, if I was more faithful, more devoted, the spirits would show up. But instead, my life collapsed again. My husband and I lost everything.

## The Invitation of Peace

*December 12th.*

*New York City.*

I walked into St. Patrick's Cathedral, not knowing what I was looking for, just knowing I was tired of fear. The city outside was loud, chaotic. But inside those walls, there was a silence I had never known. The marble floors stretched endlessly, the candles flickered without demand, and the air felt thick with peace.

For the first time in years, I wasn't performing. I wasn't chanting. I wasn't bargaining. I was just sitting. And in that stillness, I felt something holy, something alive. Not in the statues, not in the rituals, just in the presence.

I began to realize: God doesn't share His glory. He is the Alpha and the Omega. He wasn't asking for sacrifices, He was asking for me.

## March 24, 2024—My Pero Dios Moment

We always used to keep money at the altar in our home. It sat at the base of ceramic pots filled with rocks and honey, meant to symbolize saints that would protect our money. But deep down, I knew they weren't saints. They were idols. Man-made symbols I had been taught to trust.

And when we finally decided to let it all go, my husband and I drove back to our hometown. We took those pots and threw them into a water pond, breaking ties with everything they represented.

But my husband didn't want to throw the $100 bill. "No," he said, "I'm going to spend it." So we brought it back home. It floated around our house for a while, almost like a relic of the past.

At one point, I gave it to my daughter to spend at the carnival.

But she didn't.

She brought it back to me.

And on that Sunday, March 24, 2024, when it came time to tithe at church, that $100 bill was the only money we had to give. We didn't think twice. We released it.

In that moment, I knew God was receiving it. Not just the money, but the gesture, the surrender, the trust. It wasn't about the amount. It was about the heart behind it.

This wasn't just an offering, it was a declaration:

We don't need altars of stone. We trust the living God.

I heard the Lord as clear as if He was sitting beside me: "I am going to bless your money. I am forgiving you."

Tears poured down my face. My body shook with a mixture of relief and regret. For years, I had poured thousands into rituals, sacrificed animals, given up my peace, all to win the favor of something that never showed up.

And here was God. No cost. No ritual. Just grace.

**The Wait & The Wonders**

The miracles didn't come overnight. They took nine months, like a pregnancy, for everything to be reborn. But during that waiting, God sent women into my life: Marie, Eliza, and Miriela. They didn't give me formulas. They didn't ask for offerings. They opened their Bibles, held my hand in prayer, and taught me how to talk to Jesus like a friend.

Those nine months were deeply spiritual. God kept sending me people who poured into me at just the right time.

Strangers, friends, even a passing conversation that might have seemed ordinary to anyone else, became lifelines for me. They gave me water when my soul was dehydrated.

A word of encouragement. A verse that slipped perfectly into the cracks of my worry. A prayer whispered over me when I didn't even know how to pray for myself. These were not coincidences; they were divine interruptions, like drops of living water falling into the desert places of my spirit. Each encounter felt like a reminder: I see you. I haven't left you. You will not wither here.

The Bible became more than a book on my nightstand; it became my sustenance. *Psalm 91* especially wrapped itself around me like armor and refuge. *"He who dwells in the shelter of the Most High will rest in the shadow of the Almighty."* Those words became my shelter when fear tried to creep in, my covering when I felt exposed. I held on to His promises: that He would deliver me that His angels would guard me, that no plague or terror would come near my dwelling. Each verse was like a drink of cool water in the desert, reminding me that I was safe under His wings.

Scripture nourished me in a way nothing else could, softening the dry soil of my heart and allowing faith to take root again. Those months stripped me of self-reliance, but in exchange, they built in me a dependence on God's presence that I had never known before. It wasn't structure that sustained me, it was Spirit. It wasn't discipline that carried me; it was grace. And in that fragile, thirsty season, I learned what it meant to be kept alive by Living Water, protected by the promises of Psalm 91, and sustained by the God who never fails.

At first, my prayers were clumsy. Simple sentences whispered through tears: "God, help me." But each day, my faith grew stronger. I learned to pray scripture. I learned to hear the Holy Spirit's voice instead of chasing after spirits who demanded fear, inviting God into the places fear once lived.

I began to pray differently. Jesus wasn't a distant figure anymore; He became my partner. I began inviting Him into every part of my life, and my prayers turned from fear to faith.

One of the first undeniable moments where I felt God's presence was while listening to the song "The Goodness of God." I felt covered. Protected. Accompanied. It was like the breath of heaven swept over me.

And slowly, blessings began to bloom:

- Our finances recovered.

- My marriage deepened in love and respect.

- My health renewed.

- My identity rooted itself in something eternal.

**Who I Am Now**

I'm not religious anymore. I'm in a relationship. Jesus is my best friend, my anchor, my light. I don't wake up wondering what the spirits are saying. I wake up knowing Who I belong to. A few years ago, I would've panicked if I couldn't predict my future through cards or rituals. Now, I rest in peace knowing that my Father already holds tomorrow.

**What I Broke, What I Built**

In my family line, there was a thread of witchcraft, fear-based religion, and spiritual bondage. Generation after generation had unknowingly passed down beliefs wrapped in control, confusion, and counterfeit power. But by the grace of God, that thread ends with me.

I drew the line in the Spirit. I broke the chains that were disguised as protection. I severed the ties that connected me to darkness, so my children would never have to question who they belong to or where their help comes from. They will not grow up in fear. They will not need to manipulate outcomes or plead with the unknown. They will not inherit the trauma of false altars. My children will inherit truth. They will be rooted in the unshakable foundation of Christ. They will know they are covered by the blood of Jesus—fully seen, fully loved, and fully protected. They will walk in peace, speak with authority, and rise with confidence in who God created them to be. They will not chase purpose; they will live it. They will not survive by rituals; they will thrive by grace.

I am not just breaking generational curses; I am building a new legacy.

One of faith.

Of freedom.

Of divine inheritance.

The curses are broken.

The silence is broken.

The shame is broken.

And now, the bounty of heaven is upon us.

We are walking into a future soaked in promise, draped in favor, and led by the Spirit of the Living God.

**To You, My Sister**

If you're reading this, caught between altars—between fear and faith, control and surrender—I need you to hear me: you are not alone.

I was where you are. I know the desperation. I know the fear. But I also know the freedom.

It's going to hurt at first. Leaving what you've known, even if it's been harmful, will feel like tearing away from a false comfort. When you've enticed the darkness for so long, walking away from it feels like withdrawal. Your soul may tremble. Your mind may question. You may even feel like you're betraying something sacred. But that's the lie: you were never meant to serve fear.

There will be spiritual warfare. The enemy doesn't want to let you go quietly. But greater is He who is in you than he who is in the world. You are not walking away empty-handed; you are walking into freedom, into truth, into a love that doesn't demand the blood of animals, silence, or suffering in return. Don't give up. Don't turn back.

God has plans to prosper you, not manipulate you, not punish you, but to prosper you. But those plans can't unfold while your hands are still tied to altars that were never meant for you. You can't carry divine blessing into a space built on deception.

Yes, the pain is real. The tears. The confusion. The lonely nights where you wonder if you made the right choice. But so is the glory on the other side.

A life where peace isn't earned, it's inherited. Where you don't chase after protection, you dwell in it. Where your prayers don't echo into silence, they're answered by a living God who knows your name.

You don't have to beg. You don't have to prove. You don't have to perform. You just have to surrender.

And when you do, you'll see: what you thought was power was just a shadow. And what God gives you? That's the real authority. That's the real covering.

Don't be afraid to strip away everything man-made. Walk into the presence of Jesus raw, real, and ready. You don't have to earn His love. You don't have to bleed for His attention. You just have to receive it.

You will be protected.

You will be restored.

You will be welcomed into a Kingdom greater than anything you've ever known.

And when the fear rises, remember these words that changed everything for me: But God. Pero Dios.

**Perla Tamez-Casasnovas**

**Instagram:** @perlatamezcasasnovas

# Chapter 2

# The Gilded Cage

*by Anonymous Contributor*

*"She is clothed with strength and dignity; she can laugh at the days to come."*
— **Proverbs 31:25 (NIV)**

### The Beginning of the End

There are moments in life when you don't realize a chapter has begun—until you're already in the thick of it. For me, that chapter began the day I said, "I do."

They say marriage is the beginning of a beautiful journey. But mine started with fear, confusion, and a growing sense that I had made a terrible mistake. I should have felt safe, not like a prisoner trapped in a cage. Things were already off to a rocky start. An incident had occurred just a few weeks after our wedding, and out of shame and embarrassment, I kept this dark secret hidden for the next eleven months. To the outside world, everything must have looked shiny and perfect. What they didn't see behind closed doors was emotional manipulation, gaslighting, and psychological abuse. I was living a nightmare I couldn't wake up from.

Two months after the nuptials, I was home alone on a Sunday and decided to take a pregnancy test. It was just a formality to silence what-ifs. I stared at the test, expecting nothing, but before the waiting time was up, the result showed an instant positive. I was in shock and disbelief. I didn't even feel pregnant. Later that week, I went to my family doctor, and they confirmed that I was, in fact, pregnant. Six weeks along, to be exact. My world completely changed in an instant. I remember feeling overwhelmed with excitement for the life that was now growing inside of me. For a brief moment, I was full of hope.

The house we were renting, our first home together, didn't have much furniture, but it felt like the start of everything we'd dreamed of. I had plans to turn the guest room into a nursery and start picking out paint colors. Weekends were spent at Barnes & Noble buying magazines, baby books, and reading everything I could about what to expect as a first-time mother.

All my hopes and dreams quickly came crashing down when I became aware of a clear little plastic bag with white powder tucked in the back of the bathroom cabinet. I wanted to believe the excuse that it wasn't his, or that this was just a one-time mistake. It was much easier to buy into the lies because the truth was too painful. I didn't know this person at all. More lies began to unravel, and I became aware we had financial problems. The rent hadn't been paid for months. He was using my pregnancy as an excuse to delay consequences, telling stories to buy time. Eventually, it all fell apart.

By December, we were evicted, moved in with my in-laws, and we put most of my belongings into storage.

This was yet another red flag. I didn't know it then, but I was bracing for survival. Why did I continue to ignore all the warning signs? Why did I believe that I could somehow fix this person and save our marriage?

**The Trap That Looked Like a Home**

Moving into his parents' house was meant to be temporary, but it turned into captivity. Promises faded. His true self emerged—substance abuse, erratic behavior, and no financial transparency. The house was grandiose, but it wasn't safe. Even though a cage is made of gold, it's still a prison.

My pregnancy had been a breeze. No morning sickness, nausea, or unusual food cravings. Just an appetite for two and a growing belly. I was probably the healthiest I had ever been in my life. I wanted to do everything possible to make sure my baby was healthy. I was lucky enough to be able to work up until the day I delivered. I remember waking up at 4:00 a.m. to go to the restroom (this became a frequent thing in my last trimester and not fun for someone who isn't a morning person). I was spotting. Could this be it? I don't feel any contractions. After a quick call to my OB/GYN, they told us to head over to the hospital. There aren't enough books or reading material to prepare you for labor. Things were happening so quickly, but I was relieved to have my mother by my side. Everything was fine until my husband decided he no longer wanted my mother in the delivery room. He leaned over and told me they only allowed one person, and I had to ask my mother to leave. That's not what I wanted. I needed her in that moment more than ever. It shattered my heart to ask her to leave, but I knew he would make matters worse if I didn't do as he instructed.

Aside from the heartache and sadness of another one of his controlling outbursts, I was hardly in any physical pain. After only four hours of labor, I felt the sudden urge to push. My doctor said, "Sure, let's give it a try." I couldn't feel anything below my waist, and I wasn't even sure if I was pushing properly, but after three attempts, my baby came into this world. The room was dimly lit and peaceful. No loud cries, just a healthy baby with amazing reflexes. It felt too easy. I believe it was God's way of showing me mercy for everything else I had to endure in my marriage.

The following night, when we left the hospital, I felt a sudden sadness take over me. The nurses had taken such great care of us. I dreaded going back to my in-laws' home. There was nothing warm or welcoming about that place. I tried to make the best of it, but my family wasn't allowed to visit. I had no say, no voice, no autonomy. I was just trying to survive.

Isolation can drive some people over the edge. For me, it was a break from the violent outbursts. Pregnancy changed my body in so many ways; I didn't look or feel like myself anymore. I would gaze into the mirror, and it felt like I was looking into the abyss. I did not recognize the woman in the mirror. What happened to the girl I knew? This person was numb, sleep-deprived, a shell of the vibrant girl she used to be—who had so many hopes and dreams for the future. I was isolated but not alone. I had my baby; it was just the two of us in our own little bubble. I was in awe of this beautiful, perfect baby and thought, *How did something so precious come from me?* I did not feel worthy, but I thanked God for giving me the greatest gift and entrusting me to raise this child. Looking back now, there's no doubt in my mind that my baby saved my life. It was a love I had never experienced before.

**The Silence of Shame**

I didn't cry. I didn't break down. I couldn't afford to, not while nursing a newborn. I did my best to suppress all negative emotions. Not just to keep the peace, but because I didn't believe I had a choice. I remember finding comfort in cooking TV shows like Gordon Ramsay, which kept me company while my baby took naps. And all the while, the shame built quietly.

Shame is a monster that will eat you alive. My self-esteem was completely wrecked. This person knew my weaknesses and slowly, over time, eroded my confidence. I felt weak, powerless, and didn't see a way out. This wasn't supposed to happen to me. I did not fit the statistics. I came from a loving family, wonderful parents who provided everything a child needs to be independent and successful in life. I was not raised in an abusive household, but my father was strict and believed in traditional values. We were brought up in the Catholic Church and attended Mass just about every Sunday. He used to say, "You don't leave this house until the day you get married." I thought marriage was my ticket out of my parents' home, as if it were so terrible. Living with roommates in college or shacking up with a boyfriend was out of the question. Living with a man before marriage was a sin and frowned upon. Since I was such an obedient daughter, that's exactly how it played out. I waited for the first person to propose to me and thought life was going to get so much better. I was gravely mistaken. It's amazing how someone's words and societal beliefs can imprint and change the course of your life. It wasn't until recently that I dissected my father's words and realized the subliminal message behind them. He didn't believe his daughter could stand on her own two feet and become successful. I needed a man to see my value and take me out into the world as if I were some prize or trophy. It was the false fairytale that my prince charming would swoop me off my feet and we would live happily ever after. Unfortunately, that's not what happened in my case. How could I have fallen for the lies? I was smarter than that.

**The God in the Thread**

The day I left, I didn't plan it. My husband offered to drop me off at my grandmother's house. Not my parents, who, after years of dating and ten months of marriage, suddenly became the enemy. I didn't fight it. I just needed to get out. I missed my family, my support system, so much, and I know they missed me, too. They grew increasingly concerned after I gave birth, and communication became less frequent. My only lifeline was my Blackberry. Family members and whatever few friends I had left with would take turns texting me every day to make sure I was ok. When he finally agreed to take me and the baby to see my grandmother, it felt like furlough. A temporary break from prison. I didn't have my engagement ring on. I thought if I left it behind, it wouldn't raise any suspicions of me wanting to escape.

However, he noticed I wasn't wearing it and was bothered by it. He told me to go get it while he waited for me in the car. My heart sank. I thought, *He's going to change his mind.* I quickly grabbed it and put it on my ring finger. What was once such a beautiful ring full of luster now felt more like an ankle monitor or dog tag that said I belong to him. I quickly got in the backseat and sat close to my baby.

That's when I saw it, a single loose thread on my baby's blanket, shaped perfectly like an ichthys. A symbol that resembles a fish. The same symbol that always seemed to show up when I needed a reminder that God was nearby. I didn't have a plan, but heaven did.

**The Collapse That Saved Me**

We arrived at my grandmother's house, and he carried the baby in the car seat while I followed with just a diaper bag over my shoulder. He said he would be back for us in a few hours. The minute he walked out and closed the door, I fell apart. Tears began to run down my face, and I could no longer hide the nightmare I was living. I didn't have the energy to keep up the facade. Like a lost child, I cried out, "Please call my mom. Don't make me go back."

That day, the truth cracked wide open. My family took me to my parents' home, and everyone knew something was terribly wrong when I ran to my parents' closet to hide with my baby. The level of fear I exhibited was proof of abuse. I truly thought he'd take my baby away or hurt me. Threats had been made in the past, and I certainly wasn't going to doubt him. When he showed up at my parents' house, my father stood firm and said I wasn't leaving. For the first time in a long time, I felt protected. But the shame lingered. The guilt. The questioning. Was I overreacting? Was I doing the right thing? Would my child hate me one day for leaving?

I had never felt so low in my life. This person really took me to the depths of hell, and I allowed it. I wanted to be swallowed up into the earth. To just disappear quietly, hoping nobody would notice I was gone. I couldn't see a better future. All I could focus on was my world collapsing and having to hang on by a thread for my baby. Whatever hopes I had of being a family and happily married were quickly evaporating. I not only had to grieve the loss of my failed marriage, but the shame and secrets that I once kept hidden were rising to the surface. Another phrase my parents used to tell my siblings and me growing up was, "I don't care what trouble you're in; we will go to the gates of hell to rescue you if we have to." As a teen, I didn't do drugs or abuse alcohol, so I never thought there would ever be a need to save me. But this was their way of telling us that if we ever made a mistake or got ourselves into a bad situation, no matter what, we could call on them to bail us out. I always knew my parents loved me and wanted the best for me. Fast forward to my late twenties I desperately needed to be rescued, and sure enough, they kept their promise.

**The Second Exit – And Rock Bottom**

At least three months had gone by since I filed for divorce. Maternity leave was up, our baby was now in daycare, and I was getting used to starting over. Things were going excruciatingly slow in family court. This was not an arena I was familiar with.

The day before a court hearing, I would have the worst anxiety and sometimes panic attacks. I felt out of place being surrounded by men and women in orange jumpsuits, handcuffed and chained together. I didn't belong here among criminals; I didn't do anything wrong! I was getting nowhere with the court system. My estranged husband was changing, though. He looked like he was getting his life together and was going to great lengths to reconcile. I told myself maybe it would work, that I owed it to my child. Maybe this time would be different. It would also give me some financial relief. I wanted to believe he could change, that he was truly sorry for the pain he caused. This wasn't a second chance; it was far beyond that. Even my therapist warned me. But I couldn't live with the doubt, so I stopped the divorce proceedings.

    Things weren't perfect, but it felt like a fresh start. We had our own apartment now, and we were raising our baby together. No more temporary custody orders. It wasn't long before the old patterns and behaviors returned, about two months to be exact. I found bottles of liquor in the kitchen. He began to control my communication with my family again. Any little thing would set him off. I thought I could outsmart him despite the legal threats he made. My soul knew I wasn't safe. I had to find a way out. It was the weekend before Christmas, and he had been up at least twenty-four hours. When I thought it was safe to leave, I put the baby in my car and proceeded to call 9-1-1. Why didn't I just drive away? I was still under his control, and he didn't even need to be present. When I turned the car on, he came out and took the baby out of the car seat. I was explaining to the female officer that the past 48 hours had been torture, and all I was trying to do was leave for safety with my baby. Unfortunately, without a court order, they couldn't intervene.

    I had to choose between walking back into danger, knowing I had shown my hand, or leaving without my baby. I was an emotional mess. To the officer, I probably appeared to be an unstable mother who was struggling to express the level of danger she was in. She asked me to phone a relative or friend who could take me to my parents' house. I can tell you that angels are real. The first person I thought of was a coworker who was also a good friend and lived nearby. It was a Sunday afternoon. She answered and came to my rescue. No questions asked, no judgment. They vouched for me to let the officer know I was not the problem. How could I return to my parents after everything I had put them through over the past few months? More shame piled on top of guilt. The harsh reality is that I left my baby with my abuser because I feared he would take my life if I stayed. A choice that will haunt me for the rest of my life. In the depths of my soul, something told me that he wouldn't hurt the baby; it was me he wanted to punish. I also knew he would have his mother step in to help him.

When I returned a few hours later, I was escorted into our apartment by two police officers so that I could gather a few of my belongings. They warned me that if I made any trouble, they would arrest me on the spot. I remember walking past my soon-to-be ex-husband and mother-in-law, who was holding my baby in her arms. How did they become the victims and I the villain? I could feel the rage building inside of me, and I gave them the dirtiest look as if saying "This isn't over, and I'm coming back for my baby."

**When the Shelter Became My Sanctuary**

That evening, I ended up at a women's shelter. Alone. Afraid. Broken. I was still trying to process the last forty-eight hours. I was an educated woman with a bachelor's degree, but the gravity of the situation hit me like a ton of bricks when someone showed me a chart and explained what the cycle of abuse looked like. For the first time, I saw the ugly truth staring right at me. I had to accept my reality. I was in an abusive relationship and a victim of domestic violence. The woman who did my intake asked if I was hungry. I don't even remember eating that day. She offered a bowl of rice and beans and a slice of white bread. I remember sitting alone in the kitchen, eating in silence. It was a sobering moment. I was depleted and needed a place of sanctuary to build up my strength again. My nervous system had been in a state of fight or flight for so long that I forgot what peace felt like.

This was nothing like the first time I left. This time it was my rock bottom. I left behind the one person in this world that I was supposed to protect. I failed. I let down my family. I knew I would be judged for leaving my child with my abuser. What kind of mother would do that? However, something in my core was determined not to accept defeat.

After I was shown my room, I sat on the floor facing a narrow mirror, thinking, *I'm smart. I have a good job. How did I get here? Is my baby okay?* As mothers, we often give so much of ourselves to everyone else until there's nothing left. I never expected to end up in a shelter, but I knew it was where I needed to be in that moment to pull myself together so I could go back into the fire and save my baby. Even in that stark room, I felt God. In the quiet. In the food. In the fact that I was still breathing.

**The Wisdom Born from Fire**

That experience forced me to break every self-limiting belief I ever carried. It forced me to become brave even when I didn't feel ready. I didn't have the luxury of waiting until I "healed." I had a little baby watching me. Depending on me. And I had to rise.

I've learned that forgiveness isn't saying what you did was okay. It's saying what you did no longer controls me.

I had to learn how to forgive someone who never apologized because my healing could not wait for their accountability. Forgiveness didn't come easy. It came after countless nights of crying myself to sleep, years of therapy, and the realization that I deserved peace more than I deserved closure. I also had to forgive myself. The person who had a chokehold on me for so long no longer had power over me. I was his source of power, and it was high time I took it back.

**The Curse That Broke, and the Blessing that Began**

Generationally, women in my family were taught to endure. To stay silent. To "suck it up." I was the first to say, *I want out.* I didn't care who I disappointed. And that shift changed everything.

Because in that bold move, I didn't just save myself. My divorce wasn't just a turning point in my life—it changed the entire fabric of my family. For me, it was about survival. For my loved ones, it was a reckoning. My father, a man raised to believe that protecting his family was his sacred duty, carried the weight of my pain as if it were his own. Several family members struggled to accept that they couldn't stop what happened to me. The truth is no one could have saved me. I had to save myself. The aftermath of my divorce showed my family that strength sometimes looks like walking away and choosing yourself. The storms that don't break us build us up for something greater. We may not see it in the moment, when we're full of despair, but one day it will all make sense.

**If I Could Hug the Woman Reading This...**

To the version of me that didn't think she'd ever make it out of the woods—I'm so proud of you. You didn't just survive. You stood up every time you got knocked down. You didn't numb yourself with vices. You didn't give up. You fought your way out of the darkness and found a path to healing. One that broke generational curses so the cycle of abuse would not repeat itself. You chose the greatest thing of all—LOVE.

And to *you* reading this, you are not alone. You being here is already a miracle. And if my story gives you even the smallest glimmer of strength to make it one more day, then it was worth telling.

To the woman who feels trapped and doesn't see a way out, God has not forsaken you. I see you. I know the weight you're carrying. The dark secrets you mask with a smile. The fear. The shame. I've been in your shoes. I walked through the fire and lived to tell the story that not many are fortunate enough to tell. Please understand that this is not your fault. You do not deserve this. And more importantly, you are not powerless.

"And finally, this question, the mystery of whose story it will be. Of who draws the curtain. Who is it that chooses our steps in the dance? Crowns us with victory when we survive the impossible? Who is it that does all of these things? Who teaches us what's real and how to laugh at lies? Who decides why we live and what we'll die to defend? Who chains us? And who holds the key that can set us free…It's you. You have all the weapons you need." **(Sweet Pea,** *Sucker Punch***)**

You've always had the power; you just need to reclaim it. You are one decision away from completely changing the course of your life. You don't have to be brave, but you do have to fight. Because someone is counting on you, and deep down there is a version of you who deserves to be free, whole, and finally at peace. Do not give up, because one day, when you're ready, you will rise.

**Held in the Dark: A Prayer for the Woman Who Can't See the Light**

God, for the woman who feels trapped, forgotten, or too broken to begin again, I ask for Your presence to flood her heart with courage. Remind her that You see what happens behind closed doors. Whisper truth to her when the lies of fear get too loud. Strengthen her spirit, steady her steps, and place the right people in her path. Let her know she is not alone, that she is worthy of peace. That her story isn't over, it's just the beginning. Cover her in Your divine protection, restore what has been stolen—her voice, guide her in wisdom, and lead her to the life You always intended for her.

In Jesus' name, Amen.

*From one survivor to another, I'm living proof that storms don't last forever and there's always a silver lining.*

# A Daughter of God

# Chapter 3
# The Soul Touch Queen: A Journey of Awakening

*by Dr. Esther Akindayomi*

*"I will restore to you the years that the swarming locust has eaten..."*
— **Joel 2:25 (ESV)**

**The Roots That Made Me**

I was born belonging—before I ever questioned where I fit, before I wondered if home could truly exist. Lagos, Nigeria—my first home. A city of movement, of resilience, of unbreakable spirit that pulsed with unending traffic, vendors calling out their wares, the hum of generators and sirens. Yet even amid that electric chaos, my soul found anchor in ritual and lineage.

In our culture, newborns are carried away from the city's rush to receive a name steeped in history and undergo rites that tether the child to ancestors, purpose, and destiny. When they placed me in my grandmother's arms, the world fell silent. She held me as if I were the answer to a prayer she had spoken decades earlier. There, in the shade of a mangrove, my grandmother—a woman who had lost her own daughter long ago, whose eyes could no longer see the world, yet whose spirit perceived everything—declared, "This is my daughter, *Abake*, who has come back to me. This time, her life will not be cut short. She has come now to stay, and she will live a long and fulfilled life." That day, drums rolled, and women sang blessings that wove through the tall grasses. A promise became woven into my marrow: I was chosen, I was tethered, I was home.

I have no conscious memory of that day, yet for years, my parents spoke her words over me with quiet reverence. My mother's voice would tremble with awe; my father's deep tones swelled with pride. Each repetition felt like a sacred promise and a spiritual mantle that invited responsibility and devotion. Every time I encountered doubt—an uncertain career twist, the pang of not fitting in, the quiet ache of everyday struggle—those words grounded me, reminding me I stood on the shoulders of generations who believed in me.

Though my grandmother seldom appeared in our Lagos compound, the few visits to her village remained etched in my memory: rough clay walls warmed by the midday sun, smoky embers rising through mango canopies, goats bleating at dusk, and my grandmother's voice booming across open courtyards. Even when I returned to Lagos's urban sprawl—the honking horns, the vendors hawking yam fritters, the scent of jollof rice simmering in roadside pots—I carried those village scenes in my spirit.

Back in Lagos life in our polygamous household was alive with energy. Six children—five boisterous boys and me, the only daughter—filled every corner with laughter. Saturday mornings meant *amala* and *gbegiri*, cooked by our mothers with tender care, then served in ritualistic harmony. My father, a prosperous man with a household full of staff, would summon us into the living room. We sat on woven mats, hands scraping the soft black yam dough and rich bean soup from one wide ceramic bowl he placed between us. With every shared mouthful, I tasted more than food—I tasted unity, inheritance, and the promise that I had come to stay.

My father taught me how to stir the pot, guiding my fingers until the dough held its form, teasing that even the mothers could learn from my technique. I reveled in his praise, seeing in his eyes a reflection of my own budding worth. Though I wasn't the eldest son, I was undeniably his daughter: his strength draped across my shoulders, his leadership pulsing through my veins. I became the glue that held us—six children, two mothers, a spectrum of voices—together.

At twenty-one, hope shimmered in the form of marriage. I walked into marriage the way so many young women do: romanticized, naive, believing stability was something another person could give me. He was my college professor, ten years older, responsible, and dependable. That's what I wanted. That's what I chose. And for a time, it was enough. When he proposed, I accepted with the same fervor that once had me clutch Grandma's hand. In November 2006, we boarded a flight to America, our hearts brimming with promise. Rhode Island's crisp air heralded the birth of our first son in 2008; Texas's sprawling skies welcomed our second in 2011. I poured love into motherhood, into the new culture, into building a life that felt like the next chapter. I loved the family we built. I still do, despite the marriage's collapse.

On our tenth anniversary, we threw the wedding celebration we had never held. White linens, candlelight dancing on the smiling faces of friends and family. Yet between vows and toasts, I sensed and tasted the irony: a beginning meant to renew vows instead marked an ending. We clung for five more years, weaving threads of pretend unity until the tapestry unraveled completely. In that unmaking, I remembered Grandma's words—an echo louder than the collapse: You have come to stay. You are chosen. And so, my journey home began, home to my roots, home to my soul, home to the woman I was always meant to become.

## When the Life You Knew Falls Apart

I believed in forever—unwavering love sealed in vows uttered before God, a ring exchanged before witnesses, binding two people until death parted them. I thought marriage would anchor my dreams and define my worth. But in August 2018, that very framework cracked. No elaborate fight, no grand gestures, no courtroom fireworks, just the quiet exit of two souls too wounded to stay. We parted ways for the sake of our sons, yet in the stillness that followed, I felt more alone than ever before.

Standing amid the debris of a life I once thought unbreakable, I realized I was a stranger to myself. The identity I had nurtured—wife, caretaker, partner—dissolved into shards at my feet. For years, I had lived within the protective walls of his provision: bills paid, maintenance handled, decisions made. He had been the architect of our life, and I had been content to live in the home he built. I never paused to acknowledge the level of dependency I had cultivated until I was forced to navigate the world alone.

I slipped into an extended-stay hotel no one could trace, a hidden sanctuary for heartbreak. Alone felt like drowning; some days, merely breathing required effort. Every day was survival, and tears fell freely: tears in empty parking lots, tears on long drives from the hospital where I worked, tears in supermarket aisles behind stacked cans. The world saw me go about my routines, but inside, I was crumbling.

Alcohol became both escape and enemy, my nightly ritual. I leaned into wine's numbing promise, one glass, two glasses, until nothing felt sharp. Sleep came only when I forced it, sinking into oblivion to silence the ache. In daylight, I buried myself in busyness: hospital shifts that spanned dawn to dusk, community events where I wore my "I'm fine" mask so tightly it felt like a second skin. Traveling for conferences offered a brief escape. Strangers applauded my professionalism, my charisma, my competence. With every handshake, every lecture hall I filled, the void inside only widened. I was restless, reckless—a woman on the precipice of collapse, masquerading as having it all together.

Yet in the midst of my recklessness, God's goodness chased me. A colleague slid a cup of coffee into my hand, their eyes soft. A friend texted, "I'm here if you need anything," just as I sank beneath grief. A scripture verse popped onto my phone at precisely the moment my heartbeat quickened with fear. Each act of kindness whispered: "You are not alone." But I remained shackled to shame, convinced I must hide or risk complete collapse.

## The Night in Jail That Should Have Been My Wake-Up Call

I never thought I'd know the cold bite of steel around my wrists. Jail was a distant possibility reserved for others, those who had spiraled out of control or wandered too far from home. Not me. I was educated, responsible, and careful. Yet on that December night, I learned how swiftly a life can derail.

Earlier that day, I had walked out of the hospital buoyed by hope. After spending nearly a year in an extended-stay hotel, I'd just put a deposit down on a new home, a tether to a fresh start. A friend invited me to his brewery to celebrate. We savored a flight of beers he'd brewed himself, each flavor tasting like possibility. When I climbed into my car, I felt lighter, believing I could finally leave the past in the dust.

The drive back is a blur. At some point, I must have blacked out behind the wheel, because all I recall is the shriek of sirens, the throb of flashing lights, and my car mangled along the roadside. At the station, I sat on a metal bench beneath flickering bulbs that buzzed like manic insects. Shame draped over me in heavy waves. I, a mother and anesthesiologist, someone who calibrated life and death with precision, had become a statistic.

Then she arrived, a fellow mother, caught in her own spiral of heartbreak. She'd been arrested for leaving her children alone while chasing her fractured marriage's remains. Her grief mirrored my own. Without hesitation, she reached across the cell, her arms wide, and pulled me into an embrace I did not deserve but desperately needed. Her coat smelled of coffee and warm spices; her touch was fierce with compassion. In that moment, I felt the weight of my shame lift as if her embrace carried the promise of redemption.

The next morning, my mother and sister appeared in the courtroom, with no barrier between us, only proximity and pain. My mother's eyes met mine with love wounded by disappointment and hope battered by reality. Her silence asked the question I had danced around for months: Who have you become?

I had no answer.

Bail came and went, a breathalyzer device was installed in my car, and my license was on probation. But I treated each restriction as an inconvenience rather than a wake-up call. I continued pouring wine at night, kept my hospital shifts heavy, and maintained my community roles when it suited my image. I had perfected the art of functioning, a polished exterior masking hemorrhaging grief.

And yet, grace persisted. Small interventions such as an unexpected text, an answered prayer, or the memory of that mother's hug kept surfacing within my shattered heart. Each became a crack in my armor, preparing me for something more than merely surviving.

## A Soul Still Searching

For nearly a year, I existed in the blur of an extended-stay suite. I was present but absent. Seen but hidden. Functioning but untethered. No one knew where I lived, not my mother, not my children, not even my closest friends.

My one-bedroom suite came with all the basic necessities. It had a small kitchen, a modest living area, and a bedroom tucked behind a flimsy door. I brought very few belongings, most of which hung in neat rows inside the closet. I rarely cooked. I rarely lingered. The dim yellow lights gave the room a tired glow, like it, too, was waiting for someone who never fully arrived. Most nights, the television flickered with reruns of Family Feud, the voices of strangers filling the silence I refused to touch.

Work became my distraction. Each morning, I dressed in crisp scrubs and walked sterile hospital hallways, calibrating anesthesia machines, consulting with surgeons, soothing anxious families. In those corridors, I found purpose, a measure of self-worth tied to competence. When my boys visited, we met under fluorescent lights in the doctors' lounge, trading small hugs and whispered stories. We never talked about the hotel. I pretended I was someone else, someone stronger, someone who could outrun the wreckage, but something inside me was unraveling.

The ache within me grew louder; it was a restlessness I could not numb. Then came the invitation. A women's retreat in Sedona, Arizona. My dear friend sent me the details with gentle insistence, not pressure, but hope. "You need this," her message said. My initial response was doubt: too expensive, too soon, too indulgent. But a deeper stir rose: perhaps I deserved more than mere survival. I booked the trip in a moment of faith, landing on a flight that carried me toward transformation.

Sedona greeted me with a hush I hadn't felt in years. The earth there seemed to hum. There was energy spiraling through vortex sites, the cliffs glowed like embers, ancient winds carried stories through juniper branches, and every breath felt charged with possibility. I did not know how this fit into my Christian upbringing, but I felt less concerned about doctrine or dogma. I only knew this place was sacred, and my spirit recognized its resonance before my mind could name it.

A doctor and her daughter guided our circle with quiet authority and grace. Their voices pierced through my defenses, their presence invited stillness, and their questions stirred something deep within me. They saw a strength I had buried, an intuition I had ignored, a calling I had abandoned.

The energy work raised my vibration, and for the first time in years, I felt spiritually awake. Not bound by rules or rituals, but freed by a sense of divine alignment. Was God meeting me here? Absolutely. His goodness had been chasing me across states, across broken choices, even into the hotel room I refused to call home. Sedona was just the place where I finally stood still long enough to hear Him.

On the final day of the retreat, I made a choice that felt both daring and sacred. I would invest in my own healing, committing to a year of coaching that cost ten thousand dollars. My father's words echoed in my mind: "Investment in human resources is the greatest asset." I realized I was worth that investment. Sedona had cracked me open. I was ready to reclaim the woman I had buried beneath pain.

**The Sanctuary of Slow Becoming**

Sedona had opened something sacred inside me, a quiet invitation to remember. I left the retreat with two versions of myself in tow: the woman I had been and the woman I was becoming, and neither could stand alone. I was different, not fixed, not transformed, but aware. And awareness is a holy beginning. It's the whisper before the thunder. The doorway before the decision. I was still drinking. Still making choices that didn't fully align with the clarity I craved. But now, I could see it. I could feel the mismatch.

My life was no longer a blur; it had edges now. Soft ones. But edges just the same. I was moving toward healing, inch by inch, even when I didn't yet know the way. I craved something stable, something soft, something that whispered, "You're safe here."

So, I rented a modest three-bedroom bungalow in South Texas. It was the first place in years that felt like a sanctuary of pause. Here, I would cultivate the gentle art of becoming. Within those walls, small moments bloomed into markers of restoration. Mother's Day dinner arrived with plates piled high, laughter bouncing off walls that had once echoed only with silence. A quiet pocket where my children could visit, curl up on the couch, and play in the backyard.

I celebrated my fortieth birthday not just as a passing year, but as a declaration: I am still here. I am still standing. I am still becoming. Friends gathered for a masquerade-themed birthday with glittering masks, silk and satin, feathers and horns. The DJ played "This Girl Is On Fire" as I raised my glass to the sky, declaring myself, for the first time, "Queen Esther." Smoke went up, fire sparklers rained, and I felt the fullness of every season of my life—rooted in Lagos, polished by pain, crowned in promise. Even in that celebration, I found stillness. After the guests departed, I breathed deep, feeling the tremor of gratitude.

That bungalow wasn't just a house, it was a pause. A holy pause. One afternoon, the boys were with their father, the hospital shift behind me, and I sat alone on the couch. Soft light spilled through blinds onto the worn cushions. In that hush, I felt my chest soften. I didn't hear God speak, but I felt His presence wrap around me, quiet and gentle as dawn.

Still, old patterns beckoned. I spent more waking hours at the hospital than at home. I donned the "I'm fine" mask for community commitments. My life remained a tightrope between survival and surrender. But now, I walked with both eyes open.

**The Year of Acceleration**

Then came 2020—the year the world pressed pause. Cities emptied, businesses shuttered, and fear spread faster than comprehension. The globe exhaled and braced itself for the unknown. But my acceleration began before the world slowed down.

In December 2019, a moment of quiet rejection set everything into motion. A surgeon I had worked with often asked for me to be replaced as his anesthesia provider. That day, I wasn't my usual playful self. I was grieving the loss of a friend's wife, 38 years old, just like me. I wasn't chatty; I was reflective, and something about that unsettled him.

I wasn't allowed to ask why. So, I quietly surrendered. I dropped my badge at the front desk and walked away from a system that no longer saw me. That decision cost me $10,000 in salary, security, and familiarity. But even then, God was already catching me mid-leap. He had been preparing my wings.

Three months later, COVID-19 hit. The world stood still, but I was already moving. My job had once been a pillar of stability. Now it felt like a cage. The rhythm that once dictated my days no longer fit the woman I was becoming. I stepped into something new: locum work, traveling across Texas, building a career on my own terms. I became the architect of my time, my energy, my future.

Then came an unexpected invitation, one so perfectly timed it could only be a God wink. I was asked to put together an anesthesia group. It wasn't just a role. It was the collision of everything I'd carried: leadership, medical expertise, spiritual depth, vision. Even as the pandemic ravaged systems, I was building, designing the structure, and assembling the team. Stepping fully into a calling that had waited patiently for me to say yes. I was no longer merely functioning within someone else's structure. I was creating a system grounded in compassion, efficiency, and grace.

But God wasn't finished. In August 2020, R.G.Vita Infusions was born. What began as personal restoration for my own anemia and exhaustion blossomed into a healing sanctuary for others. I crafted infusion menus rich in electrolytes, vitamins, and amino acids, designing treatment rooms with soft lighting, cushioned seats, and calming playlists. Patients arrived worn thin and left glowing with renewal. Hydration was no longer transactional; it was transformational.

Stories unfolded in those infusion chairs: a teacher wept as she felt energy return, trembling hands clutching the IV pole; a veteran choked up at the sense of being nurtured after years of silent endurance; a bride-to-be laughed with vibrant clarity as wedding chaos melted away. Each story stitched together science and soul, grounding me in the synergy of healing.

COVID had halted the world, but it had propelled me into purpose. I was no longer surviving; I was creating, I was leading, and I was healing. Above all, I was stepping into the fullness of who I was always meant to be.

**Reckoning and Rebirth**

By early 2024, I had become adept at curating my image, poised, empowered, and spiritually attuned. But the mirror reflected only a polished surface. Clarity became an illusion when I refused to look beneath the gloss. Then came New Orleans: three days that cracked every illusion wide open.

The first night I got lost, physically, emotionally, spiritually. Bourbon Street swallowed me in neon blur and thunderous bass. Every drink tasted like rebellion, every face a stranger, every dollar a fleeting thrill burned in regret. I felt both hyper-visible and unseen; my internal chaos amplified by the city's carnival chaos.

The next two days passed in a haze of overspending, tension with my boyfriend, and the mounting weight of regret. I moved through crowds like a ghost, searching for solace in drinks, corners of shadowed streets, and none came. But beneath the glitter of escape, something sacred was cracking.

On the flight home, I stared out the window at the patchwork earth below, numb. Walking through my front door on the morning of January 29, 2024, I sank into my home office chair, fragments of my life collapsed around me. In the stillness, a question rose: "Shall I continue in sin and ask that grace may abound?"

And in that moment, I felt it clearly, not in my mind, but in my gut that something had to change. God had been gracious with me for so long. Too long. My spirit trembled; I felt my knees buckle under the weight of mercy squandered. I knew if I didn't make a change, I would lose everything.

So, I made a decision. No grand proclamation, just a resolve typed out in simple black ink on white paper. Thirty days without alcohol. One day at a time. I printed a calendar, wrote my *why* in bold letters, and taped it to the wall where I could not miss it, a covenant rather than a goal. It was a turning point and a spiritual line drawn in grace.

Something shifted in that moment, not merely in habit, but in spirit. It wasn't just self-discipline. It was divine, and I believe God whispered that calendar into my heart. He met me in my recklessness, in my exhaustion, in the quiet hum of my office that morning, and said, "Come back to Me."

The first sober morning felt raw as an open wound. Cravings pounded like old regrets, my body warring with muscle memory. But in that tension, I heard other whispers: the hush of early dawn, the steady pulse of a healing heart, the memory of Sedona's red cliffs cradling my tears. Those whispers wove into a new rhythm, with sober days stacking into weeks, weeks crowning into months. Today, I haven't touched alcohol since.

Now I see it all. The entire landscape of grace beneath my story. In the orbit of sobriety, I saw glimmers of every tender mercy collected in my spirit—small acts I once missed: a coffee delivered, a prayer unbidden, whispers in the canyon winds of Sedona, the embrace of that stranger in jail. Those moments were reflections of light, not the source. The source was always more radiant: love that refuses to let go.

New Orleans was the unraveling. January 29th was the reckoning. And this—this is the rebirth. I am not the same woman; I am no longer hiding; I am no longer performing. I am home.

**Called Home: When Soul Touch Came Alive**

It was a Sunday morning. I awoke drenched in sweat, heart pounding against my ribs, something pressing deep into my spirit. It was urgent, weighty, not just a thought, not a memory, but a command. A whisper with divine force behind it. "Go find your journal."

I searched my shelves, rifled through notebooks and cluttered corners, digging through remnants of old chapters, none of which held what I was looking for. But I knew it was close; I could feel it. And then, tucked away in the corner, untouched, were the boxes. Among half-forgotten notebooks, a bluish silk spiral surfaced, dust-coated and tender.

I hesitated; it stared back at me like it had been waiting. Like it hadn't given up on me. Like it knew this moment would come. I ran my fingers across its surface and felt memory rush into my palms, knowing that opening those pages meant confronting hopes I had buried beneath survival. But when I peeled back the cover, breath returned to my lungs. Page after page revealed the younger woman I once was. The girl who dreamed boldly, believed fiercely, wrote clearly. She carried fire and called it faith. She had no doubt that her life would be used by God. She had named the vision Soul Touch.

And that vision hadn't faded; it had waited. She hadn't disappeared, she had simply been buried under survival. I read, I wept, and I knew: that journal wasn't just a record but a resurrection. A return to the assignment I had received when

I was twenty-two years old. A ministry born from a divine whisper, tucked into pages that held my becoming. That morning wasn't emotional nostalgia; it was a moment of activation.

I closed my eyes and felt the weight of every step that brought me here. Grandma spoke life over me. Sedona cracked me open. South Texas gave me stillness. New Orleans stripped the illusion. January 29th baptized me in truth. And this journal, this sacred invitation, brought me home. Soul Touch wasn't just meant to live in me. It was meant to live through me.

Today, Soul Touch Wellness stands as a living witness to that promise. It is no longer just a calling. It is a living, breathing movement that honors the connection between body, mind, and spirit. Through one-on-one coaching, restoration experiences, tailor-made products, and weekly Harmony Hour gatherings, we offer spaces where souls remember their worth, bodies reclaim health, and spirits renew hope.

Soul Touch is not just my business. It's my surrender. God is the Founder. I am the steward. It's bigger than me. Holier than me. And yet, graciously working through me. This isn't about perfection; it's about presence. About offering others what I had to fight to reclaim in myself: truth, alignment, and freedom.

If something stirs within you as you read this, know it is sacred. You have not missed your chance. You are not too broken, too dishonored, or too distant. You are being called home, into whispers of grace, into healing beyond ritual, into the crown of your becoming.

There were moments in my journey that didn't look or feel religious or happen in church, but they were holy and they were light. And though I didn't know to call it God back then, I see now that He was there; in the desert, in the silence, in the love of strangers, in the chaos, in the whisper that pulled me to the journal, and in my surrender on January 29th. He was in every breath of return.

None of those moments was the Source of light. But all of them reflected it. Sometimes we miss the presence of God because we're looking for pulpits. But He's in the whispers, in the shifting, in the longing, in the healing we didn't know we needed. In the journal we forgot we wrote. Even when we're not calling on Him by name, He's still calling us by ours.

This is not the conclusion. It is the crown. Soul Touch is here, and so are you.

**Dr. Esther Akindayomi**
**Instagram:** @soultouchqueen
**Website:** www.soul-touch.net

# Chapter 4
# When Breath Returned

*by Dr. Nina Golde*

*"He reached down from on high and took hold of me; he drew me out of deep waters. He rescued me from my powerful enemy, from my foes, who were too strong for me."*
— **Psalm 18:16–17 (NIV)**

**The Weight of That Day**

It had been exactly one year since we buried my little brother.

On Mother's Day 2023, he passed away suddenly at just sixteen years old. No signs. No sickness. Just here one day and gone the next. And as if that grief wasn't enough, we laid him to rest on Father's Day. Two holidays meant to celebrate life and love now stand like tombstones on the calendar.

This year, the grief returned quietly, but fully. I felt it pressing into my chest as Mother's Day approached. I decided to spend it in Houston with my family. I didn't want our parents to be alone. I tried to stay strong for them, but sorrow still lived in my bones.

I asked God why. Why did He take him so soon? Why without warning? But even in the questioning, I never stopped believing that God is good. I just didn't understand His ways.

**The Battle Before the Miracle**

The night before it happened, I couldn't sleep. There was a heaviness in my spirit, a weight I couldn't shake. I didn't know if it was a dream or a vision, but I remember waking up and placing my hand over my son as he slept, covering him in silence, as if something unseen was trying to come for him.

I didn't know what it meant, but I knew enough to stay in prayer.

The next morning, I was exhausted, but I stayed in worship. That's how I fight. That's how I survive. My family was visiting and we planned to drive to Progreso for the day. Even in the car, I felt the Lord pulling on me: *Stay in praise. Don't stop worshiping.*

I didn't know why, but I listened. My spirit stayed awake.

**The Scene That Changed Everything**

Later that afternoon, back at the house, Noah's swim instructor was on his way to our home for a lesson. I went upstairs to change out of my swimsuit quickly so I could sit outside and watch the lesson. He was just five years old—playful, fearless, and always trying to keep up with the big kids

He usually stayed in the kiddie pool, where it was safe. But lately, he'd been taking swim lessons and gaining confidence. That day, he saw his older sister and cousin splashing in the deep end and he decided he wanted to be where they were.

He wanted to prove he could do it too.

I was upstairs when I heard my sister shout, "Where is Noah?"

Something in me snapped. I didn't pause. I didn't ask questions. I just ran. My body was moving before my mind could catch up. My heart was racing. My spirit was screaming.

I ran through the house and into the courtyard, and that's when I saw her. My sister. Pulling Noah out of the pool. His body was lifeless and limp.

I screamed.

I dropped to my knees and took him from her arms. There was no breath. No movement. His eyes were fixed. I held him in my arms and cried out the only name I could: "Jesus!" Over and over. It was all I knew to say.

**When Faith and CPR Collided**

Somewhere between the panic and the pleading, my medical expertise and instincts finally kicked in. I laid Noah on the ground and began chest compressions, my hands shaking, my mind racing, my heart barely holding on. I was saying his name over and over, louder each time, like maybe my voice could drag him back to me.

"Noah... Noah, come back to me!!" I sobbed, pressing down, counting in my head, trying to keep the rhythm while everything around me was falling apart.

But he didn't respond.

His eyes were wide open. Lifeless. Fixed. He wasn't there.

The air around us felt thick. The sound of my hands on his chest was all I could hear, just that and my own gasping prayers. I felt like I was outside of my body, like I was watching myself from above, a mother trying to save her child and failing.

*Why is this happening?*

*God, where are You?*

*Not again - not on this day.*

My sister was on the phone with 911, my mom was screaming behind me, people were running, shouting, crying, but it all felt muffled, distant, like the world had paused on the edge of something sacred and terrifying.

And then I began to slip.

The lie crept in like a fog: He's gone.

I started to believe it. My hands slowed. My breath caught in my throat. The world started spinning. I stopped the CPR and sat there frozen and in disbelief.

And then, my ten-year-old daughter stepped forward.

She had been watching the whole time. Wide-eyed. But now, something shifted in her. She looked at me with a kind of strength I'll never forget. Her voice didn't tremble. It didn't shout. It just cut through everything:

**"No."**

Just that one word, sharp, clear, commanding.

She stepped in front of me, gently moved my hands aside, and dropped to her knees beside her brother. She didn't ask what to do. She didn't flinch. She just started pressing, deep, firm, steady. Her little hands, so small, so brave, doing what needed to be done.

I watched her push with everything she had, fighting for him like a warrior. She had this fire in her eyes, and I knew God had placed something holy inside of her for this very moment.

Still, he didn't move.

At one point, I worried her compressions were too rough. Her small hands pressed down with such force that I thought she might break one of his ribs. But she didn't stop. She was fierce. Focused. Unshakable. Her whole body moved with determination, as if her soul knew what her mind couldn't fully grasp, *I have to bring him back.*

Something in her faith reawakened mine.

I leaned down and began to breathe into Noah's mouth. Again and again. His lips were cold. His skin was pale. I felt the edges of despair trying to choke me out, but I kept going.

My daughter kept pressing. I kept breathing.

We called his name like a lifeline.

We begged. We fought. We prayed.

And then…

A cough.

Faint. Weak. But it was there.

And then another.

Water began to pour from his mouth. His chest began to tremble. His eyes fluttered, just barely at first, but then he blinked.

He turned his head slightly, and looked right at me. His lips quivered and he whispered:

**"Mama."**

Then he burst into tears. And so did I.

**Held in Chaos**

Everything around us blurred. My mother came running out, shaking, and draped something over me. I hadn't even realized I was still in my underwear. I didn't care. I just held him and refused to let go.

When the ambulance arrived, they had to lift both of us onto the stretcher. I couldn't stand on my own.

At the hospital, I looked up and saw the words "near drown" written on the whiteboard. That moment broke me. I fell to my knees and wept, clutching my son, breathing him in, whispering, "Thank You, Jesus."

Everyone kept telling me how lucky I was. But this wasn't luck. This was God. He showed up. He stood between death and my baby and said, *Not today.*

That day, Psalm 18 came alive in me. I had cried out and my God came for me.

## Grief, Mirrored in Her Eyes

My younger sister, who helped raise Noah, stood beside us, shaking. She didn't speak. She just held him, kissed him, and cried a cry that was so deep, so broken, it didn't even make a sound.

She was mirroring me. I could see it all in her eyes, the terror, the relief, the grief, the gratitude.

We had almost lost our baby. But God had mercy.

## The Devil is a Liar

The first lie that crept in was the loudest: *He's dead.*

My heart wanted to believe it. My body had started to give up. I looked at my son and thought, *God, why would You let this happen?*

But then something deeper pushed through me.

I've always believed in spiritual warfare. I've always known that what happens in the physical often starts in the spirit. This time, I saw it with my own eyes.

The night before, I had sensed the enemy lurking. That day, he tried to strike again, on the anniversary of my brother's death. But God intercepted him.

## God, My Shield

I am always praying. Always covering my children, my husband, and my family. I plead the blood of Jesus over them. I rebuke the spirit of death and confusion. And I trust God to be who He says He is—our Defender. Our Shield. Our Rescuer.

That day, it all made sense. This was an assignment from the enemy and God intercepted it. Just like He said He would.

> Psalm 18:16–19 (NIV)
> *He reached down from on high and took hold of me;*
> *He drew me out of deep waters.*
> *He rescued me from my powerful enemy,*
> *from my foes, who were too strong for me.*
> *They confronted me in the day of my disaster,*
> *but the Lord was my support.*
> *He brought me out into a spacious place;*
> *He rescued me because he delighted in me.*

When I read these words now, they are no longer just verses on a page. They are my lived experience. They are what happened by the pool. He reached down from on high. He drew my son out of deep waters. The enemy was too strong for me, but not for Him.

The Lord supported me when I collapsed. He brought us out. And He did it, not because we were perfect, not because we had it all together, but because He *delights in us.*

I didn't just witness a miracle, I lived inside a promise. Psalm 18 didn't just happen that day. It continues to unfold in our lives, over and over again, as a reminder that God still rescues.

**A New Way of Living**

Everything in me shifted.

I don't rush through life anymore. I don't waste time on things that don't matter. I don't hold onto offenses. I give more grace because I know everyone's walking through something unseen.

I'm more present with my family, and my purpose. I don't want to miss a single moment.

Losing my brother started the shift. Almost losing my son made it permanent.

My life is not built on hustle anymore; it's built on assignment.

**Two Stories. One Faithful God.**

Every time I look at Noah, I think of my brother. Their stories are woven together now.

It's a strange duality, grief and glory holding hands.

But I don't ask why in bitterness anymore. I ask in faith. I know my brother's life had purpose. Even in his short time here, he changed our family. His absence still echoes but it has also awakened something holy in us.

And now, with Noah, I live more intentionally.

I honor my brother by remembering him. I honor Noah's miracle by raising him with the knowledge that his life carries divine purpose.

Two different stories.

One faithful God.

And I trust, fully, that there is purpose in both.

**Elohim Shomri—God My Protector**

God showed me who He truly is. Not just in concept, but in reality. He is my Rescuer. My Shield. My Defender.

He brought breath when there was none.

He showed up when I screamed His name.

He stood between my family and death.

I call Him Elohim Shomri - God, My Protector. And I will never stop telling this story.

**A Blessing for You, Beloved Daughter of God**

From one woman in the fire to another, this is for you.

If you are holding grief in one hand and gratitude in the other,

If you are carrying the weight of questions that may never be answered on this side of heaven,

If you have ever looked at someone you love and wondered if breath would return…

I bless you with the peace of God that surpasses all understanding.

I bless your spirit to rise up even when your body feels weak.

I bless your voice to speak the name of Jesus when fear tries to steal your words.

I bless your home to be covered in the blood of the Lamb—sealed in praise, guarded by angels, and filled with a presence so thick that no darkness can linger.

I bless your ears to be tuned to heaven's whispers.

May you hear the warnings before the waves rise.

May you sense the shift before the storm even begins.

And when the enemy dares to knock, may you be found worshiping.

I bless your motherhood.

I bless every prayer you've ever whispered over your children's beds.

Every tear you've cried into your pillow.

Every "God, please" you've spoken through trembling lips.

He heard them all.

He bottled every one.

I bless your daughters-eyes, those childlike parts of you that still long for answers, still ache to be held, still wonder why certain losses came so early and so hard.

May you know that even in the unanswered, you are deeply loved.

May you find strength in surrender and beauty in becoming.

If you've ever wondered if God would show up for you, let this story be your reminder:

He still breathes life into dead things.

He still rescues.

He still stands between us and death.

He still answers the cry of a mother's heart.

So, beloved, may you rise.

Not just in strength, but in softness.

Not just in fire, but in faith.

Not just for survival, but for purpose.

I bless your next breath,

Your next battle,

Your next breakthrough.

May the same God who saved my son remind you that nothing is ever wasted, not the pain, not the silence, not even the years that feel lost.

And if the devil dares to come again, may he find a woman clothed in worship, surrounded by angels, and whispering the most dangerous name she knows—Jesus.

**Dr. Nina Golde**

**Instagram:** @GrowthStudioPodcast

**Website:** thepodcaststudiorgv.com

# Disclaimer

This chapter contains personal and sensitive experiences, including themes of abuse, addiction, spiritual warfare, mental health struggles, and suicidal ideation. While the story reflects the author's true journey and testimony of redemption, healing, and faith, some content may be triggering or disturbing to readers.

The experiences shared are not intended to diagnose, treat, or replace professional medical or psychological support. If you or someone you know is experiencing abuse, trauma, or a mental health crisis, please seek help from a licensed professional, trusted spiritual leader, or crisis center.

For immediate help in the United States, please contact:

- **National Suicide Prevention Lifeline**: 988
- **National Domestic Violence Hotline**: 1-800-799-SAFE (7233)
- **Substance Abuse and Mental Health Services Administration (SAMHSA) Helpline**: 1-800-662-HELP (4357)

Names and identifying details have been changed to protect the privacy of individuals. Any resemblance to actual persons, living or deceased, is purely coincidental.

This story is a testament to the transformative power of God's grace and is meant to offer hope to those who feel unseen, unheard, or broken. **Reader discretion is advised.**

# Chapter 5
# From Poles to Purpose

*by Tracey Castillo*

*"Am I now trying to win the approval of human beings, or of God? Or am I trying to please people? If I were still trying to please people, I would not be a servant of Christ."*
— **Galatians 1:10 (NIV)**

**Childhood Questions and Early Awareness**

Have you ever asked yourself, "Who am I?"

"Where did I come from?"

"Why am I even alive?"

I did. I remember sitting on the sun-warmed concrete outside my family's home in South Texas, the kind of place where playing outside was the norm, the air smelled like fresh-cut grass in the summer, and in the distance, you could hear cars rumbling down a worn-out gravel road. As I looked at my hands—small, thin, trembling—I silently asked, "Where did I come from?"

At the time, I didn't know that our hands are tools. They are tools of either purpose or destruction. Every decision we make, even the smallest one, holds weight. They open doors, not just in the physical world, but in the unseen, spiritual realm too. Those little hands had already carried more than most people knew. Within a child's hands lies more than innocence, there is power. These small hands can build, heal, create, and worship. In the physical, they shape tomorrow's world; in the spiritual, they carry prayers that move mountains. I remember walking into the living room and seeing my father watching a pornographic cartoon, as if it was nothing. I didn't know how to react. When my mother walked into the house and caught us, her anger was indescribable; she yelled and screamed at my father for allowing it.

**Growing Up in Hardship and Faith Flickers**

I was raised in a home that knew hardship like a close companion. And yet, despite the struggles, flickers of faith still remained. My mother was a very outspoken woman. Her face bore the weight of years of worry, no fear. She worked multiple shifts at a hospital—always exhausted, her back aching from caring for patients who couldn't even remember her name.

My father, when he was around, was a man whose charm slowly gave way to chaos. Addiction had chained him, and I watched the light in his eyes fade. Our home shifted from laughter to emotional numbness to closed doors and heavy silence.

We were raised Catholic. We weren't taught about God; we were taught about the Virgin Mary, so honestly, I didn't even know God existed for a period of time. Without a personal relationship with God, I was left vulnerable to the world's version of who He was, or worse, the lies whispered by the enemy.

Pain was woven into our bloodline: emotional, spiritual, even physical wounds that were never healed, only handed down. When parents don't heal, their trauma becomes our inheritance. We call them generational curses. And they didn't skip me.

**Rebellion and Running from God**

Eventually, I rebelled. I acted out, ran from the law, and lived recklessly. There were so many times I could've died. I should've died. But I didn't.

Times of breakfast, driving, alcohol, views, drug abuse—you name it. Sin was rooted deeply in me. Now I know why, because even then, God's hand was on me.

I used to tell myself, "I wasn't born broken." I was born breathing, crying, living, just like everyone else. But somewhere along the way, between the innocence of childhood and the bruises of adolescence, something cracked. It didn't happen overnight. It was gradual, like a slow fade. A dimming of the girl I was meant to be.

As I got older, I sought validation from the world because that's all I had ever known. By fifteen, I was already a young woman desperate for direction. I thought affection would fill the emptiness, so I clung to relationships, hoping love would heal what was broken.

But instead of healing, I opened spiritual doors I didn't even know existed. No one ever taught me that what looks physical often carries spiritual consequences.

**Toxic Love and Motherhood in Chaos**

By sixteen or seventeen, I was deep into the nightlife scene. I became a well-known bartender, partying every night, chasing temporary highs, ignoring the permanent damage. That's when I entered a toxic relationship with a man I thought was love. But it wasn't love, it was lust. Brokenness disguised as passion.

We'll call him "Carlos". Carlos was infatuated with my beauty and charisma, but never cared to understand my soul. Caught up in the rush, drugs, alcohol, fast money, reckless choices, I ended up pregnant. And I was still a child myself. I thought having a baby would change things so that he would grow up and our love would deepen, but it didn't. He cheated. He lied. He manipulated. And like many naive girls, I took him back again and again.

I had a second child with him, thinking maybe another baby would rekindle our relationship. But nothing changed. The pattern only worsened.

I'll never forget the day I went into labor with my second child. I was excited to meet my baby, but Carlos didn't even believe I was in labor. Instead of supporting me, he told my mother to meet us halfway. He dropped me off at her location and went to the gym, not caring if I made it on time to the hospital or not.

That moment crushed me, but it also woke me up.

To every woman reading this: Don't believe a man will change just because you have children with him. If he wants to change, he will, and it won't be because of you. It'll be because of God.

Now I understand why most Christians wait on marriage. It's not just tradition, it's a life-changing covenant. Only God knows your perfect soul mate. He knows what we need, how we need it, and who we need to live a peaceful life in covenant with Him.

**The Move Back Home and a Dangerous Neighbor**

Years passed. I eventually left and moved back to my hometown in South Texas, hoping for peace. A fresh start. A safe place to heal with my children. But what I found wasn't peace, it was warfare.

We met a couple who lived across from us. At first, they seemed kind, friendly, and welcoming, but behind that surface was something much darker. The man had deep emotional instability, violent tendencies, and a controlling spirit.

He introduced me to someone new, someone I believed was just a friend. But he was far from it. He was a very tall, disfigured man that only a mother could love. We'll call him "Tobi."

Yet I got closer to him. I wasn't focused on his appearance; I was drawn to the fun, the danger, the rebellion. Coming out of a toxic relationship, that kind of chaos felt familiar.

Ladies, please hear me when I say: Heal before you seek connection, even friendships. If we don't learn to heal with God, we will continue depending on broken, imperfect men—men who damage us, slowly and silently. And all because we never learned our worth as daughters of the King.

**Control, Stalking, and the Mask of Wealth**

This man carried deep rejection wounds and extreme hidden insecurities that he masked well. It's clear now: he wasn't sent by God. He watched me obsessively. Took photos. Made notes. Paid to get me drunk. When I was asleep, or thought I was, he took pictures of my personal documents: my ID, my Social Security card. He ran my background and credit reports. He claimed I was applying for a job at one of his businesses as a manager, but I never did.

Tobi was so scared of being accused that he even forged my signature on many documents which were mailed to an address where I had never lived; later, I found out it was one of his many addresses. It was all a lie. He used his wealth and connections to control, stalk, and manipulate me. Even now, he still stalks my social media, calls me through an app that changes the caller's number, and tries to reach out on my birthday, like nothing ever happened.

He even manipulated my daughter, tricking her into handing over my phone while I slept. He searched for anything he could use against me. He took screenshots of private text messages that he manipulated in his own head, accusing me of cheating. He took screenshots of private photos that I had for myself and kept fabricating for his own proof to try and gain that leverage against me. He even tracked my whereabouts through my cellphone using a fake email account he created, all while thinking I had no idea.

And yet I still stayed with this man, why, because I chose to see the good in him. In reality, there was no more good in him. The truth is, he was already a beast on the outside. But eventually, the beast on the inside came out too. A man full of rejection from every woman who had ever denied him. I believe at the time he finally found someone who genuinely loved him, yet he pushed me away. All because of trust issues and fear of losing his wealth.

You can have all the money in the world and still be completely alone. So now, there he is: a lonely man, living in a lonely world, surrounded by money and always living in fear of losing it. He lives in fear, masked by ego.

No matter what this man did to me, he will never know to this day how much I pray and intercede for him. Later on in my journey, the Lord revealed to me "That man will never bother you again," in Jesus' name, which means if this man ever tries to do harm against me, he would eventually have to deal with the God I serve (Exodus 23:22).

And still, I pray for him. I pray for his salvation. That God would break the bondage the enemy has over his life because his life is driven by fear and control. When God reveals sins, visions, or promises—it's not to boast—it's to pray. Just as I've already forgiven all my abusers and accusers, so has God forgiven me of my transgressions.

**The Lure of Fast Money and the Neon World**

Having two children and living a fast life, I really never had help. I tried looking for quick jobs here and there, but nothing. Thanks to social media, I came across a post for promo models working for a major alcohol beverage company in South Texas. I contacted them for an interview, and, of course, they hired me. Who wouldn't? I have an awesome personality. I'm very fun, loving, and outgoing; I have the whole package.

But of course, just like every other job. I didn't know the evil behind the allure. The manager was a smooth talker in front of many, but behind closed doors, he was something else entirely. He'd convince us to go to his house to "try on swimsuits," then pressured us to take private photos, something clearly against the rules.

Naive women like me at the time, desperate for work and lacking boundaries, didn't question it. No one complained or questioned it. Everyone was silent. He was one of the head managers at the company, so he pretty much had enough seniority to blind others to the truth, and he was a master manipulator. Who would believe us? At the end of the day, we were just a couple of young girls who were promoting a brand. Too often, women like us are dismissed and judged long before anyone bothers to know our story.

So many nights after promos, this manager would buy drinks to intoxicate the women, then later take photos of them without their consent. Unfortunately, I was one of them—waking up in a hotel room next to him with my pants half off not knowing what happened after he offered to give me a massage and being so intoxicated, I fell asleep right away, heavily knocked out. No one could prove it.

But we all knew, he would drive the company Hummer with a sunroof open and convince us to wave out of it while taking pictures of our underwear in the dresses that he picked and chose for us to wear for each promo appearance.

Eventually, I knew we would never win with him. We all started catching on.

But the truth is, I wasn't just looking for a paycheck; I was looking for validation. I only knew one way to get it: by using my looks and learning how to manipulate the attention they brought me. So, when another opportunity came along, one that promised fast cash and a false sense of power, I convinced myself it was the next best step. That's how I found myself under neon lights, trading dignity for dollar bills, telling myself I was in control.

**Life in the Club: Power, Pain, and Predators**

I remember those neon lights like it was yesterday. The buzzing. The way the colors painted everything in seduction and despair. The pole stood like a cold, metallic idol in the center of the room. The music throbbed so loudly it shook my ribcage, but it could never reach the silent ache in my soul.

I can still see their faces. Perverted men who looked at me like I was a toy. Judgmental women who walked in acting superior, knowing the men they were with wanted us instead of them. Let's be real. Most men don't go to strip clubs for fun. They go for false attention. They're running from their problems, looking for something temporary to mask the pain. They lack accountability and compassion.

You'd think they'd see a woman on stage and think about their daughters or wives at home, but they don't. They're high, drunk, and lost. But honestly, I was so numb with all my suppressed feelings that I eventually convinced myself I was in control. A single mom doing what she had to do to survive.

But survival turned into slavery, spiritual slavery, in stilettos and lashes. I stepped into that world thinking I had made a choice. But in truth, that world had already chosen me. There was no community. No support. Just trauma, dressed up in glitter.

Every night, I put on a costume, not just makeup and heels, but a fake smile that physically hurt. My heels didn't make me powerful—they made me numb. I moved like I was alive, but I was dead inside. I performed for crowds, but no one ever really saw me. But God did.

One night, I stepped into the dressing room of a club I was working at, and I saw something I'll never forget: a young mother pumping breast milk before taking the stage. She worked night shifts at the club and a day shift somewhere else. She stayed sober for her baby. I remember her saying, "I just delivered him. I have to work to support him." That broke something in me.

People judge us without knowing us. They don't understand that many women dance not because they want to, but because they feel like they have no other choice. I was constantly surrounded by pimps and drug dealers. I was not owned by them, but I knew them.

I lived in the fast life, even often accused to this day that I was owned by a pimp, but no, no pimp had the satisfaction or glory to own me. Thank you, Jesus, but I was surrounded by them. I knew the majority of the women who were owned by them.

These women were full of fear and chaos for many reasons. If they did not make their goal, which is money that their pimps require every night, they would get tased, yes, tased. Why? Because if they were to get beaten, bruises would show. So throughout the night, as they slept, they would get tased in the middle of the night to teach them a lesson not to come home empty-handed or disobey their pimp, in other words, "their daddy".

Every time pimps would yell at a woman in front of me, for some reason the strength within me would yell back at them, not realizing they could have easily gotten rid of me in some way, by beating me, drugging me, or worse. But because of God's grace in my life and the purpose He has now so graciously revealed to me, I understand why He protected me through my past and the hardships I faced.

I watched girls dance with fear in their eyes, terrified they didn't make enough money to bring back to their "owners." I even got robbed. One night, I was on stage with a full party throwing hundreds of ones at me. Another dancer came up and started collecting my money off the floor. She ran out with it.

And I wasn't the one to play with. The next day, I ran into her again. Let's just say, it took two grown men to pull me off her, with one hand punching her face in like it was a punching bag, and the other hand wrapped around her hair. Her face was bleeding uncontrollably. I was pulling out large chunks of hair, breaking and tearing off my fingernails as I squeezed my hands into a fist.

That wasn't my only fight. I had to fight two women at once, more than once. Survival of the fittest, they said. And I chose me, every time. The strip club had a range of women. You had the "wives", women owned by pimps and dealers who operated by strict, unspoken rules. They trusted no one outside their circle.

Then there were the undocumented women, those who feared the system but didn't fear degrading themselves for scraps. Then the "barely-of-age" teens—naïve girls who thought they were in control, weaponizing beauty but completely unaware that grown men were waiting to mistreat and discard them.

And then there were women like me. I had the reputation, the look, and the power to walk into a room, spot the weak ones, gain their confidence, and use their attention. I became everyone's "favorite." I was the one everyone invited, respected, and protected—the homegirl. But I hadn't always been that girl.

It started when I became close friends with sin. Little by little, I grew more open, more outgoing, and more dependent on attention. Later, God revealed to me that what was really driving me was a deep root of performance and ego. It blinded me, and eventually, it took over. But all that attention just made me a bigger target.

Behind the scenes was even worse. The predators didn't wear masks, they wore charms. Pimps with smooth words. Traffickers with cold eyes. Clients who saw me as property, not a person. But they could NEVER claim me. Darkness wrapped around me like a second skin. And I didn't even know I was drowning.

I thought I was free. But I was in chains, chains I couldn't see. The enemy doesn't always strike with force. Sometimes, he walks through the doors we leave open, doors of pain, trauma, and compromise. I had opened many. I thought the stage was my battlefield. But the real war was spiritual, and I was being devoured without even knowing it.

## Wake-Up Call: Human Trafficking in Plain Sight

Then came the night everything changed. I showed up early for work, something I didn't usually do. Now I know, it wasn't a coincidence. God had a plan.

I walked into the dressing room, placed my things on a mirrored table, and looked up. Behind me, in the reflection, I saw a woman in the corner, curled up, shaking, crying uncontrollably. A manager rushed in behind me, comforting her. He bought her a bus ticket. I didn't know at the time, but she had been trafficked, kidnapped, and forced to dance. She had been taken from her home, miles away. That was my wake-up call.

So, before you judge a woman whose name you don't know and whose story you've never heard, ask yourself, what if you had to become her just to make it out alive? What if she didn't choose this? What if she doesn't even know how to leave?

In fact, across the globe, an estimated **4.8 million women and girls** and **1.2 million men and boys** are trapped in situations of commercial sexual exploitation, most coerced, deceived, or manipulated into environments they never intended to enter *(International Labour Organization, 2022)*. Some don't escape. Some don't even know they can.

That night, I still worked. But I wasn't the same. I began noticing things I had ignored. Like the "house mom" at the club. Except ours wasn't a mother. He was a gay man, married to another man, working behind the scenes. And something about him felt off. I caught him watching me through the mirror again and again.

He called me over, and that was my chance to finally confront him. That confrontation, what came next, would unravel things I wasn't ready to face, but I had to. Because God was allowing the darkness to be exposed slowly. The more I saw, the more I began to go deeper into the rabbit hole of sin. I didn't even know I was about to walk into it.

**An Invitation into Darkness**

He started to open up to me, saying, "I've been watching you." His words caught me off guard. My attention stayed focused on him, surprised and silent, trying to understand what he meant. As I stood there in shock, all I heard were comforting words, words of validation that, later, God revealed were never meant for me.

He continued, "I've been watching you. You keep to yourself, mind your own business. You work and then you leave. We're in need of a roommate like you." At the time, I was in desperate need. I was sleeping in my car, working, and traveling back and forth. I danced outside of South Texas because the income was higher. The more up north, the deeper the pockets. So to me, it felt like the start of a blessing in disguise, or so I thought.

As we got closer, I eventually moved in. That's when I noticed a large statue—La Santa Muerte—an altar of death. Immediately, I was drawn to it due to the powerful gifts that God has blessed me with. The enemy lured me in to manipulate those gifts.

The house "mother" said, "Come, come meet Mama," referring to the six-foot-tall statue surrounded by cigars, candies, money, and even blood offerings. I didn't realize it then, but that moment opened multiple spiritual doors I should have never walked through.

**Spiritual Doors Swing Wide Open**

As I began believing in the power of the statue, more spiritual doors swung wide open. Demonic oppression began to rise in me. I unknowingly idolized and welcomed witchcraft. Lighting candles and talking to the enemy day and night. Over time, things got worse. I began to suffer spiritually, physically, emotionally, financially—you name it. I was always sick, tired, losing weight uncontrollably. My health deteriorated fast.

Eventually, I was diagnosed with hyperthyroidism, an overactive thyroid, and severe nasal congestion and allergies. That's when things really spiraled. I walked into a doctor's office expecting treatment, but was told I needed immediate surgery to remove half my thyroid. But when I woke up, I discovered they had removed all of it. Just weeks later, I had to undergo another surgery, a hernia repair in my belly button. Years of back-to-back pregnancies, weight loss, and stress had taken their toll. I had been less than one hundred pounds, pregnant, and carrying a toddler at the same time. It was too much.

Both surgeries were deemed successful, and I went home to recover. But what followed was a new kind of torment. I began to lose weight rapidly. I couldn't eat or digest food. My body was weak, but worse, my mind was under attack. Darkness began to rise in the house. I started seeing demonic figures in my room, shadows that moved, whispers that chilled me. Six-foot-tall Apache-looking demons dressed in rainbow-colored garments would surround my bed at night.

I couldn't sleep. I was haunted. Delusions crept in. I couldn't tell what was real anymore. My identity? Gone. My beliefs? Gone. I was empty, confused, and under constant spiritual warfare. My family began to believe I was losing my mind, and truthfully, I felt like I was.

The enemy doesn't just attack your body; he goes after your identity. I even began fantasizing about women, something I had never dealt with before. Eventually, I gave in to the delusion. While downloading a dating app, the enemy plotted in my mind. I allowed a woman to spend the night, thinking maybe it would calm the storm. That night, for the first time in a while, I slept.

But when I woke up the next morning, I saw her staring at me. She said, "There are two large demons in your room. They want to take you to hell. They told me to leave so they could continue attacking you. "It shook me to my core.

Still, it wasn't over. While I battled spiritual warfare, my family, far from God, was plotting behind my back, and then came betrayal. The family I once trusted turned on me, not to help me, but to hurt me. I was institutionalized, labeled mentally unfit. And worst of all, my children were temporarily taken from me. I was shattered.

Drugged with medication I never consented to. Pills that opened more spiritual doors. Doors to torment, to bondage, to despair. The system didn't just break me; it tried to erase me from my children's lives, and my family was helping them.

Eventually, Carlos found out because of my family, who stayed very close with him behind my back. Since he was also a nurse, he manipulated them into believing he was the best person to "help" me, which allowed him to eventually force me under his care.

He finally convinced a family member to allow him to keep me at his apartment, and he eventually took me into a room and began injecting me with multiple injections and giving me pills. He would steal pills and medical equipment from the hospital, and he even partnered with other medical personnel at different facilities to take additional hospital supplies.

As time passed, my delusions worsened, and so did my physical condition. One night, I pleaded with him, warned him to stop, and begged him to leave me alone. He was trying to sleep with me claiming we should have another child. His excuse was that if we had another child, we could rekindle our relationship.

I even asked him to call 9-1-1 because I knew and felt something was wrong. But instead, he kept me in the room. He mocked me, recording videos of me while I hallucinated and struggled, sending those clips around to others as entertainment. He finally gave up on trying to sleep with me as I begged him to leave me alone because I was scared and I didn't understand what was going on.

He got so upset, picked up a bottle of whiskey and a bottle of pills, and ended up drinking himself to sleep in the living room. In a panic, I locked him out of the room and stayed inside with my children asleep on the bed, but my mind kept wandering in and out of the hallucinations, so I eventually called family, asking them to come pick us up.

The side effects of the substances he kept giving me were worsening by the minute. The delusions became so severe that I feared for my life and for my children's safety. Eventually, terrified and desperate, I made a decision: I took my children and climbed out of the window of his one-story apartment bedroom window. We walked outside, waiting in his parking lot. Praise God, no harm came to my children or me.

**Escape and a False Rescue**

In my desperation, I turned to a family member I thought I could trust. I told her I needed help. But instead of taking me to a regular hospital or simply calling 9-1-1 for medical attention, she chose to paint me as insane. She took no responsibility for what Carlos was doing, knowing well she was the one in control, how he forced drugs into my system, how he manipulated my mind.

No one asked what caused my breakdown. No one cared to consider the source. Instead, they added more medications, stacked more labels on me, while Carlos and that one relative who should have been held accountable got away with it.

That same family member even tried to take my children from me. They tried to lure my children into the CPS system, taking photos and videos of them instead of helping. They mocked my children the same way they mocked me, all in an attempt to gain custody for themselves.

And yes, that same disfigured man Tobi mentioned earlier—the one never sent by God—was still lurking in the background, working against me. Plotting. Lying. Claiming he wanted the "best" for my kids.

To this day, I still have no idea why they allowed him anywhere near my children or me. We were no longer together, and he was not part of our family to begin with. But little did they know, God was at work; nothing can stop Him.

## Institutionalized and Silenced

Eventually, I was forced, against my will, into a behavioral hospital. A CPS worker showed up, sent by a family member who had been conspiring behind the scenes. They gave me two choices: go to the behavioral hospital or go to jail. Just like that, my own blood, my own family, turned against me without shame because they wanted a paycheck so bad that they were willing to rip children away from their mother.

But what they didn't realize was in all my darkness, and even when I was forced to be silent, even when no one stood by me, God never let go of me.

I was forcefully court-ordered to stay three days in the behavioral hospital and temporary rights were taken from me and my children by that same family member who kept calling the CPS worker. Later, I found out the real reason: that family member was determined to take my kids because Carlos promised her payments if she helped him remove them from my custody.

And Tobi, the one who had been tormenting me, was still hiding in the shadows, working with them too. To this day, I still don't understand why he made up false accusations against me and yet stayed in my life just to destroy it. It doesn't make sense, does it? A man who wasn't my partner, who wasn't even part of my family, was so determined to break me.

The first day in the behavioral hospital, my mind was numb. My body was swollen and trembling uncontrollably. Multiple nurses injected me with sedatives, yet nothing worked. My eyes stayed wide open as I lay in bed with chaos racing through my mind. I could see demon figures running along the walls. I could smell death in the air. I could taste it. Voices tormented me, whispering commands to run, to give up. But my body wouldn't move.

Eventually, I felt like a vegetable, my mind screaming for life, but my body too weak to respond. Tears rolled down my face as I silently asked myself, "What did I do so wrong to deserve this? Why do they want to destroy me?" Nurses came and went without care. They looked at me with cold eyes, smirked, and walked away. That's the problem with healthcare nowadays. You can easily tell the difference between those who work for a paycheck and those who truly care.

**A Supernatural Encounter in the Common Room**

As time passed, I eventually found enough strength to get out of bed. I walked to the common room, sat alone at a table, and opened the Bible in front of me. That's when an elderly woman sat across from me.

She had Alzheimer's and was full of delusions, fixated on the TV. But something about her pulled my attention. While all the fear, the noise, and demonic torment swirled around in me, she started muttering to herself over and over: "He only looks at the heart. He only looks at the heart. He only looks at the heart." Tears welled up in my eyes. I didn't understand why those words pierced me so deeply.

Then, as she turned her attention away from the TV, she looked straight at me and asked, "Who are you?" Looking back, I've often asked God if she was an angel in disguise, sent to remind me that help was on the way. Because at that moment, her words were like a quiet rescue.

But no one else saw what I saw. Across the room, a nurse sat watching me—laughing and mocking—completely unaware of the supernatural moment I had just experienced.

## Demonic Attack and the Moment of Repentance

The demonic torment returned quickly after. I walked back to my room and lay in bed when a voice whispered: "You are a horrible mother. You'll be back." Suddenly, a demon appeared, a long, tall figure that crawled into my mouth and exited again, playing tricks on my mind. That demon spoke: "Go get a marker. Cut your wrist. End it."

In my brokenness, I obeyed. My body felt numb; I couldn't feel the pain. I started bleeding out, and no nurse was in sight. That demon knew exactly how to plot, how to isolate me, and how to destroy me in secret.

But in the middle of it, something snapped. I came to my senses. "What am I doing?" Then something unexplainable happened. My heart started speaking. Not my mind, because it was filled with noise, but my heart. I heard it clearly, like a whisper from within: "I'm sorry. Please forgive me. I'm sorry. Please forgive me. I don't want to live like this."

At the time, I didn't understand who was speaking, me or someone else. But now I know: that was the moment of repentance. That was the moment I hit the end of myself. God brought me to that breaking point so I could choose: surrender my life to Him or stay forever in bondage, in misery, in hell.

And let me tell you, from someone who's lived through hell, please, please don't wait until you're cornered to understand what grace truly means. At that moment, I felt completely worthless. I felt like I didn't deserve forgiveness. But somehow, my heart still knew there was something more. It was like my heart was speaking directly to God.

I repented with everything I had left.

## God Clears My Name

And not long after, a doctor came in and told my nurse, "Good news. You're going to be okay."

All along, that family member, Carlos, and Tobi had been lying to CPS, claiming I was a drug addict and struggling with mental issues. But the tests didn't lie. The tables turned. And the doctor cleared my name.

Eventually, coming out of the hospital, my heart was seeking more of God. As I continued through life, God made a way for me in many ways. I kept thinking about the next big step in my journey, not knowing what I would be stepping into.

Most people love to blame God for all the wrongs in their lives, but the reality is, it's usually a blessing in disguise, or simply the result of our own decisions and choices in life. Sometimes those choices are shaped by poor teaching as we grow up, or by being guided down the wrong path.

They say, "You are who you hang out with," and often, that's true. I believe we don't get to choose the families we're born into, but later in life, we can decide whether or not we want to change.

In my case, my life changed in so many ways because of my hunger for the Lord. I was so distressed and depressed that I would travel to multiple churches, but eventually went back to my roots and visited my old childhood church.

**The Religious Manipulator**

Through that church, I met a woman I truly believed at the time had been sent by God to help guide me in my walk with Him. She even said God had sent her. At first, I welcomed her counsel, but over time, I began to notice red flags.

We'll call her "Mrs. M." She was extremely religious and often told me, *"If God didn't show me what you received, then it never happened."* I've since learned that while God can confirm things through others, He reveals His will to whom He chooses, when He chooses. He created each of us uniquely so He can use us in unique ways.

What I once saw as spiritual authority eventually revealed itself as control. I realized I had been too quick to hand over trust, sharing parts of my heart and testimony with someone who wasn't able to steward them well. That experience taught me one of the most valuable lessons in my walk with God: not everyone who talks about Him is speaking from His heart.

I could have stayed bitter, but God showed me the power of forgiveness, even for those who hurt us. Today, I'm thankful for that encounter because it sharpened my discernment, strengthened my boundaries, and reminded me to take everything, good or bad, back to God for confirmation.

**Lessons from Misguided Leadership**

Because of my connection with Mrs. M, I was introduced to a second church. At first, it seemed so on fire for God. But over time, I began to see patterns of control and fear that didn't line up with the heart of the Gospel.

Looking back, I can see how my own unhealed wounds and the "performance ego" I had once lived with in the clubs followed me right into the pews. The same desire for approval, the same need to be seen and valued, made me vulnerable to environments where leadership wasn't healthy. I didn't realize it then, but I was still looking for affirmation from people instead of my identity in Christ.

There were leaders who struggled with their own insecurities and unhealed rejection, and I often sought their counsel for confirmation of what I felt God was showing me, but instead of encouragement, my gifts were silenced. I understand now that God allowed me to walk through that season as a training ground to learn what spiritual manipulation looks like, to develop discernment, and to understand that even in church, people can lead from wounds instead of healing.

One pastor once said to me, *"When you get to heaven, you can tell the Lord you served a righteous man."* At that moment, I stayed silent, but in my heart I knew I didn't want my life to be about serving the image of a righteous man. I wanted to be a righteous woman God could use for His glory.

The truth is, churches are filled with people, and people are imperfect. When leaders or members haven't healed from their wounds, they often end up leading from those very wounds. That doesn't make church unsafe, but it does make discernment necessary. God created the church as a safe place, a hospital for the hurting, but even in a hospital, people are at different stages of healing. Some are still bleeding, some are still blind, and some are still finding their way. That's why it is so important to follow God, not man. And today, I can truly say I'm grateful to have found a church family that is aligned with God's heart; a place where I can grow, serve, and worship freely in truth.

That experience taught me that God doesn't just want our service; He wants our surrender. And when we heal, we stop repeating cycles, whether on a stage under neon lights or in a pew on Sunday morning.

**A Lesson in Spiritual Boundaries**

There was a co-pastor in church who openly admitted he wasn't willing to pay the price to fully follow God. At the time, I didn't fully understand the weight of those words, but I would soon learn that his life reflected that truth.

What began as a conversation quickly crossed boundaries and revealed an unhealthy and manipulative spirit.

In my own brokenness, I trusted his position instead of testing his words against the Spirit of God. That misplaced trust opened a door to shame and confusion, but God was faithful to close it and deliver me.

I now see it for what it was: a seducing spirit that thrives where boundaries are weak and discernment is lacking. That experience deepened my commitment to guard my heart, test every spirit, and keep my trust anchored in God alone.

## The Revival and God's Direct Call

It was during that season that I attended a revival service. I was serving, smiling, and doing all the "right" things on the outside, but inside, I was empty and tired of the performance. An evangelist had come to visit the church, and immediately I felt the Spirit of the Lord urging me to go to the altar.

Instead of moving when God spoke, I made the mistake of messaging the pastor for permission. He rudely replied, *"You're already saved."* The crushing weight of guilt and shame hit me as I realized I had obeyed man over God. I could see how often churches have people serving who aren't fully surrendered, operating on fumes. Religious teaching may tell you to serve no matter what, but a true relationship with God shows you that you cannot serve Him fully if you are spiritually and physically sick.

That night, I lay in bed and poured my heart out to the Lord:
*"I know You can hear me, Lord. If You don't help me, I'm going to give up on You. I'm stuck. No one believes me when I say I can hear You, and I want to seek You. If You don't help me, I'll give up."*

Suddenly, I heard the sound of glass shattering, as if it had been thrown to the ground. Later, the Lord revealed that something had broken in the spiritual realm. My spiritual ears had been awakened.

It hit me like a wave. I realized I had been seeking permission from people to follow God when all I needed was His approval. I had been repeating the same pattern, trying to earn worth in the eyes of man instead of walking in the identity God had already given me.

The next day, I stepped down from ministry, choosing obedience to God over the approval of man. When the evangelist invited people to surrender their lives the following night, I walked boldly to the altar. In that moment, the Lord reminded me that He alone sees the true intentions of every heart. Later, He promised He would cover my mind with the blood of Jesus, heal my heart, and surround me with people who would reflect His love.

It was the moment the cycle finally broke. I chose to stop performing, stop seeking affirmation in the wrong places, and start following God's voice above every other.

**Forgiveness, Freedom, and Moving Forward**

To this day, I carry no regrets. I have forgiven, repented, and renounced every wrong, both the things I've done and the things done to me, whether willingly or unknowingly. My heart overflows with gratitude to the Lord. Every trial, every tear, and every challenge has become a tool He can now use in His perfect timing to guide me in what to do, and what not to do, as I help others.

I believe the old saying, "People will fail you," can be rewritten as, "With the Lord guiding and realigning my steps, I will not fail." My confidence no longer rests on the opinions of people, but on the voice of God. I encourage others not to lean on my words alone, but to always pray for confirmation from Him. I no longer speak from a place of defeat, but from the power of realignment and the unshakable hope that comes through God's revelation and guidance.

The world may believe God doesn't exist or that He requires perfection, but my life says otherwise. I am living proof that He doesn't need perfection; He simply wants us to show up for Him with honesty, truth, and a willing heart.

Yes, I have been in places where many would judge a woman for putting herself on display. But today, I stand as a living testimony that God can redeem anyone, restore anything, and rewrite any story. My life is no longer marked by where I've been, but by the One who pulled me out and set me on solid ground.

**A Blessing for You**

I share my story so you can see not just where I've been, but the God who met me there, lifted me up, and set my feet on a new path. Every moment, the good, the bad, and the broken, became the reason I chose to change. And when I finally said "yes" to Him, He showed me a truth I now speak over you:

No matter how far you think you've gone, no matter how deep the pit, no matter what labels or lies have been spoken over your life, God can still use you. He can redeem every chapter and turn it into a testimony that points to His glory.

God does not require perfection. He is not waiting for you to clean yourself up before you come. He wants your heart. He wants your "yes." And when you obey His voice, you will see His promises unfold in your life in ways you could never imagine.

I hold tightly to this promise, and I declare it over you today: *"If God is for us, who can be against us?"* **(Romans 8:31)**

May this truth settle deep in your spirit: you are not too far gone. You are not disqualified. You are not forgotten. The same God who fights for you will also restore, redeem, and realign your steps.

I bless you to rise up with courage, to walk boldly into the life He created you to live, and to believe with all your heart that if He could do it for me, He can do it for you too.

## Tracey Castillo

**Instagram**: @evangelistinheels @polestopurpose

# Chapter 6
# Two Carrots & an Apple

*by Magdalena Aguinaga*

*"And we know that in all things God works for the good of those who love him, who have been called according to his purpose."*
— **Romans 8:28 (NIV)**

**The Knock That Carried Grace**

In the delicate hush of an ordinary afternoon, the knock on my door carried the sound of something sacred.

I had just laid my baby down after rocking him through yet another restless stretch. My arms were sore from holding, from carrying, from becoming. The house was still. No TV. No music. Just the occasional creak of the walls and the hum of the refrigerator, a song of loneliness I had come to know too well.

The doorbell startled me. When I opened the door, there she was, Mrs. Lugo, my next-door neighbor. Her face, lined with years and kindness, wore the kind of softness women inherit after decades of quiet endurance. She held out a small plastic bag, inside were two carrots and a single red apple, slightly bruised but vibrant in color.

"You can make papilla for your baby," she said gently, almost whispering. "Boil these… sweeten the apple with cinnamon… maybe add some chicken to the carrots, if you have some."

There was no chicken. But there was her. There was this. This gift. This moment. I could feel she understood.

We didn't say it aloud: I didn't have much in my fridge. In those days, instant noodles were my best friends in all their varieties. I had learned to "upgrade" them with some frozen vegetables, lime juice, and a splash of Tabasco—yum! Those were also the days when I kept wondering how long I could keep pretending everything was okay.

My hands trembled as I took the bag. "Gracias," I managed.

She didn't stay long. She didn't need to. Her gesture carried enough grace to last the rest of the day. We didn't speak of shame. We stood, unknowingly, on sacred ground— the quiet place where women meet at the intersection of despair and divine provision.

When I fed my son that afternoon, watching his tiny hands reach for the spoon and his eyes light up, it felt like I was feeding a king. The steam from the papilla rose in front of his chubby cheeks as he opened his mouth wide with excitement. He didn't know the miracle in his bowl. He just knew he was loved.

## Before the Storm—The Free Spirit Years

In my twenties, I was told I'd never have children. The words were clinical, delivered across a sterile desk with a tone meant to soften the blow. But nothing could soften that kind of finality. Of course, I cried and adjusted the dream.

I poured myself into building a life that looked full enough to forget the quiet ache. A life that sparkled.

Growing up, I wasn't the prettiest or the most popular, but I was always "la buena onda"—the one with the best stories, the open heart, the honest laugh. I had friends from every continent and dinner tables that stretched across languages and wine bottles. I lived in Europe while completing my master's, and our apartment, "el de las mexicanas" con Rox & Gloria, became the meeting point for expats and dreamers.

Later, my passport was filled with stamps from Tokyo to Cusco, from Paris to New York, interacting with people from all walks of life, and among them, I was someone who made people feel safe. Loved. Celebrated.

Back home, the same pattern followed. My place was always open for Sunday brunches, midnight talks, spontaneous road trips. I dated men who would travel hours just to see me for one evening, who sent poems, brought flowers, and made grand gestures. I once broke the heart of a wonderful Italian man who adored me and had even proposed. I didn't know then how to receive that kind of love. Not because I didn't want it, but because I didn't believe I deserved it.

Through it all, there was one constant: my best friend. The most handsome, stylish, funny, fiercely loyal man God could have given me. He was my rock. My chosen brother. His family became mine and mine his. He was the one who carried my suitcases and my heartbreaks. Who made me laugh on balconies overlooking beaches and cities far and close. Eliazar became more than blood, my silent partner. We learned together, grew together, and evolved to the best version of ourselves while dancing and laughing, and so many miles in between dreams. He later became the godfather of my son. Of course he did. Who else could it have been?

That version of me, the globe-trotter, the "buena onda," the one who danced in high heels until sunrise and cried with friends in candlelit cafés, feels like another life. And yet, she still lives in the stories I tell my son. He laughs when I say, "Back then, your mom was a little *loca*, but full of life." He can hardly picture me as anything other than "Mom." But I see his eyes light up, and I know he's proud of the woman I was before, and even prouder of the woman I became after.

For all the fun, all the independence, all the champagne-flavored memories—I was still running.

Running from the ache. From the diagnosis. From the quiet voice that whispered, *"This isn't all there is."*

Then came the night that changed everything.

## The Perfect Day and the Prayer that Changed Everything

It was, by all appearances, the perfect day. The kind of day that makes you pause and think, *"I made it."*

It was a period in my life where I divided my days living between the Valley and New York, the city that always made me feel electric and alive. In those trips, I had discovered the "salsa clubs" under the Brooklyn bridge and had spent a few weekends either on Broadway, shopping on Long Island outlets, or at my boss' Hamptons home.

I was now home in my brand-new house in a foreign land, one I'd bought on impulse without legal residency, but full of hope. I remember the realtor raising her eyebrow when I handed over the documents. I smiled and told her, *"Sometimes, you leap before you land."* And I meant it. I believed that the house was a new level in my life.

The weather that day was just perfect, Autumn in the valley—not too hot, not too humid. The kind of sunshine that filters through palm trees and makes everything bright. I had lunch at my favorite restaurant with one of my mentors, someone who always poured into me with wisdom, laughter, and the occasional glass of good wine. Work was going well.

I was driving my Jeep, windows down, music playing, hair dancing in the breeze. I felt like the leading lady of my own movie.

I remember glancing at the sky through the sunroof and smiling. *"God, thank You. You've been so good to me."*

But later that night, after dinner, something shifted.

I took the trash out, barefoot, wearing one of those oversized T-shirts that mean home. The night air was cool and quiet. The sky above me was velvet and glitter, stars blinking like tiny messengers. And then, in the middle of that peace, it hit me.

A sharp ache. Not in my body, but somewhere deeper. A hollow spot I hadn't noticed before.

*What's the point of all this if I have no one to share it with?*

The house felt too big. The silence, too loud. The perfume of accomplishment that had lingered all day began to fade, replaced by something rawer. Loneliness.

I looked up at the stars and whispered the kind of prayer that doesn't come from the lips, but from the soul.

*"Lord... I am ready to share my life."*

That was all I said. Seven words. Soft, simple, surrendered. But heaven heard me. Let me tell you, our prayers always get answered; they get answered *God's way*.

## The Love that Came Fast and the Life that Changed Everything

Love arrived almost like a reply. He treated me like a queen. Said all the right things. Held doors open. Sent sweet texts. He listened in a way like I was the center of the universe and not just another beautiful distraction.

It felt like something real, or at least something I wanted to believe in.

We moved quickly. Too quickly. We started building a life together, without a plan, but full of passion. I wanted it to work. I wanted the prayer I whispered under the stars to manifest into a fairytale. I clung to that hope even when the cracks began to show.

Then came the pregnancy test. Two lines. Bold. Undeniable. I stared at that tiny strip like it was a doorway. My breath caught in my throat, and tears—heavy and hot—fell before I could speak.

I cried for hours. I cried for joy, for fear, for the ghosts of every diagnosis I'd ever been given. I cried because the impossible had happened.

But I also cried because no one knew.

Not my parents. Not my closest friends. Not even my best friends who had always known everything before I did. It all happened so fast that I hadn't had time to bring anyone into the fold. And now here I was, pregnant and profoundly alone with the truth.

When I finally shared the news, it was as if a bomb had gone off in every direction. The sweetest reaction, I must say, was from Norma, my roommate, best friend, and accomplice. She remained quiet on the phone, but the next day, when she arrived home, she carried the biggest bags of fruits and vegetables I have ever seen. Her actions, as always, spoke of her enormous heart, the kind of heart that now carries the badge of Godmother and forever sister in our lives.

My parents, silent at first, processed it in their own heartbreak. Their daughter, who had once hosted dinners in Paris and worn blazers to boardrooms, was now carrying a child no one had expected, with a man they didn't know. There was no engagement. No ring. No plan.

Still, I clung to hope. Maybe love would catch up to the blessing.

But instead, things got complicated.

I started noticing the gaps, promises that slipped through his fingers, phone calls that made me uneasy, shadows behind his smile. Then came the truth: financial trouble. Debts. A job lost. Lies I hadn't wanted to see.

But I thought I was in love. And when you're in love, especially when you're carrying someone's child, you bargain with yourself. I told myself it would get better, that this was just a rough patch. That we'd make it through. That love could carry us if I carried everything else.

So, I drained my savings to help pay off his debts. I covered the birth expenses. I tried to protect him from the world while protecting our child from the instability that had now entered our home.

Eventually, my job couldn't support my absence, and I was forced to resign. He found temporary work, just enough to pay for the basics. I returned my Jeep to Mexico, a painful goodbye to my independence, and we drove a car he had bought at auction. It had no air conditioning and rattled every time we turned left. But it moved.

And so did we. Barely.

There were happy moments. Ultrasound appointments. Baby kicks. Laughter that floated through the cracks on the days we pretended nothing was wrong. But those were exceptions, not the rule. And many nights I cried myself to sleep, holding my belly and praying for strength. I clearly remember those times I offered my tears to God; I used to say, "Please use these tears so my son's life is filled with laughter and love, please drain all my energy and use it to make him smart and fierce." So I cried without shame.

And I stayed. Because love is patient, right? Because families stick it out. Because I wanted to believe the prayer I had prayed under the stars would lead me here for a reason.

Because I had already given so much, I didn't know how to stop.

## Choosing Single Motherhood and Becoming Stronger Than I Ever Knew

When I finally chose to leave, the label single mother clung to me like a scarlet letter. The decision didn't come with thunder or a dramatic ending; I was just a woman who refused to drown.

The decision came with stillness. With the quiet exhaustion of one who has given it all. With the clarity that crept in after rocking my baby to sleep while his father slept in another room, disconnected, indifferent. It came when I realized I had become both anchor and sail in a ship that was going nowhere.

And so, one summer, just before my baby turned four, I made the decision: I would do this alone. It wasn't heroic. It was survival.

I remember the first person I talked to was my paternal grandmother, Mami Mary. My only living grandparent. I was afraid of the scandal and, to be honest, of the family judgment. But her response was kind and filled me with the courage I needed so desperately: *mejor sola, tú puedes.* No questions, no drama, just reassurance. So I did.

While my son was spending the summer having a blast with my parents in Saltillo, I made arrangements, and he was gone. And in that moment, everything changed. My label changed. My friendships changed. My world shifted.

Some people, especially those who once spoke of grace and faith, withdrew their love quietly, as if my decision had contaminated the purity of their beliefs. To them, *"Good Christian women don't give up."*

But I hadn't given up. I had risen up. And while some doors closed, others opened. Wide.

My chosen family stepped in like an army of angels. My best friend, already my son's godfather, became a daily presence, even in the distance when I was on the verge of tears. New friendships unfolded like the secret troops any new mother needs. We met at the early development classes for babies, and the "gymboritas" became my family. We learned to be moms together, most of us away from our roots, so we depended on each other from sunrise to school and graduation, even to this day.

My new circle didn't judge. They didn't preach. They just showed up.

It was in those days that I began to redefine what family really meant. Blood is sacred—but love, *love is divine.* Love that sits beside you in silence. Love that drops off diapers without asking questions. Love that says, *"You don't owe me an explanation. I'm here."*

And through it all, there was my son.

Mikel.

He was barely out of toddlerhood, but something in him shifted the moment I stood up and claimed our peace. His spirit expanded. His gaze changed. His little arms hugged tighter, as if he knew I needed anchoring.

He became "the little man" of the house overnight.

He started checking the locks at night, making sure the kitchen light was off, reminding me, "Mommy, don't forget your keys." And later, when he was barely tall enough to reach the counter, he would ask to learn to cook with me. Who would have thought that was the beginning of something so big? His little hands, his words, and his actions reminded me, "You can do it, mamá."

He knew.

Even now, he doesn't always remember the details of those early years, but his protective instinct never left. He walks on the street side of the sidewalk. He says, "Text me when you get there" with a tone that echoes something deeper, something inherited from the weight we carried together.

He grew up faster than other kids. He had to.

And while that truth aches sometimes, I also know this: the boy I raised is becoming the man I once prayed for.

**God in the Details—The Miracles in the Mundane**

We often imagine miracles as thunderous events, dramatic and undeniable, announced by angels. But in my life, God came softly.

He showed up in the gentle details. The quiet timing. The unexpected kindness.

I was raised in a good home. My father, a provider in every sense, gave me a childhood wrapped in security and soft privilege. I was the *niña bien* among my friends, the girl who changed cars every couple of years, who didn't know what it meant to go without. My parents built that world for me with sacrifice and love. So when life flipped, and they saw me struggling as a new mother without a partner, their heartbreak was silent but fierce.

They lived in Saltillo, three hours away, and made the trip often. My mother would bring groceries from Mexico, things that reminded me of home and dignity, and invite us to eat out, saying "our treat," even when I knew they were stretching to do so.

But what broke me every time was what I found later: a folded bill tucked between Psalms and Proverbs in my Bible. A silent blessing from my mamá. She never mentioned it. She never needed to. It became her sacred tradition, to leave a little hope in the Word when words failed. It was her way of providing without provoking shame, of honoring me as a mother while protecting me as her child.

There was also the worship song that came on when I wanted to give up, just as I was praying in my car, tears spilling, hands gripping the wheel as if that grip could hold together my life. The lyrics spoke of surrender, of strength not our own, of a God who restores. And in that moment, I didn't just hear the song, I felt it fill the cracks inside me.

There were Scriptures taped to my fridge, words written on sticky notes in exhausted handwriting during nights I couldn't sleep.

*"The Lord is close to the brokenhearted."*

*"Be still and know that I am God."*

*"I will never leave you nor forsake you."*

I would recite them aloud while washing dishes, folding laundry, or staring into the mirror, wondering if I would ever feel like myself again. Over time, they stopped sounding like promises for someone else and started becoming truths I could stand on.

There were friends who dropped off groceries without calling, others who messaged late at night just to say, *"Thinking of you. Keep going."*

Even the cinnamon on the boiled apples became holy. The smell reminded me of home, of tradition, of something sweet still possible. I would watch my son eat, and I'd whisper a gratitude prayer over him, a declaration that he would grow up to be kind, to be protected, to be different.

Little by little, the girl who had once been buried under bills, heartbreak, and silence began to rise again. Not suddenly. Not triumphantly. But steadily. My healing came in layers.

In therapy sessions where I finally said the words I was afraid of. In budgeting spreadsheets that made me feel in control again. In laughter with my son at the park—the kind that bubbles up out of nowhere and makes you forget the weight of the world.

In holding him through the night when he had nightmares or when he was sick, and in realizing that I no longer feared.

And I would be remiss not to mention the gift God gave me through my work. For over fifteen years, my job has been one of the few constants in my life—a source not just of income, but of dignity, growth, and grace. My boss and coworkers became part of my quiet safety net. They offered support when I didn't have words to ask for it, and stability when everything else was crumbling. Through every season, my work anchored me. Looking back, I now understand, it wasn't just a job. It was divine provision.

God was not in the earthquake. He was not

in the fire. He was in the whisper. And that whisper

was enough.

**Legacy and the Woman I've Become**

Twelve years later, I sit at my desk with a cup of coffee and a heart that has learned how to hold both grief and grace in the same breath.

Sometimes, I catch a glimpse of myself in the mirror and barely recognize her, the woman I've become. She is softer in spirit, guided by logic but still with the honest laugh, and her eyes hold both strength and tenderness.

Now, writing these pages, I wonder: if the girl from the perfect day under the stars could see me now, what would she think? Would she be proud? Would she be afraid?

I think she'd be surprised. Not because I survived, but because I've learned to thrive.

That woman who once danced through airports and rooftop parties now hosts healing circles and business strategy calls. She helps other women reclaim their voice in multicultural workplaces, using every story she's lived as a tool for transformation. She no longer hides the cracks. She lets the light shine through them.

And at the center of it all… is Mikel. My son. My miracle. My legacy.

He is not just the reason I kept going; he is the living proof that love can rebuild anything.

There's something sacred in the way he looks at me, not just with affection, but with reverence. He knows our story. He's heard the late-night anecdotes, the travel tales, the heartbreaks. He knows who I was before and who I chose to become. And in his eyes, I see pride.

He knows how to make a bed, cook his own meals, and walk a woman safely to her car. He holds the door open not because he was told to, but because he watched his mother do everything with honor. He's the kind of young man who prays before exams, who cries during heartfelt speeches, who hugs without rushing.

Mikel didn't grow up with a traditional father figure, but he was never without strong male love. My father and my brother became his examples of what real men look like. Gentle, but bold. Protective, but kind. Faithful in their words and actions. My brother has always been my anchor. He's the one I call when I'm scared, when I'm confused, when I need truth spoken with love but without hesitation. He's my mother's favorite (and rightfully so), a devoted father, and one of the most brilliant minds I know. His strength and clarity have carried me through more storms than I can count, and to Mikel, he's not just Tío. He's a blueprint. A mirror of what's possible. A man who proves that masculinity can be holy.

Thanks to both of them, Mikel knows that strength has nothing to prove.

I've also taught him what I wish someone had taught me: That God isn't waiting for us to be perfect, He's waiting for us to be willing. The world will try to define us, but we get to decide who we become. That asking for help is not a weakness. It's holy.

And above all. I've taught him that love—real, love—is not performative. It doesn't abandon you when things get hard. It doesn't shame you when you fall. It picks you up, wipes your tears, and stays.

That is the legacy I want to leave: that I turned survival into service. That I rose, and then I reached back to pull others with me.

## To the Reader—A Love Letter to the Woman in the Valley

To the woman holding this book with trembling hands, unsure whether to laugh or cry, I see you.

You, who smiles in public and weeps in secret.

You, who feels like you're failing but keeps waking up anyway.

You, who once had a vision for your life that looks nothing like what you're living now.

You are not alone.

I wrote this for you.

Not because I have it all figured out, but because I've stood where you're standing. I've sat on the bathroom floor asking God, *"Why did You choose me for this?"* I've stared at the ceiling in the middle of the night, wondering how much longer I could keep going.

And still, I'm here. And still, you're here. That means God isn't finished.

Please don't believe the lie that your mistakes disqualify you, that your past defines you or that you are behind.

The truth is: You are chosen. You are being rebuilt. You are the daughter of a King who sees you, even when others look away.

Let Him meet you in the ordinary.

In the sink full of dishes.

In the crumbs on the car seat.

In the bedtime story, you read even though you're exhausted.

In the neighbor's knock.

In the cinnamon on the apples.

You don't have to wait until you feel holy to be held by God. He will hold you as you are.

And one day, not too far from now, you'll tell your own story. You'll carry your own torch. And another woman will walk by the light you leave behind.

So here, querida mía, take this:

You are loved.

You are worthy.

You are enough.

And sometimes, it only takes a glorious sister to give you the courage to tell your story, and with it, the reminder that God also comes in the form of two carrots and an apple.

*"And my God will supply all your needs according to His riches in glory in Christ Jesus."* (Philippians 4:19).

**Magdalena Aguinaga**

**Instagram:** @thecqcoach

# Section Two

# The Altar

*"Present your bodies as a living sacrifice, holy and acceptable to God, which is your spiritual worship."*
**– Romans 12:1**

The altar is where everything shifts. It's the moment we stop clinging and start releasing, when our hands open and our hearts whisper, *"Lord, have Your way."*

Surrender does not always come easy. It often comes after we've exhausted every other option, after pride has failed us, after control has slipped through our fingers. And yet, in this vulnerable posture, God does His greatest work.

The women in this section know the weight of surrender. They've laid their dreams, their fears, their mistakes, and their grief on the altar of God's love. And what they discovered is this: surrender is not the end of you, it's the beginning of Him in you.

As you step onto the altar with them, may you find the courage to release what you've been holding too tightly. Because the altar is not where you lose your life; it's where you finally discover it.

# Chapter 7
# Erica's Road to Surrender & Mercy

*by Erica Hernandez Castillo*

*"But he said to me, 'My grace is sufficient for you, for my power is made perfect in weakness.' Therefore I will boast all the more gladly about my weaknesses, so that Christ's power may rest on me."*
— **2 Corinthians 12:9 (NIV)**

**Opening Prayer**

Dear Heavenly Father, I want to thank you for giving me the courage and opportunity to share my personal testimony with the people reading this book. I ask that you give me the right words and details, so that I can touch their hearts. I ask that the Holy Spirit comfort them as they intake my words in hope that it helps lead them to You. Instill in them that they are not alone, for You are always with them. Father, I promise to always give You all praise and glory. In Your name I pray. Amen!

**When Innocence Meets Reality**

Mini minds run wild with imagination, often dreaming about getting married and having a family. Innocence possesses a light brighter than a sunny spring morning, so we don't stop and think about the possibility of divorce or being single moms.

Unfortunately, it happens to the best of us. But if only at a young age we were taught that not all things last forever, we would be able to mentally prepare ourselves for when seasons run dry. How is it that some find their way out of murky waters and others get stuck in the mud? Could faith have something to do with it? Glory be to God that I am one of those who is learning how to navigate through headwinds. I continuously grasp how God's love is merciful and everlasting, even when I fall short. Staying steadfast in my faith has helped me overcome adversity, and surrender has been the golden seed that has been patiently waiting within me for the right light to blossom, thus helping me bloom into who I am today.

Inevitably, getting there has come with challenges; however, nothing God didn't think I could handle.

**The Summer Everything Changed**

Sadly, many years ago, in a scorching summer month, my family fell apart. Although it was disastrous, it was the start of a growing faith. Learning that my ex-husband had filed for divorce was devastating. Contrary to the sadness, it was the rise of my personal relationship with God. Be certain that I am not going to speak ill of my children's father; in fact, because of his bold move, I was able to change many things about myself that weren't pleasing to God, which turned me into a better person.

Years after the divorce, I started to reflect on my own conduct during the marriage and began to take accountability for self-inflicted shortcomings. I started to focus on the things I had done wrong in the marriage. When I pivoted towards my own bearing and concentrated on the things that I contributed, I began to heal and no longer felt resentment towards him. Shortly after that, my life began to change. Had I done that earlier, my relationship with my kids could have been healthier, stronger, with more pleasant memories, but it didn't happen that way. Unbeknownst to me, I was in desperate need of change. For that reason, God needed to work on me first before I could serve others.

**When I Started Recognizing His Hand**

God began to reveal His love for me in different fragments in my life, but it took me a while to comprehend that it was Him. It takes getting to know Him to understand. I would say things like "what a coincidence" because I was oblivious that it was Him; because of that, I didn't realize the significance of giving credit to the One who makes it all happen. In Proverbs 3:6, it proclaims, "In all your ways acknowledge Him, and he will make your path straight." This declares that giving God praise for His work, will lead to a righteous path, and a plow of blessings.

Without a doubt, I believe that there is a seed planted deep in our core waiting to be accepted and nurtured; so, when fully grown, it can fulfill its purpose. In my opinion, life is not supposed to be easy. We are not guaranteed a perfect life. Loss, turmoil, and setbacks are a must to grow stronger in our faith and rely on God for strength. My life turned upside-down in July 2009. Well, now I can say it turned the right side up. That sneaky summer, I trampled into a new chapter of single motherhood. I had four kids, three of whom were teenagers, plus a house to maintain. My job was not equipped to financially support a family of five; the child support was not enough. But even with that uncertainty, God put it in my heart to enroll in college full-time. It's truly remarkable how I convinced myself I could pull it off without having a clue. I was working part-time, only bringing home $7,000 a year—on top of which I didn't even own a computer! I was clueless as to how I was going to pay my bills, but something deep inside of me whispered that everything was going to be okay- the Holy Spirit, indeed. At that point, nothing anyone would have declared could have convinced me otherwise. In my case, I had no one cheering me on, no women's support group like the ones we have now. God rooted the idea of college within me because it was all part of one big plan. To the world, it was impossible, but to Him attainable.

The Bible reads in Matthew 19:26, *"With man this is impossible, but with God all things are possible."* Listening to Him was life-changing! Bachelor's in English and a minor in Reading with a concentration in middle school education. Fast forward, I now have a real estate license and own a trademark for a golf business I started as well. Through many prayers of hope and strength, I was able to overcome many obstacles. Faith is an undeniable force that can move mountains and overcome all the negative noise that says you can't, simply by believing in Him.

**No Gas. No Food. No Light. No Problem.**

No gas, No food, No light. No problem! College life felt like a permanent splinter piercing right underneath my feet. Emailing my professors that I couldn't make class due to no gas in my truck was like playing Russian Roulette. My gas was sacred; therefore, I needed every drop.

Fortunately, my professors understood, but despite that, life continued to be a battlefield. I had to keep myself fueled to be able to keep marching- affordable food brought some comfort to the situation. The two-for-one burritos were life-changing! Unhealthy, but enough. There were times after football games when I managed to take my kids to McDonald's for a happy meal; still, I didn't have enough money to get myself something from the menu. When the kids would ask why I wasn't eating, I convincingly replied that I had eaten earlier.

Watching them laugh and have a good time was plenty for me. We weren't always that lucky. There were moments at home where I had to get creative with the meals or dig to figure it out. During one desperate moment, I searched my kitchen for food, determined not to ask my ex-husband for another $5 Little Caesars pizza. I remember crying out, "Oh my God, what am I going to do?!" Then, as I opened the kitchen cabinet door, there lay a brand-new sealed loaf of bread. I remember it so vividly; I could not believe my eyes! I vowed that I didn't have any bread. In that moment, I knew it was a miracle and just carried on. But as I grew stronger in my faith, I realized from whom that miracle came, it was God's mercy displayed right before my eyes.

Now I understand, in that moment God wanted me to rely on Him and no one else. A couple of times our light was shut off, and I stayed home alone or at a friend's house. I once sent my kids to their grandparents, who lived down the street. I didn't want to ask, but I had no choice. Each time I prayed, each desperate time God provided.

**God in the Dark**

With just a candle on, I silently lay in the dark. Truly, it was one of the best times I had with God. Often, when we struggle and God provides, we are so caught up in the misfortune that we fail to recognize the good He has done. I was blind in those moments. He wanted me to be tranquil and believe in Him. Philippians 4:6 teaches us to ask, it says, *"Do not be anxious about anything, but in everything by prayer and petition, with thanksgiving, present your request to God."* Calmness is not a superpower; it just requires individual will and faith that God will provide. It can transform uncertainty into a crystal-clear kaleidoscope.

**Provision, People, and Purpose**

In retrospect, all the people I connected with during that time were meant to be in my path. For example, Mr. and Mrs. Lizcano, whose house I was renting, were part of that blessing. They guided me by showing me how to apply for Housing and were very patient in the process.

Not only was I able to keep my kids in the same schools and house we were currently in, but it also encouraged me to stay in school. It still amazes me that I registered for college before even applying to the housing program! It's all about trusting the process. The Lizcanos, God rest their souls, played a pivotal role in my life. I was also blessed with amazing neighbors who helped me with one thing or another, and they did it gracefully and willingly. It was the perfect spot for us. God knew the desires in my heart, and He provided. *"For I know the plans I have for you," declares the Lord, "plans to prosper you and not harm you, plans to give you hope for the future."* (Jeremiah 29:11)

Roadblocks will be constant in our lives, but they are there to mold us into who we are meant to be; everyone He places around us plays a significant part in one way or another. Even though the Lizcanos' home was a blessing, I still faced many challenges. For example, the divorce affected my kids tremendously, each in different ways. If only I had the right tools during this loss, I could've helped carry their cross.

Often, when we are going through a divorce, we unintentionally focus on our own feelings and the struggles we are facing in that moment, and we tend to forget the warriors who are experiencing it right next to us, our kids. When there are children involved in a marriage and that marriage is headed for divorce, it is no longer between A and B. The divorce now involves A, B, C, and D. It affects the children emotionally, financially, and it disrupts their routine. On top of which, they need time to mourn and somewhat heal. Don't minimize their hurt. We must break the chains that hold us down in the relationships of those we love. Inevitably, their innocence gets apprehended somewhere in the middle of the storm. Adults get caught in barbed wire trying to get loose at the same time, heal from the bleeding wounds; they become entangled trying to physically, emotionally, and mentally survive. How is this intentional?

**Resilience or Survival?**

Most say that kids are resilient, but in times like this, I don't think they have a choice. Kids are great at hiding their feelings, and what looks like "resilience" may just be an empty facade. Some become overachievers, and others may turn to addictions, whatever that may be. They dangerously suppress their feelings by staying busy. I learned that while we are praising them for all their hard work and achievements, their pain lingers on like a plague. I wish I knew then what I know now. There are many situations in my life that I regret, but the one that has taken the longest to get over has been the lack of awareness of my kids' torment and everything they faced during and after the divorce. It was reckless! With an enormous amount of regret, now I understand what my daughter Ashley meant when she poured her troubled heart out to us while she lay crying in her closet on the cold floor, "What about what we want?!" I remember it like it was just yesterday.

Sammy went from being the top reader to being withdrawn and took on his own way of healing. Andrew was small and was confused about what was going on; he became extremely discouraged. My oldest, Allison, was almost a mom to them and carried so much weight on her shoulders. I hate that my kids were left to deal with their emotions all on their own. If I could turn back time, I would stop everything just to ask how they are doing or what I could do to help them heal. If this is your current situation, I pray that our misfortune changes the narrative in your kids' lives. If I can spare a mom from future heartaches with her children by sharing, then I know that my regrets were fate to spare someone else's. Kids deserve their feelings to be acknowledged; mine deserved it too. I long for forgiveness. This was a time when they needed me the most, and I failed. See, God blessed me with four kids, and it was my duty to make sure they were okay, and I fell short. However, in my belief, it's never too late to make things better. Don't quit because of some rejection. Remember that everyone copes and heals differently. Keep an open mind. Everyone has a right to be heard. Don't wait, seek out your kids. God granted me mercy, and he will do the same for you-progressively.

**When Church Wasn't Enough**

I believe that the aftermath of a divorce sometimes leaves people walking around like zombies- living without being alive. At the time, I thought I was doing my part in helping my kids feel better by taking them to Sunday Mass and CCD. Now I know that attending church had nothing to do with what my children needed from me. I had an obligation to fulfill, but I was emotionally unaware. While my kids were doing their best to live in the moment, even making it to Mass took everything I had. They never knew that sometimes I could hardly wait to get home from church, lock myself in my room, and bawl until I couldn't anymore. I took them to church because I was terrified that if I didn't, they would fall apart, but they had no idea what I was up against. I was trying to save them while no one was trying to save me, that's how it appeared to be then. Silent sacrifices sometimes go unnoticed. It was difficult for me to attend the same church as my ex-in-laws, but I did it for my kids. I tried my best not to interrupt their entire being, especially in that regard.

    People's body language and stares at church were one of "why are you still here?" But on the other hand, God had placed a constant desire in my heart to attend that specific church- it was a divine thread and spiritual connection in which I had absolutely no clue about at that time. Just like God was molding me in that moment, I know He was doing the same for my kids. Flashbacks about my tough church experiences back then are slowly becoming foggy; that confirms that God heals the wounded. Doing what's best for the kids requires attention to all aspects of their lives. I've come to realize how important it is to take time for the kids' mental well-being, just like we do for their physical health. It's part of keeping them whole. Psalm 127:3 states, *"Children are a gift from the Lord; they are a reward from Him."* Yes, life becomes overwhelming, but focusing on what you can do to make the kids well might help you in the process. My depression and anxiety attacks encouraged me to continue attending church. I was desperate for help from the scary thoughts that poisoned my mind. I sought medical help from a doctor, and he put me on medication, but they gave me worse thoughts, so I decided to get off them and try to do it on my own. But this is me; everyone is different and has different medical needs. *Please seek your doctor's advice.* I prayed, but not as intentionally as I do now, yet it still worked. My coping strategy was to keep busy with the kids, work, and college. Just like church, I continued to allow my girls to participate in cheer, band, drama, etc. My boys, Andrew and Sam, continued with football and basketball.

Somehow, I managed to do so financially. This reminds me of when I was little and desperately wanting something yet knew we couldn't afford it. Mom would always say, "Si Diosito quiere." She still uses it! That small phrase gave me so much hope because I knew Diosito was something big. My heart managed to hold on to it, especially when times were tough. I know this because as I continued to struggle and was mentally drained, I remained praying for strength and patience, and everything according to His will. Because of Him, I was able to keep all four in extracurricular activities and sports. Through prayer and church, I found the inspiration and charge I needed to keep going and continue to do what we were already used to doing as a family.

**The Retreat that Changed Everything**

One day, my church announced an all-women retreat. The desire to go was deeply planted in my heart, but there was one big problem—money! When I realized that there was a fee to attend, suddenly that urge no longer existed- so I thought. The human mind plays tricks on us, especially when our current situation is delicate. Evil thrives in darkness; therefore, it tries to sneak in to confuse us, especially when we are striving for righteousness. For this reason, we tend to think that things are impossible, but God's plan overrides all of ours. His commands contradict the human mind. Therefore, He places people in our path to assist in making things happen, like my friends and Sisters in Christ, Sandy and Gina.

One day at Mass, they both offered to help pay a deposit for the retreat so I could attend. I can't remember who I hesitantly said *okay* to, but I feel God purposely blocked that from my mind because He wanted me to focus on their kindness and nothing else. Although I felt embarrassed to take the money, when one reached and touched my shoulder, she gently grabbed my hand and placed the cash in it; I couldn't help but confirm with a "thank you." They had me hooked like fishermen!

Once again, God provided and made what I most needed happen. For that reason, it was essential that I keep my faith strong, especially when things went wrong. Bumpy roads can sometimes be unavoidable and can make life confusing, causing people to lose faith, but learning to rely on God can shift the whys to why not.

Unfortunately, there are tidal waves that creep up when God is working on us; they try to drown us, hoping to paralyze His will. The day of the send-off, I had no sitter and no money. I had to pay the remaining balance of the retreat. I felt defeated and incredibly sad. About an hour before it was time to set sail, I asked my oldest daughter, Allison, to please ask her dad one last time if he could watch them for the weekend, so that I could attend, and by the grace of God, he finally agreed. However, there was one more hurdle to overcome—the bank! I knew there was no cash in the account sitting around at my disposal, and I was reluctant to check. Looking back, I now understand that it was the Holy Spirit encouraging me to call and check my balance. check my balance. There's no other explanation since, without a doubt, I was broke. When I finally had the courage to call and learned that I had the exact amount I needed, excitement swam through my veins, parting them from everything within me like the Red Sea did the Israelites.

In that moment, I seized anything I could get my hands on and dashed my way to St. Anne's. I had less than thirty minutes to get there. When I arrived, I sprinted in, wrote a check, and off I went to one of the most memorable spiritual experiences of my life! Romans 8:28 explains, "And we know that in all things God works for the good of those who love him, who have been called according to His purpose." Unfortunately, like the Israelites, it took many more downfalls for me to understand that God's love is not to be taken for granted. I remember hesitating when I handed the check to the church lady because I was still in disbelief. Why me?

**The Power of Forgiveness**

God has been so merciful and loving, even at times when I have felt unworthy. This demonstrates how forgiving He is, and the reason why I am working overtime trying to master how to forgive those who have hurt me. It's a struggle and very challenging most of the time because my Earthly ways get in the way, but that's why I'm determined to learn. Although I was so upset at my kids' dad for not saying yes, the first time, I learned that forgiving him was part of my healing, and essential for my eternal salvation. I am not perfect, but neither is the world we live in; therefore, I must remind myself of God's grace to me. What I am most grateful for is being subconsciously aware of my failures because it reminds me to be patient with others. Accountability has helped me heal by learning that EVERYONE makes mistakes, and in turn, it has brought some peace to my family. In my belief, it has shown my kids that I take responsibility for where I went wrong. Although I am working on the right words, my actions now are an unspoken, remorseful way of expressing my sincere apologies. In my belief, it shows them how much I love them, hoping to heal the broken heart. Moreover, when we heal old wounds, we can better serve those around us.

Letting go of the past assisted me in creating a more peaceful way of life with my kids and their father; we can coexist. It's nice to be able to get together for celebrations and see that my kids are comfortable and enjoying the moment. It creates that emotional shift that most parents long for after a divorce. We will always experience disappointment, especially from those we love. But in time, it leads us to a much better place where we see a warmer reflection of ourselves in our children's eyes, no matter how long it takes. God wants us to love and be loved. Confirmation is evident in the people He unites. People get discouraged at times, but I promise it is all done at the perfect time and moment. When I learned to concentrate on my own mistakes, work on myself, and then forgive myself, that's when God knew it was time. He waited for me to finish college because He knew a huge distraction was about to enter my life.

**Betrayal Before Bliss**

Two months after I graduated, I met a guy who later played a significant role in my life. It didn't come easy; I had to experience betrayal before bliss. In July 2013, a friend unexpectedly invited me to dinner with a group of ladies. I felt out of place because they were professionals, and I was just getting started. Still, I got out of my comfort zone and went.

 During the meal, I started feeling uneasy and saw dark clouds creeping in. A strange conversation began among them; the body language was loud—the cues foreshadowed betrayal. See, at the time, I was getting to know someone who appeared to be a "nice guy." It wasn't serious, but my friend knew there was some interest because of the details I shared with her. Immediately, one began by asking another if she was "talking" to anyone, and the other one responded yes.

 The instigator persisted in announcing his name, but the accomplice hesitated to do so. At that point, I looked at my friend and signaled with confusion. She gestured to wait and observe; right when she did that, I knew I was being set up. When the lady began the unnecessary details, I knew exactly who she was talking about. By coincidence, it was the same guy I was having conversations with. In that moment, it felt like I was sharing a meal with Judas Iscariot. It wasn't like I was in love or attached to him. **That wasn't the point.** My heart was shattered! Betrayal is a girl's worst enemy. It paralyzes us. I could have said something to join the conversation, but my defense has always been to sit, observe, and learn. I wasn't hurt by them because I barely knew them; however, because I loved my friend like a sister, I felt wounded. Still, I continued my friendship with her.

This is why forgiveness is necessary and should be a way of living. She, too, has committed herself to serving God and has been a great prayer friend whom I have joined at church every now and then. The details of what transpired at dinner are not as important as what happened later that night, and sharing this with you is not to gossip, rather to explain my personal testimony about how God sometimes presents love in the most unpredictable times, even times when it's a bit painful. Amazing things happen when you surrender to God, especially when you are the most confused. This should be drilled at a young age. In moments of despair, surrender occurs naturally because we have no other choice, but afterwards we experience God's blessings.

That same evening, my friend convinced me to go to a country club called *Hillbilly's* (Hill's for short) to listen to live music. I conditioned only if she would drive all the way back to my house for my boots, hoping it would discourage her since we lived in a different city, but she agreed, and there we were.

On our way to Hills, I kept thinking about what I had just experienced. Instantly, I realized how naive I was. I was dumbfounded about how well this guy played his cards. What a gift! Either way, deception wasn't going to ruin my night. Feeling defeated and a bit overwhelmed, I stopped right outside the door of the honky-tonk and prayed. I said, God, if you want me to be single for the rest of my life, I am perfectly okay with that. I promise. I will do as you please, but please take the wheel. I will never forget this prayer and moment. We walked in and stood in the center talking. Five minutes later, I see a couple I knew at the entrance paying to get in. They came straight to say hi, walked away, and five minutes later, the wife came back and introduced me to the man I would marry two years later. The details that transpired after that will be written later in a memoir.

For now, God's love and mercy are the focus. We have to learn to trust Him in every situation, even if it's painful. It is not easy to do. That's why you need to ask God to show you the way, and He will. Pray for patience in everything and anything. That's what brought me to where I am today. Is my life perfect? No. Is my marriage perfect? No. Only Heaven knows where life will take us and where we'll end up. Are adult children a walk in the park? Absolutely not. But through prayer and surrender He makes everything right according to His plan. We don't know what the future holds and the rest of God's plan; the only thing that's certain is His love. Did you know that the tougher life gets and the hardest things we endure are building us into the warriors God needs us to be? I used to question Him all the time when terrible things happened.

Now I say, "I trust you, Lord." The journey leading to Him has been long. There's been curved roads with many stop signs, long stoplights that never turned green, dark alleys with no light in sight, and several thunderstorms. But no matter how difficult the situation, I have always turned back to Him.

**A Relationship Like No Other**

I have learned that a relationship with God is very personal, and it is one that is between Him and me and no one else, just like a marriage, a parental relationship, or someone very dear to you. Those relationships we love and hold so close to our hearts that we don't share the most intimate details are the perfect example of what your relationship in faith should be between you and Him. Because I have risen in light about people being created with a purpose and know that the Holy Spirit lives within them, I think twice about judging others or making them any less than what God created them to be.

Looking down on others is like looking down on Jesus. This concept has truly made me think twice about being hateful and judgmental. Yes, because I am human, I will have moments where my feelings take over. I am not perfect; only God is. But through prayer and repentance, God has shown me grace and mercy. I don't worry like I used to, nor do I sit around praying that God show those who hurt me a lesson. I just worry about fixing myself and taking responsibility for where I went wrong. Life always has consequences for bad behavior, so I just let God handle things at His own time.

My concentration has shifted to evaluating my actions and what I can do to better serve others. I don't let others dim the light He ignited. I do it for Him. I take the punches for Him. I receive the ridicule for Him. I take the rejection for Him. Because I know He protects those who love Him, none of those things scare me. Does it make me feel bad, or at times break my heart, of course. I have human emotions, and I walk on land where evil exists; for that reason, I always remind myself to run back to the Holy Father.

**God's Plan > My Plan**

I have concluded that the more I endure, the bigger plan He has for me, which excites me with anticipation for what's to come. It took me forty-eight years to get to where I am, and I'm still learning and growing, so don't get discouraged with anything and everything. Pray and give your time to Him, so that you can get to know him. Give him a chance, the way you want others to do for you. The difference between our plans and His is that His leads to Purpose. Open your heart to the wonderful possibilities that He has already connected to your name.

Remember that "He knew you before you were born." Evaluate that one and see where it leads you. There are more blessings God has granted me through the years. In quiet moments and throughout the day, I give thanks and praise. Just as I have learned to acknowledge Him in all things good and bad, I have learned to confess my weaknesses, which lifted some weight off my shoulders. I am taking accountability and walking in a brighter light.

Because rewriting the past is not an option, I am learning how to humble my way back into my children's hearts by changing how I do things now. I've learned that change is a delicate process, yet a powerful one.

In my heart, I know my grandchildren are my second chance to make things right, my hope for a better tomorrow, and they mean the world to me. People often say that the love for grandchildren is unlike any other. Well, I can attest to that. I see rainbows and butterflies when I am with them. They make me feel alive and will continue to do so when I am no longer here.

Remembering all the people who helped me throughout my seasons has inspired me to do the same for others. I am taking the knowledge and skills God has blessed me with and adopting philanthropy in my philosophy about doing His work for His people on Earth. In addition, the opportunity for a second chance at love has reminded me of the ways not to be and the things that are right.

**Mercy Through Surrender**

Forgiving myself and others has helped me heal, and in doing so, I have experienced His mercy. Learning that surrender is not just an abstract idea, but an action that leads to all Godly goods, such as love, patience, forgiveness, self-awareness, and the ability to serve His people. Philippians 4:13 confirms, *"I can do everything through Him who gives me strength."* This testifies that He was the One who made it possible for me, thus making it possible to share it with you, so that you can do the same for someone else. Do your part and surrender all your burdens to God and experience His grace poured onto you.

**Closing Prayer**

I hold your hand. I invite you to my past. I grant a season of my life. Be still... Inhale, Feel. Release my hand. Lead with your own light. No more rose-colored film. We share, but He leads. Our hearts need Him to see. Listen... Follow, Repeat.

With Sincere Love & Hope—Your Sister in Christ,
**Erica H. Castillo**

**Erica Hernandez Castillo**

**Instagram:** @ericah492

# Chapter 8
# From Doing to Being: My Journey to Surrender

*by Giselle Dominique Mascarenhas – Villareal*

*"You will seek me and find me when you seek me with all your heart."*
—Jeremiah 29:13 (NIV)

### Eliza's Introduction

I grew up in the church, not just attending services, but absorbing a culture that, while rooted in the Word, often centered more on caution than compassion. We were fluent in Christianese - phrases like "guard your heart" (Proverbs 4:23), "test every spirit" (1 John 4:1), and "come out from among them" (2 Corinthians 6:17). All scripture. But sometimes, scripture delivered without the proper context turns into fear instead of freedom, wounding instead of healing.

I was taught to be wary of people who spoke differently about faith. If someone said "the Universe," I was told it meant they didn't really know God. But the truth is, many people are still searching. They're trying to describe a divine presence they haven't yet encountered personally. Romans 1:20 says that "since the creation of the world, God's invisible qualities... have been clearly seen, being understood from what has been made." So maybe when someone says "the Universe," they're responding to that quiet pull of creation, still groping toward truth, still waiting for someone to show them that the force they feel has a name, a face, and a heartbeat: Jesus.

I was also taught that meditation was dangerous. That it would open the door to deception. And yet, scripture calls us into meditation. Psalm 1:2 says the blessed one is the one whose *"delight is in the law of the Lord, and who meditates on His law day and night."* Joshua 1:8 says, *"Keep this Book of the Law always on your lips; meditate on it day and night."* Psalm 46:10 calls us to "Be still, and know that I am God." Stillness. Reflection. Intimacy with God. These are not new-age ideas, they are ancient Biblical commands. We've just forgotten them.

And then there was the distortion around love. Especially self-love. Somewhere, I absorbed the belief that loving yourself was selfish. Maybe even sinful. But when Jesus said, *"Love your neighbor as yourself"* (Mark 12:31), He made it clear: you can't give to others what you've never received for yourself. If we can't learn to see ourselves through God's eyes, how can we reflect His love to anyone else?

Oh, and money. *"You cannot serve both God and mammon"* (Matthew 6:24) was used to scare away from success, as if every financial blessing was a spiritual risk. But mammon isn't only money, it's misplaced trust. The problem isn't abundance. It's allegiance.

Then came Giselle.

A woman full of color, passion, and light who practiced many of the things I had once judged: meditation, self-love, manifestation, the "Universe." Had I still had my head buried in the religious sand, I would've missed her entirely.

Giselle wasn't just a new friend. She was a divine assignment. A soul too radiant to ignore. And instead of pulling her into my world, God used our friendship to meet her in hers. Not through rules, but through relationship. Not through fear, but through love. I didn't hand her a sermon; I gave her space to experience Him.

This is the story of that encounter. Of how a God who breaks every box used a deeply imperfect vessel like me to reach one of His fiercest, most vibrant daughters.

Thank God He had already started peeling away those religious blindfolds. God was showing me that we don't introduce people to Him by shrinking their light—we do it by reflecting His.

And through a friendship, not a sermon, Giselle met Jesus. Not the one religion warned her about, but the One who had been pursuing her heart all along.

This is her story.

**Giselle's Story**
**The Resistance**

For as long as I can remember, I've had a knowing. A quiet certainty in my spirit that what I dreamed of, what I felt, would eventually come to life. I didn't grow up with perfect peace, but I had something better: a divine calm that wrapped around me like a whisper. I didn't have the words for it then, but I know now... that was God.

He lived in the stillness, in the secret places of my heart, in the way I'd feel safe even when the world around me felt unstable. It was a presence, steady and sacred, that held me in a way nothing else could. I had no doubt that I was connected to something greater than myself.

But when I got married to my daughter's father, I lost myself in a toxic relationship. That inner knowing, the clarity I had carried since childhood, was consumed by fear, shame, and self-doubt. I may have looked put together, even glamorous from the outside, but inside, I was drifting. I had lost my anchor. I had lost my connection to God within me.

Still, I never stopped praying. I've prayed to God for as long as I can remember. I've always been spiritual, intuitive, grounded in something bigger. But if I'm being honest, I didn't trust religious people. The performance of it all made me deeply uncomfortable. The big, showy prayers felt like auditions. The scriptures are thrown around like weapons. The energy was off. It didn't feel holy. It felt strategic.

Whenever someone quoted scripture or prayed out loud like they were on a stage, I'd roll my eyes and think: You're probably having an affair. Scamming someone. Doing something shady behind closed doors. I just didn't trust it. At the church I sometimes went to as a kid, I'd see families I knew secrets about acting like saints. It felt fake, like church was just another place to be seen, to impress, to posture.

I learned early on that religion could be used as a mask. A weapon. A way to control others or elevate oneself. I didn't reject God; I rejected that version of Him.

My grandmother, on the other hand, prayed constantly. Her house was filled with crosses, rosaries, novenas, and whispered blessings over meals and moments. One afternoon when I was about nine, I remember her kneeling in the living room, clutching her rosary like it was her only lifeline. Tears streamed down her face as she prayed out loud with such conviction that I could feel it in my bones. It felt real. I felt safe. Seen. Loved.

But not even an hour later, I heard her in the kitchen screaming at my grandfather, spewing venom and hate that shook me. I stood behind the hallway wall, heart pounding, trying to reconcile the woman pleading with God moments before with the one now tearing someone down. That contradiction didn't just confuse me; it wounded me. It planted seeds of distrust in my spirit. It taught me that prayer could be performance, not presence.

The same was true in my home. My father tithed 10% of everything he earned and meditated every day. But he lied. He womanized. He manipulated. And that left me with one loud, lingering message: The people who used the most God-language often lived the least God-like lives.

There was a massive disconnect, and I carried that weight for years.

By the age of 12, I told my mom I wouldn't be doing my confirmation. I didn't want to go to church ever again. I couldn't explain it fully then, but I had a knowing that God was real, but He wasn't there. At least not in that space. Not in the way it was being presented to me. I felt God in my own prayers, in gratitude, in quiet moments of hope. But not in religion. Not in those people. That wasn't my place, and those weren't my people.

Still, even in that disconnection, I never stopped talking to God. I thanked Him every time something good happened. I whispered prayers in the dark. I held onto that faint thread of connection, even when it felt like I had drifted too far to find my way back.

**The Guide God Sent**

And then years later, God sent me a guide. Ruben.

The man I would marry 14 years ago. The love of my life. He wasn't religious. But he walked with such unwavering certainty that I couldn't help but be moved. He never questioned what he faced; he simply surrendered. He lived in trust. In goodness. In grace.

I grew because of that. Slowly, steadily, I began to believe again, not just in God, but in a version of faith that felt authentic. That felt real. That didn't require a performance or a stage. I wanted to learn how to pray, how to connect to God in the way He desires from us, not out of obligation or guilt, but from love.

## The Bridge Back to God

And when I was ready, God gifted me Eliza. A woman who bridged the gap between my mistrust and my return. Through her, scripture no longer felt like a sword; it felt like a lifeline. Her presence was truth. Her words softened the walls I had built, and slowly, I walked home.

It was a knowing. A profound one. That God had placed her in my life to lead me back to Him, not just to believe in Him, but to trust Him again. To rest in Him again. To love Him again.

Curiosity crept in. Quietly. Subtly. Through the back door of my life.

Eliza was different.

She didn't try to convert me or correct me. She didn't open with scripture or close with advice. She just was. Present. Grounded. Real. She showed up with her heart wide open and her flaws right there with it. She could be a hot mess on Monday and still walk into Tuesday declaring God's promises with unshakable certainty.

And I watched. Closely.

Because there was something about the way she carried her faith. She didn't wear it like a costume; she lived it like oxygen. Not for applause. Not for attention. Just for God.

Until Eliza…

No one had ever shared God like her.
Not with conviction. Not with love. Not with zero judgment.

That was the moment I felt spiritually safe with her. Because she wasn't trying to fix me, she was just inviting me back to myself.

I leaned in.
And when I did, my world expanded.

Eliza taught me what it meant to walk with God, not for show, but for survival. For surrender. She used scripture like a flashlight in the dark, not a megaphone on a stage. I watched her walk through storms, not quoting verses to be holy, but to stay sane. Her faith wasn't polished; it was practical. And that moved me.

That was my person.

I knew in my spirit that God placed her in my life to help people like me, people who had been burned by religion but still craved God, to come closer without shame.

And when I finally gave myself permission to learn how to hear God's voice on purpose, not just in hindsight, everything shifted.

My life expanded.
My heart felt light.
My knowing, the one I thought I had lost, became crisp again.

Because now I understood: it was never gone.

God had always been in me. That whisper I followed as a child? That gut feeling that guided me? That was Him. I just didn't have the language for it yet.

But now, I do.

And once I opened myself to the fullness of that relationship, I didn't just heal, I quantum leaped into intimacy with Him. And I am never looking back.

**The Surrender**

I've always been a doer. A fixer. A builder. I've lived much of my life with structure, strategy, and solutions. I was the one who showed up with the plan. The vision. The next step. I helped others transform. I coached them into clarity. I held space for breakthroughs.

But behind the strength was a quiet ache.
Because while I had helped others find peace, I hadn't yet tasted it for myself.

Then, somewhere in the quiet, God whispered something that changed everything:

**"I don't just want your outcomes, I want your obedience."**

That truth stopped me. Because I had always measured my worth by what I could do, build, or achieve. But God wasn't asking me to do more. He was asking me to let go.

Surrender didn't come to me in a grand moment; it came like a soft unraveling.
It looked like allowing.
Allowing the pain. The loss. The change. The unknown.

Letting go of the timelines.
The control.
The need to know how or when, or why.

And in the stillness… God met me.

Not with a list. Not with a punishment.
But with love Gentle. Patient. Certain.

He started showing up in the smallest ways, yet they felt like the biggest miracles.
Prayers answered the same day.
Encouragement spoken through strangers.
People placed in my path with words I hadn't dared speak aloud.

He knew my thoughts.
He knew me.
And more than anything, He wanted me to know that He was proud of me.

That realization broke something open in me.
All the lies I had believed about God, that He was distant, conditional, or disappointed, began to fall away.

In their place came truth:

**God is near. God is kind. God is not performance; He is presence.**

My prayer life shifted from obligation to intimacy.
I stopped praying to check a box and started praying to check in with the One who had always been with me.

I started my days with prayer not to feel holy, but to feel at home.
I began to study, not to gain more wisdom for myself, but to become more like Him.

I made space for His voice.
And He filled it.

Psalm 46:10 says, "Be still, and know that I am God."

And in that stillness, I knew Him.
Not through a priest. Not through a ritual.
Through a relationship.

I realized something else, too:

When people say "the Universe," they're often just reaching for God.
They're using the language they have for the longing in their soul.
And I believe God hears them, long before they know how to say His name.

Because He knows what we mean, even when we don't have the words yet.
And He's not waiting for performance, He's waiting for surrender.

**The Breakthrough**

There was a moment in the shower—raw, primal, and sacred.
No music. No candles. No gentle scripture playing in the background.
Just hot water, steam, and a mother on her knees.

My son had just endured a betrayal so gut-wrenching it felt like my own soul had been cracked open. His entire life's work, years of sacrifice, devotion, discipline, was taken from him. Just like that. In a single blow.

And something in me snapped.

I wasn't crying. I was commanding.
I wasn't pleading with God; I was confronting Him.
Not in rebellion. But in relationship.
The kind of relationship where you know you're allowed to show up unfiltered.

I stood under that stream of water like it was holy ground, fists clenched, heart pounding. I spoke to God out loud, furious, certain, desperate, bold.

"You know who my son is. You see him. Don't you dare act like You don't.
He's not out here quoting scripture, but he lives it.
He shows up with integrity. He protects, he leads, he sacrifices.
He's never asked You for anything. But I'm asking. Right now.
No—I'm declaring.
You show up for him. NOW."

There was no performance in that moment. No polite language.
It was holy fire.

And the crazy thing is, God didn't flinch.
He didn't silence me or shrink back.
He answered.
Immediately.

Within days, my son, who had just lost a multimillion-dollar company, was invited into the very work his soul was made for. Something even greater. Even more aligned.

God had been preparing the way all along.
What looked like devastation was actually divine positioning.

That moment changed me forever.

Because it wasn't just a breakthrough for my son.
It was a breakthrough for me.
I realized: God is not fragile. He can handle our rage. Our honesty. Our audacity.

He doesn't want our polite perfection; He wants our whole selves.

And in that moment, I knew:
God saw me.
God saw him.

God trusted me with that prayer. And I trusted Him to answer.

**The Becoming**

Before, my life looked pristine on the outside, organized, high-achieving, efficient. I was the one with the answers. The one who made things happen. But internally, I was exhausted. Constantly striving, overthinking, anticipating. I lived in a mental loop of protection, performance, and perfection.

I was addicted to productivity—to proving myself and to being praised.

I needed the outcome to feel worthy. The recognition to feel real.
And yet, I had no peace.

Now, I live differently.
I still build. I still lead. I still create.
But it's not my project anymore.
It's His.

Today, my mornings begin at 4 or 5 AM. I wake up early, not to get ahead, but to get aligned. I pray for an hour. I move my body. I study truth through the Bible, Kaballah, the wisdom of leaders who walk with God in authenticity, not performance.

My life flows in a sacred rhythm now.
Because I'm no longer the source, I'm the vessel.

And when things feel shaky, I ask myself:
**"Am I the Light?"**
**"Am I building or destroying?"**

Those two questions center me instantly.
They pull me out of reaction and back into reflection.
Back into God.

I've released the need to explain myself. To be validated. To be understood.
I don't chase acknowledgment anymore.
I don't need credit.
I no longer compromise on my values, my faith, or my purpose.

Peace now lives in my body.
I breathe more deeply. I feel lighter. My discernment is sharp. Even when pressure builds in my chest, I know how to release it.
Prayer is my medicine. My center. My calm.

I used to want certainty.
Now I want alignment.

Those around me feel the difference.
People have always told me, "I love your energy."
But now?
Now I hear: "I love how your energy gives me peace."

My husband, my children, my team, they all see the shift.
I'm more present. More tender. I listen without rushing to fix.
I lead with honesty, even on the messy days.
I no longer pretend to have all the answers. I model what it means to fall and rise with grace.

And when I support other women, I do it by sharing my truth, raw, open, without filters.
But I also protect my energy. I protect my time.
Because this life I've been given, it's sacred. And I don't take a single breath of it for granted.

This is what becoming looks like:

It's waking up each day and choosing to show up without excuses.
It's owning every moment, every joy, every heartbreak, as

either a **lesson** or a **message**.
Period.

## What it Feels Like to Be Loved by God—With Nothing to Prove

It feels like exhaling after a lifetime of holding my breath.
Like unclenching my fists after years of trying to hold it all together.

It feels like finally taking off the armor and realizing I was never in a war to begin with.
Like silence that doesn't shame you.
Stillness that doesn't scare you.

It feels like being known.
Not the curated version of me. Not the high-performing version.
But the real me, the one that's still healing, still becoming, still figuring it out.

To be loved by God with nothing to prove is to feel safe in the middle of your questions.
It's to be seen at your messiest and still be chosen.
It's realizing that you don't have to earn what's already yours.
That grace was never a transaction.
That worth was never up for negotiation.

It feels like walking into a room and not shrinking.
Not performing. Not posturing.

It feels like being wrapped in a kind of peace that doesn't make sense.
A peace that doesn't come from the absence of chaos but from the presence of God.

It's freedom.
Freedom from the addiction to validation.

Freedom from needing to be the strong one all the time.
Freedom from the lie that love has to be earned.

When you're loved by God with nothing to prove, you stop hustling for your identity.
You stop building towers to prove your greatness, and start building altars to remember His.

You start living from overflow, not emptiness.
You begin to ask better questions.
You no longer ask, "Am I enough?"
Instead, you whisper, "God, how can I serve You today?"

Because love like this—real, unconditional, God-ordained love—changes everything.
It makes you bold.
It makes you still.
It makes you whole.

And if I could go back and whisper something to that girl inside me, the one hiding in the hallway, the one walking away from church, the one trying to find her way, I would say this:

**Trust that every challenge is God preparing you for the overflow He desires for you. Be excited for those moments. Surrender all of it to God: the good, the bad, and the confusion. Show up every day and BE LOVE. And allow God to handle the rest.**

### Eliza's Reflections

If there's one thing I've learned, it's this:

People aren't transformed by your opinions. They're moved by your example.

They're not watching how many scriptures you know, how often you go to church, or your theological debates.

They're watching how you live. How you love. How you listen.

And the truth is, nobody's walk with God is perfect. Mine sure isn't. But when your heart is truly centered on Him, even in the questions even in the mess, that's what draws people in.

That's what Giselle saw in me.

Not a perfect Christian.
But a present one.
A real one.
Still learning, growing, and stumbling toward grace.

God doesn't want your performance. He wants your presence. He wants your surrender. He wants you, as you are, not as you pretend to be.

We don't need more "church people." We need surrendered people. People who stop performing for God, pick up their cross, and start walking with Him.

People willing to take off the religious masks.
People who let others witness what a real relationship with Jesus looks like:
Messy. Beautiful. Raw. Healing.

Because real transformation doesn't come through judgment.
It comes through love.

We must learn to see people the way God sees them, through the lens of mercy, not moral superiority. Through the lens of story, not shame. Every person you meet is carrying a past you can't see. They are a culmination of wounds, culture, trauma, survival, longing, and divine purpose.

And sometimes, the holiest thing you can do is simply give someone the dignity of being seen.

Seen without a sermon.
Loved without a label.
Met right where they are.

And let me tell you something true:

If I had looked at Giselle through a religious, judgmental lens, if I had clung to fear instead of love, I would've missed out on one of the greatest gifts of my life.

God didn't bring Giselle into my life for a moment.
He gave me a sister.
A soul-friend.
A woman who reflects Him back to me in wisdom, laughter, light, love, and raw truth.

Her journey doesn't look like mine, and it's not supposed to. Everyone has their own God language. And just because someone uses different words or walks a different path doesn't mean God isn't the One leading them.

Giselle is on her own God journey. She's discovering the many beautiful, faceted ways God reveals Himself. Her God language is practicality. She learns through movement, through wisdom, through spiritual frameworks like Kabbalah. And I will never judge her for that, because I've seen it enhance her relationship with the Lord. Not diminish it.

Now, I know for some, the word Kabbalah can feel unfamiliar or even unsettling, especially within Christian spaces where it's often misunderstood. But let's be clear: Giselle isn't chasing other gods. And Kabbalah, for her, has become a personal development tool, not a replacement for Scripture.

Kabbalah, at its root, is an ancient Jewish mystical tradition that seeks to understand the nature of God, the soul, and divine purpose. And Giselle always takes what she learns back to The Bible.

**God can use anything to draw His children closer to Him.** And I've watched Him do that in Giselle's life. The fruit speaks for itself—peace, clarity, surrender, and an ever-deepening hunger for His truth.

God speaks through many forms. And sometimes, the unfamiliar is simply a different language He's using to reach someone's heart.

It's not my job to police Giselle's walk with God. It's my honor to walk beside her. To pray with her. To lead her by example. To pour into her when she's hungry

I ask questions. I stay open. I don't close myself off to learning.

Because God doesn't call us to bring people to Him and then abandon them, He calls us to disciple them. To walk with them. To love them as He loves us.

I was honored to bring Giselle to Jesus and baptize her in the South Texas ocean. To meet with her every week (for years) for Bible study and prayer. To walk beside her, not as a spiritual authority, but as a sister who believes in her calling.

I try my best to lead by example, and to cultivate God's truth in her through my own messy, honest, imperfect walk. But I've also learned this:

It's not my job to control Giselle's relationship with God.
It's not anyone's job. That is sacred ground, and only He gets to stand there.

So, if you take anything from this chapter, let it be this:

Let's stop leading with ego and start leading with empathy. Let's stop chasing the image of "holy" and start choosing honesty. Let's stop expecting people to look and learn like us before we love them like Him.

Ask God to break your heart for what breaks His. Ask Him to show you people the way He sees them. And be willing to walk down unfamiliar roads if it means meeting someone exactly where they are. That's what Paul did in *1 Corinthians 9:20*: he met people in their world, in their culture, in their language. Not to compromise truth, but to connect through it. He didn't change the message. He simply honored the person and the level of consciousness they were at. And that's the heart of God.

We don't have to look the same, talk the same, learn the same, or worship the same to walk each other home to Him. I deeply believe that is the kind of love that really changes the world.

— **Eliza M. Garza**

**Giselle Dominique Mascarenhas-Villareal**

**Instagram:** @giselleempowers

# Chapter 9
# Broken but Restored

*by Cynthia L. Hernandez, M.Ed.*

*"When you pass through the waters, I will be with you; and when you pass through the rivers, they will not sweep over you. When you walk through the fire, you will not be burned; the flames will not set you ablaze."*
— **Isaiah 43:2 (NIV)**

### From Stillness to Suffocation

The whole world had shut down during COVID. Schools were closed. Living rooms turned into offices. Life outside stopped, but inside my home, the pressure only intensified. What looked like stillness to the world was suffocation to me. Work was a place that I could go to get away; now work was at home. A place I looked forward to escaping.

My world narrowed to my children, a cousin, and two close friends, both of whom were slowly pushed out of my reach. But isolation wasn't a coincidence. It was intentional. It was control in its cruelest form, disguised as care. I was not allowed to have friends. He had ensured to cut off pieces of my family a little at a time. Years of emotional manipulation had taught me to second-guess everything: my instincts, my worth, even my prayers.

During those months, the silence was sharp. I wasn't just isolated from people; I was isolated from my own voice. I moved through each day like a ghost, doing everything I was supposed to: meals, meetings, laundry, schoolwork, all while suppressing the growing ache in my chest. I laughed when expected. I cried when no one was watching. I was breathing, but I was not alive. I had not been happy for decades.

Every morning, I woke up with one question: "God, is today the day something changes?" What I didn't realize then was that sometimes we think we're waiting on God, but really, He's waiting on us to trust Him enough to take the first step.

The days came and went. And nothing changed. It only intensified; things only got worse.

Some nights, I lay in bed long after everyone had fallen asleep, eyes fixed on the ceiling, trying not to feel the sting of another prayer that felt unanswered. I didn't just feel tired, I felt hollow. My body moved, but my spirit felt stuck, locked behind invisible bars. I had been living in a prison I allowed him to create for me, and I was starting to see it.

**The Breaking Point**

There were moments I wanted to run, to just pack up and go. But go where? With what? And how could I take my children into an unknown future when I wasn't sure I had the strength to lead them? The kids had already been moved from place to place to try to start over somewhere new when things got really bad.

Still, I clung to God, barely, but I did even when my prayers felt small. Even when the Word looked blurry through tears, even when I questioned if He saw me at all, I clung to Him like a child clinging to the hem of a parent's robe, hoping He wouldn't let go. I never stopped praying, but it felt as if I had gone unnoticed.

**The Surrender That Saved Me**

Then came the day when the breaking couldn't be postponed anymore.

I could not wait until everyone was asleep. I could not hold it in any longer. I wanted out of a world shaped by domestic violence and the chaos of alcoholism. The person I once trusted with my youth, my future, and my heart was now the source of my deepest pain.

I got down on my knees in the middle of the living room, floor rough against my skin. I didn't care. My body trembled, not from fear, but from the weight of finally laying it all down.

"God..." I cried out, barely audible. "I'm sorry." Those were the only words that seemed to come out.

The words came out raw, from a place so deep I hadn't touched it in years. All the pain was just rushing out. It had been suppressed for decades. I knew I had felt the Holy Spirit for years; He had been telling me to get out. I wanted to hold my family together, but it had become total hell on earth for the kids and me. I knew I had to trust God and finally let go.

"I'm sorry I haven't listened, even when I've felt You speak to me. Even when I've begged, and You were already answering. I kept trying to fix it myself. I thought if I stayed quiet, if I worked harder, if I did everything right, it would get better. But it didn't."

The tears came without permission, without shame.

"I can't carry this anymore. I don't want to. I surrender. Take the wheel, Lord. I trust You. Even when I don't understand. I'm Yours. I promise not to doubt Your will any longer. Just get me over this wave of the unknown. I am ready. But I cannot do this without You."

**Walking through the Fire**

At that moment, something shifted. Not outside, but within. My circumstances hadn't changed. The room was still dim. The fear hadn't magically disappeared. But there was peace, an unfamiliar, holy calm that covered me like a warm blanket. For once, I felt I would be ok.

God didn't speak with thunder. He didn't show up in fire. But He came close. Closer than He had ever felt before.

I exhaled, really exhaled, for the first time in years.

*"Come to Me, all you who are weary and burdened, and I will give you rest."* (Matthew 11:28)

There had always been threats, chilling warnings spoken low enough to haunt me but loud enough to keep me in line. The kind of words that made me fear for the people I loved most. Slurred promises of what would happen if I ever dared to leave. He told me no one else would want me. He warned that if I ran, he would find me. That I'd never be safe. That death would be the only escape. He threatened to kill my mom and my nephews during his drunk episodes. I had stayed because it seemed easier than running and hiding. And at one point, I believed him. The kids and I lived in fear. He would pass by my home to see if I was home. He would call hundreds of times—literally.

But something changed when I gave my pain over to God. The death threats no longer scared me the way it used to. Not because I wanted to die, but because living like this was worse. Death wasn't the worst outcome anymore. Staying in that house, allowing my children to believe that this was what family looked like, that was far more terrifying. I sat my three younger kids down and told them, "If he kills me, it will all be over. I will wait for you all in heaven, he will go to jail, and the nightmare will end. I am no longer living in fear, and I would rather he kill me."

I realized then that I wasn't just surviving for myself. I was surviving for them. I was not alone; the kids were just as much prisoners as I was. Their friends could no longer come over because their parents knew bits and pieces and did not feel that our home was safe for their kids to visit. The children were isolated, too.

In that moment, I made a quiet, fierce vow: **We will live,** even if it meant risking everything. Even if I had to walk through the fire alone, but I wouldn't be alone. God had shown me that. He had been there when I cried on the floor, when my daughters lifted me up, when my son stood between me and a man who should have protected them all. He was there in the silence, and now He was guiding me into the light. I had realized that even though I felt like I was walking through the fire for my children, they were actually walking through the fire for me.

The threats didn't stop immediately. They echoed in voicemails, in text messages, in rumors whispered through mutual acquaintances. He sent pictures of himself with a mask and a gun to intimidate me, but I had made up my mind - death was better than ever getting back with him. My fear no longer held power over me. It had been replaced by something stronger—**faith**.

I leaned on scriptures as if they were oxygen, inhaling promises and exhaling the lies that had held me hostage. *"Even though I walk through the valley of the shadow of death, I will fear no evil, for You are with me"* (Psalm 23:4). I repeated that verse over and over. Sometimes aloud, sometimes in my heart, but always with conviction.

I had Scriptures written all over my home. Every time that I saw one, I said it out loud. I put my whole trust in the Lord to help me through it.

Leaving wasn't just a decision. It was an act of holy rebellion, a refusal to let evil win. I began reaching out quietly. I clung to my two best friends and my cousin. I had confided in them over the years. Not fully, but enough. My friends had gone to save me and the kids many times from his rage. I found a counselor, connected with women at church who had walked through their own storms. One of my really close friends was a pastor. She had taught me the Word for many years, but now I needed her to help me put it into action. I built a safety plan that I protected with fierce determination. My family, though hurt and distant, slowly began to understand. And when they saw I was truly done, truly ready, they opened their arms again. They had stopped talking to me for two years. The emotional roller coaster was too much for them to handle, but seeing that I had left him for a couple of months, they slowly started coming back into my life. I needed them more now than ever.

There were still moments when I questioned myself. Nights when I cried into my pillow and wondered if I was doing the right thing. I had grown up in a "broken home" and did not want the same for my kids. But had he been what he was supposed to be for them? I was confused. But then I'd hear the laughter of my children, light, free, real, and I would remember why I left. I would remember why surrendering to God wasn't giving up; it was finally standing up. They had a place that now felt like a home. Something they had never felt before.

I wasn't running. I was rising.

They were rising together.

I remembered that for years, the kids had begged me to leave him. The kids were happier. The house was calm. No one was afraid anymore.

I stopped hiding the truth that I had been embarrassed by for years. I let myself speak it. My story was ugly, but it was mine. And in that story, God was not silent. He had been present through it all. He had grieved with me, stood beside me, and now, He was rebuilding me. I felt it from within.

From brokenness, beauty.

From ashes, resurrection.

From fear, a holy fire that would no longer be extinguished.

Resurrection didn't come all at once. It came slowly, like the first warmth of spring thawing the edges of a long, brutal winter. It came in the form of ordinary days, of cereal bowls on the kitchen table, of silence that wasn't heavy with tension, of children who began to sleep through the night without flinching in fear. We were now able to sit around and laugh and talk without having to fear that the person who once controlled our home would begin suspecting things. We slept in the same room together for months. We listened to music full blast, danced, laughed, and just healed piece by piece.

I woke up one morning and noticed I was breathing easier.

No more checking the driveway for his vehicle at all hours of the night because he was out drinking and with other women.
No more wondering if my children had hidden the phone fast enough, trying to document his actions or call for help, even though I would not accept it.
No more jumping at the sound of keys turning in the door. What mood would he be in this time that he got home? What version of him would walk through the door tonight? Who would take most of it this time?

No more body checks when I got home from work, as if he were a warden. He inspected me when I got home from work, and the kids knew what he was doing. I never passed his inspections and would be trapped in hell until it was time for work the next day. He constantly accused me of the things that he was doing. His best form of manipulation.

## Learning to Breathe Again

Freedom was unfamiliar at first, awkward, like learning how to walk again after a long time of crawling through broken glass. I was not sure what I enjoyed doing. I had spent too long surviving that the simple joys that a hobby brings did not fit into my life. I was finding my life again, though lost. But it was mine. **And I knew exactly who had given it to me.**

*"So if the Son sets you free, you will be free indeed."* John 8:36

I didn't pretend everything was suddenly perfect. The trauma didn't evaporate overnight. My children still carried the weight of what they had endured. Each is facing their own aftermath. Each healing in their own way and at their own pace. My son was learning how to be a young man again instead of a soldier. He had distanced himself and was now in his own healing process. My daughters were relearning safety, that love did not mean tiptoeing around rage, and my youngest son was shielded from most of it by his older siblings. He was the youngest, and the others tried to take him to the room during fights, so he would not hear or see. To prevent him from facing the fear that they had for years.

There were lots of conversations with lots of tears, and plenty of questions. Why? Why didn't you leave when we asked you to? Why did you let him? There were hard conversations that I had with the kids. I apologized over and over. I promised them that they would never live life like that ever again. I had promised them before, so they were still unsure that this was ending forever.

## The Home We Built Together

What had once been a house full of fear was gradually becoming a home filled with healing. The kids were not angry anymore. Life was coming back little by little.

I worked hard. I started rebuilding, emotionally, spiritually, and financially. I found strength in my independence, but my true power came from God. He had brought me out of the grave. And now, I was walking in resurrection.

I still had the journals, pages filled with prayers, pain, and pleading. I read back through them one night and wept. Not from grief, but from gratitude. Because God had answered—every word. Maybe not in the way I expected, but exactly the way I needed.

I looked around the room that night, at the sleeping faces of my children, and realized they had never been safer. Not just physically, but emotionally. Spiritually. Together, they had survived something that could have destroyed them. But instead of being crushed, they had been **reborn**. It was not something that I could have done alone. I looked back and was grateful that my mom, siblings, and oldest son used tough love and stopped talking to me. The ultimatum that they gave me saved my life.

My daughters had grown bold in their faith. They prayed with me, read Scripture with me, and leaned on God the way they saw their mother do. There were times that we were broken, but the Christian music never stopped playing at home. It brought peace and healing for us. My oldest son, the protector, the shield, was beginning to rest. He was no longer living in the same house, but he knew that his siblings were no longer facing a monster. Because of the brave choices made by his older siblings and me, the youngest was spared from years of more terror. He had been spending lots of time away from home with his oldest brother. It is where he felt safest.

The resurrection wasn't just mine. It was theirs.

And one day, I knew I would tell this story. Not because it was easy to relive, but because someone else needed to know that survival is possible. Someone else may need to know that it is not easy, but it is definitely worth it. That *resurrection* is real. That *"God still lifts the broken from the floor and breathes life into dry bones"* Ezekiel 37:5.

I would tell them that I had once begged for death. That I had once doubted God's silence. That I had cried so hard on the living room floor that I thought I'd never rise again. But I did. Because He never left me.

Not once.

Even when I felt abandoned. Even when the threats were loud and the silence from loved ones was louder. Even when shame wrapped around me like chains, God was there.

And now, I would no longer whisper.

Now, I would speak loudly.

He had been speaking to me loudly, but I chose to ignore Him. It was not the answer that I was looking for. Now I see, it was what God knew was best for me.

For the mother still kneeling. For the daughters still hiding. For the son standing at the door, trying to be stronger than any boy should have to be. For the youngest, having to watch all of them face a battle that he was being protected from. May your scars become stories of strength, and your survival a legacy of unshakable love and resilience. May every step echo with the power of your survival. Safety is not too much to ask for. Love should never come with fear. You deserve more - and that "more" is possible. *"There is no fear in love, but perfect love casts out fear. For fear has to do with punishment, and whoever fears has not been perfected in love"* (John 4:18). Through Christ there is always more—more strength, more healing, more hope. What feels like the end is often just the beginning of redemption.

We had endured the storm—every ache, every silence, every shadow. But God, in His mercy, was not finished with our story. Love without fear was possible. Through Christ, we found the courage to breathe again - and God gave us a place to do just that. God didn't just rescue me from the storm; He brought me into a safe harbor. He did not bring me back alone; He rescued my children, too. We each needed a place to exhale. For me, that place was a street called Acacia.

I went back to my childhood home. I had grown up on Acacia Ave. The only place that I had ever been safe. I was reminded of my best childhood memories as I walked through the house. I felt the presence of my grandmother. Just like the Acacia tree that survives harsh conditions, grows strong, and never forgets how to bloom, I realized I was doing the same. My children were doing the same. It was not a coincidence that I was born and raised on a street with such symbolism. God gave me daily reminders that He was with me all along. I was never alone.

The kids are thriving. Everything I tried to teach them about believing in themselves has taken root. They are so close, so full of love. They have grown into the most beautiful and handsome people, inside and out. They know they have each other. They know they have a happy and healthy mom. I soak up the moments with them now. The kids are grown now, but they know I did the best I could.

**Legacy of Love**

They are proud of me.

They are proud of me for regaining my financial stability.

They are proud of the resilience that I showed, while staying disciplined when the weight of everything felt impossible.

The peace they have now is real. It is tangible. They are proud of the battles, sacrifices, and struggles that shaped them into the young adults that they are today. They are proud of each other and themselves, too.

The children had every excuse to take a different route in life. By God's grace, they chose to find peace and love. They all healed in their own way, but not one did it without their faith and without having to lean on God for strength and understanding.

They have forgiven me. They have transformed through my surrender.

**Thriving After the Storm**

After years of surviving chaos, I never thought I'd know the feeling of being cherished. But God, in His perfect timing, brought someone into my life, a man who didn't flinch at my brokenness. A man who loved gently, with steady hands and a quiet strength. A man who knew he hadn't caused the wounds, but was willing to help carry the healing.

My children didn't need more words or promises; they had heard too many of those. What they needed was consistency. Calm. Safety. And he gave them that. Not by force, not by trying to replace what was lost, but simply by being there. By staying. By choosing love over ego, patience over pride, presence over power.

He helped rebuild their lives, one prayer, one dinner table laugh, one moment of peace at a time.

The woman who once whispered, *"Take the wheel, Lord"*, now drives down quiet streets with worship music playing, my children laughing in the backseat. Sometimes, I glance at them and tears well up, not from pain, but from deep, overwhelming gratitude.

I remember the woman who cried on the floor, the girl who prayed to a God I could barely hear, and I smile.

That woman survived.

And because I survived, I now **thrive**.

My home is no longer haunted by fear. It's filled with laughter, healing, and sometimes still a little chaos, but the good kind, the loud family kind. My children know what it means to be loved without strings. To be spoken to without yelling. To be held without fear.

My story didn't end in brokenness. It was reborn in surrender. And it lives on in freedom.

**To the Woman Still Waiting**

So, if you're that woman reading this, just know you're not alone. It's okay to feel embarrassed, it's okay to feel ashamed. But what's not okay is staying in a situation that isn't safe and is doing more harm than good. And when you finally step into the life God has for you, you will understand why every battle had to be faced.

Not just to survive.

But to come home to yourself.

Have faith. Let go.

It's going to feel so good; you are going to wish you had done it sooner.

*"I can do all things through Christ who strengthens me."* (Philippians 4:13)

**Cynthia L. Hernandez, M.Ed.**
**Instagram:** @cyn.thialhernandez

# Chapter 10
# When the Tomb Becomes Your Womb

*by Eliza M. Garza*

*"You prepare a table before me in the presence of my enemies; you anoint my head with oil; my cup overflows."-*
—**Psalm 23:5**

### The Dream and the Disillusionment

Every entrepreneur begins with stars in their eyes, fueled by passion, purpose, and the promise of possibility. You believe, with every fiber of your being, that your journey will be a steady climb upward. Much like falling in love, you view your new venture through rose-tinted glasses, dreaming only of what *could* be, certain you'll conquer every obstacle that stands in your way.

You give it your all, your time, your heart, and your faith, doing the best you can with what you have, where you are, and with what you know.

But what no one prepares you for is the *ugly*.
The loneliness.
The heartbreak.
The moments you question everything.
The days when your dream feels more like a burden than a blessing.

### When Ego Dresses Like Purpose

I was green in business. I didn't come from a family that talked about money, especially in my Hispanic culture, where those conversations are often avoided. So, I moved forward in ignorance, trusting my business partner because she was my friend. And in my mind, *friends don't fail you*, right? What could possibly go wrong?

What started off as an innocent dream, pure and full of possibility, became quietly convoluted with old wounds, unhealed insecurities and buried pain. And by the time I realized it (or maybe before I even could), ego had taken the lead.

I told myself I was chasing a dream from the heart. But deep down, it wasn't just purpose; it was pride. It was the part of me that needed to be seen, validated, applauded. I didn't know it then, but my ego had dressed itself in ambition. I wanted to succeed not just for the mission, but to feel like I mattered. To prove people wrong. To finally feel like I was enough.

Maybe you're there now. Maybe it's not your purpose pushing you, it's your ego disguised as drive.

The ego doesn't always scream; sometimes it whispers, *"If you just achieve this one thing, then you'll be enough."* But here's the truth: you already are.

**The Fall and the Fire**

Then came D-Day. The day everything unraveled. The day I lost it all. My business partner turned on me. Our relationship severed and with it, the dream we built.

I've never been through a divorce, but that must be what it feels like, when something you love dies while you're still alive. A silent, devastating death. The death of a dream. It hit me like a wave I didn't see coming. One moment, I was swimming toward the shore, and the next, I was drowning.

I had poured everything into this, my heart, my blood, my sweat, my tears. I drained my savings, used every ounce of my financial cushion just to keep breathing while I built something I believed in.

My family was in it with me, working themselves to the bone because I asked them to believe. My staff counted on me. They had mouths to feed. They had dreams of their own.

And me? I was running on fumes, on midnight drive-thru meals and too many energy drinks, on adrenaline and suffocated prayers. I didn't rest. Didn't pause. Didn't care for the woman behind the dream.

I gained fifty pounds, but it wasn't just the weight. It was the stress, the pressure, the pain that had nowhere to go. I worked myself to the bone.

Self-care? That wasn't even on my radar. My motto was simple: "Sacrifice now, celebrate later." Hustle now, rest when it's all done. That's what hustle culture does, it tricks you into thinking you're building your dream. But really? You're just chasing an invisible finish line, one that keeps moving farther away every time you think you're close.

And for the first time in my life, I can say I gave *everything* to something.

That's the thing about talent: it can trick people. It can look like excellence when really, it's exhaustion. It can look like confidence when really, it's a shield. You can give fifty percent, and the world will still applaud because it looks like someone else's one hundred. But you know. *You* always know. This time, I gave it all. And it broke me. Because when you finally give your full one hundred, when you finally go *all in* with no safety net, no backup plan, no pretending, that's when the cost reveals itself. And the world? The world rarely sees that part. But *you* do. And so does God.

**When God Says Fight**

I was going to walk away from it all. I thought, my peace is too valuable for this. I am the hands and feet anyway. I can rebuild this again. But God spoke. Not just once, twice – it seemed like a hundred times. The messages and confirmations that kept coming through were very clear. "This is your business. I gave it to you. Now <u>fight</u> for it."

**How God Speaks**

People sometimes get confused when I tell this part of my story.
The question always comes up:

**"Wait, you heard God speak? Like, an actual voice from heaven?"**

No. Not like that.

I didn't hear a booming voice from the clouds. I didn't see writing in the sky. But yes, I *heard* Him. Loud and clear.

Here's the thing: **God is always speaking.** He doesn't just use one method. He knows how to speak to each of us in a way our souls will understand. He brings himself to our level.

Some people hear Him in a whisper, a thought that cuts through the noise. Others feel Him in their gut, a deep knowing, a conviction that won't go away. Some hear Him in dreams.

Others hear Him through Scripture, where a verse leaps off the page like it was written just for them.

God speaks through people, nature, a song lyric that hits you in the exact place you're struggling, a scene in a movie that makes you cry for reasons you can't explain, through a sermon, or a clip that shows up on your feed at the exact right time.

**But you have to be paying attention.** You can't pass it off as if it were just a coincidence, because it's not. It never is.

For me, my communication with God is like a direct download into my spirit. It's not external, it's internal, almost like a whisper that bypasses logic and lands straight in my soul. Sometimes it feels like a thought that wasn't mine, but carries too much wisdom to ignore. Other times it's a strong impression, like someone handed me instructions I didn't ask for but can't shake off.

And then there are the signs. I get *a lot* of signs. Sometimes it's repeating numbers. Sometimes it's someone saying a phrase I just prayed about, a friend or random stranger telling me the exact encouragement I needed, or something as simple as a feather on the ground or butterfly in the sky.

But here's what I want you to know:

**You might not hear Him the same way I do, and that's okay.** Your communication with God is personal and sacred. He knows how to reach *you*. He knows how your mind works and how your heart processes. He will always speak in a way that aligns with His nature, loving, guiding, never shaming or condemning.

So, if you've ever wondered, "Why doesn't God talk to me like that?" Maybe He *is* talking. But it might sound different from what you expected.

Slow down. Ask Him to show you. Sit in stillness and say, "Speak, Lord. Your servant is listening." Pay attention to what bubbles up, what keeps repeating. To what tugs at your heart and what won't let you go.

Because He's never silent. He's never distant. He's simply waiting for you to tune in.

## The Fire I Didn't Want

God telling me to **"fight"**?
It felt... peculiar.

I thought, *Isn't God the God of peace? Of rest? Of love and grace and turning the other cheek?*
Why would the Prince of Peace tell me to stand up and fight?

It made me question everything.
Was that really Him? Was it just my pride?
Was I trying to justify holding on when I was supposed to let go?

But the confirmations wouldn't stop. They came one after another—undeniably clear, unmistakably divine. Scripture, conversations, songs, sermons, circumstances—each one echoing the same message: **"Fight."**

Still, even with all the clarity, I hesitated. Because let's be honest, just because we *hear* God doesn't mean we always *listen*.

I pushed back. I wrestled. I started to debate with the One who knows all things.

**"No. I don't want to,"** I told Him.
*"This is too much. It hurts too much. I've already lost so much."*

We went back and forth like this. Me resisting. Him waiting.

Until finally, He answered me in a way that shook me to my core.

He said,
**"Fine. But if you don't fight, don't come back to Me later and say I didn't give you what I promised. Your promise is *through* that fire. Not around it. Not above it. *Through* it. Now go. You won't get burned."**

And in that moment, I knew. The instruction wasn't just about saving a business. It was about saving *me*. It was about confronting the very thing I wanted to run from.

This was no longer about the fight itself; it was about obedience, trust, and surrendering my comfort in exchange for my calling.

God wasn't punishing me. He was preparing me. Not to survive the fire, but to come out of it *refined*.

I did. I pushed back, and so did the community; they rallied around me to help get my business back. The fight was felt from the other side, so much so that they retreated... but not for long.

**The Weight of Rebuilding**

I began rebuilding in the middle of COVID, not just the business, but everything that had collapsed in the fallout. I was resuscitating my employees, who had been displaced for two long, uncertain weeks—some of them afraid they had lost their jobs for good. I was trying to regain the trust of my customers, who didn't know if I was still open, still standing, or if I had disappeared without a word. I was fielding calls from landlords who were confused, and unsure what was going on.

I was trying to hold up my family, who had absorbed the worst of the chaos emotionally, physically, and financially. They did everything they could to help me stay afloat while silently carrying their own exhaustion. I was staring at finances that were shattered, every safety net gone, every number screaming *survival mode*.
I was trying to salvage a relationship that had been placed on the back burner, because my dream, my crisis, had taken center stage for too long.

And then there was *me*.

The woman behind the dream.

Running on fumes.
Barely sleeping.
Crying in private and performing in public.
Operating in overdrive, just trying to survive the daily whip lash of recovery—emotionally, mentally, and spiritually.

I wasn't just rebuilding a business.
I was trying to put myself back together like Humpty Dumpty, piece by broken piece

And the hardest part?
The world expected me to carry on like nothing had happened because on the outside, it looked like I had gotten my business back.

But behind the scenes, I was still bleeding.

## The Lawsuit that Birthed My Becoming

Just when I felt like I was finally starting to catch my breath, like my head was bobbing just above water after months of drowning—*bam*.

I get slapped with a $1.5 million lawsuit that's riddled with lies. A lawsuit designed not just to wound, but to *wipe me out*.

And so began the legal circus:
**One attorney... two attorneys... three attorneys... floor.
One retainer... two retainers... three retainers... more!**
I was draining accounts I didn't even have, trying to keep up.

Finally, my third attorney looked at me with sincere, almost apologetic eyes and said, "Eliza, this case is a mess. I'm so sorry, but I think if I stay on, I'll end up doing more harm than good. I can't help you."

Just like that, I was defenseless. In the middle of a red-hot legal battle. Facing not one... not two... but three attorneys on the opposing side—all of them seasoned, sharp, and well-funded. Some would even say the best in the region.

And I sat there thinking, How did this happen? I just went through *three* attorneys and came out empty-handed, and she's over there acting like this is the most ordinary day in the world.

Why? Because she had *money*. And I didn't.

This was my **"What the blankety blank blank blank is going on, God?!"** moment. Like, for real. I'm out here trying to obey You, and this is how You play me?

Make. It. Make. Sense.

## The Stations of the Cross

One morning, I woke up heavy. My mind was clouded, and I just needed to *breathe*. I didn't have a plan. I just needed to be somewhere quiet, somewhere sacred, anywhere I could clear my head and hear from God.

There was a small church park across the street from one of my stores. That's where I went.

I wasn't intending to walk the Stations of the Cross. I had only done that once before in my life. The intention wasn't ritual. It was desperation. I just needed to *pray* and *listen*. To somehow make sense of the chaos I was drowning in.

But God had other plans.

I got to the first station. Christ, leaned over, carrying the cross. His body heavy, face weary. You could see the weight of it—the pain, the exhaustion. I stood there, frozen. Tears began to fall, and I whispered through the lump in my throat, **"Lord, that's how I feel."**

And I heard Him, so gently, **"Keep walking."**

So, I did.

Walking. Praying. Walking. Crying.
I made my way to the next station.

There He was: Christ on the ground. Crushed under the weight. Surrounded by those trying to console Him, but clearly in agony.

Still crying, now with my jaw clenched and my chest tight, I looked up and whispered again, **"Lord, this is how I feel."**

And again, I heard, **"Keep walking."**

So I kept going. With every step, my legs felt heavier, like I was dragging years of disappointment behind me.

**Get Ready to Lose It All**

Then I reached the last station—Christ crucified. There were no words left in me. I just stood there in silence, sobbing, staring up at Him on that cross. And in that quiet moment, when I wasn't even trying to pray, God interrupted my thoughts.

    I heard Him say:
**"Get ready to lose it all."**

    I sniffled.
Wiped my face.
And stared up at the cross with disbelief.

    **"I'm sorry... what?"**
**"Lose it all?"**
**"No. No, no, no. That can't be You. I *listened*. I *obeyed*. I *fought*. I did everything You asked me to do, and *this* is how You repay me?!"**

    And then it all came out.
Raw. Unfiltered.

    **"Is this some kind of cruel joke? Do You think I'm Your puppet? Can't You see I am in pain?! What kind of God does this to someone who's trying to follow You?"**

    I was fuming. And I knew I was being disrespectful, but I didn't care. The pain was too real.

    And here's the thing: I learned in that moment that God can *handle* us. He's not intimidated by our questions. He's not offended by our honesty. He doesn't want the performance; He wants the *real*.

    He wants your heart just as it is.

Broken.
Messy.
Confused.
Crying.
Screaming.
Mad.
He wants *all* of it.

Because it's only in the real that healing can begin.

And just when I thought I'd gone too far, He answered me again so gently and lovingly.

**"It doesn't end here. It ends over there."**

And my eyes were drawn to the final station—the tomb of the resurrection.

That was it. That was the moment everything broke wide open.

Whatever knot had been lodged in my throat was finally released, and I wailed. Not a quiet cry. A deep, soul-rattling kind of cry.

If anyone was in the park that day, I probably scared them. But I couldn't hold it in anymore. It all came rushing out.

Because in that moment, I *knew*: I was at a crossroads. And God was asking for a deeper level of surrender, a level I had never given before.

And it hurt. It didn't feel spiritual or peaceful. It felt like *death*, and it was. The death of control. The death of comfort. The death of ego. The death of a dream.

## The Confrontation

Then I heard Him say,
**"Are you going to let Me use you, or not?"**

That question landed like a brick. Because it wasn't just a question, it was a confrontation. It carried *three revelations* at once.

First, the obvious:
Was I going to obey?
Was I going to pick up my cross and keep following, even when it hurt? Even when I didn't understand?

Second, it revealed my **ego**. I had been making this entire journey about *me*.
My pain.
My image.
My business.
My reputation.
But there was a *bigger picture* at play—souls, legacy, purpose beyond anything I could imagine.

And third, it exposed my **hypocrisy**.
I pray every day, "God, use me. Use my life."
And here He was—*actually doing it*—and I was trying to tap out because it was uncomfortable.

I realized then how quick I was to say "Yes, Lord" when the call felt exciting, but how fast I crumbled when it required suffering.

What a brat. I wanted the crown without the cross. The calling without the crushing. But God, in His mercy, was refining me. He was peeling back the layers of pride, self-reliance, and performance, and all He wanted was *my heart*. The real one. Not the filtered, public-facing one. The bruised, bleeding, doubting heart. The one He died to save.

I answered Him, and said, "I don't know. I'm going to have to think about this and get back to you because I didn't know we were going this way."

## Silence

The silence was palpable. Not an absence of God, but a silence so thick it spoke louder than words. It was correction wrapped in stillness. It felt like God saying, *"This next part requires a deeper level of spiritual maturity. I'm not going to chase you. I've done My part. Now you need to choose."*

And just like that, I stopped talking to God and started talking to myself. I said, **"Eliza, why are you so resistant? What are you running from?"**

And Eliza—the inner version of me, the child in me—answered swiftly without hesitation.
**"Pain."**

So I sat with her. The little girl who had been trying to stay safe all these years. The one who believed that if she could just control everything, she'd never get hurt again. I counseled her.

**"Eliza, pain is part of life. We can't avoid it. Not even with God. But without Him, the pain multiplies. It gets darker. It lasts longer. And it leads you to places that rob you of your joy, your peace, and your light.**

And I knew that was true, because I had lived it. I had walked without God before. And that pain? It didn't refine me, it *wrecked* me. It led me into dead-end relationships, toxic environments, and deep spiritual confusion. It swallowed me in darkness until He miraculously stepped in and pulled me out.

But the pain *with* God? It was different. It still hurt, but it produced something valuable. It birthed strength. Character. Wisdom. Purpose. It came with a promise. A **return on investment**. God never wastes our pain. Pain always leaves a gift… if you *allow* it.

And in that moment, the decision seemed obvious: **Pain with God.**

But I also knew, I had only made that choice in my *mind*. God wasn't asking for intellectual agreement. He was asking for *surrender*. A decision of the heart.

**My Yes**

So I paused.
Sat with it.
And really let it sink in.

This wasn't about religion anymore. I had already gone through the phase of *"God, if You're real, show me."*

I knew He was real. Not because of a sermon or because of a perfect life. But because He had become my **best friend**. He had walked with me in silence. Held me in pain. Sat with me when no one else could understand what I was going through.

I didn't want to live another day without Him. Not because I feared the consequences, but because I *loved* Him. I truly *loved* Him.

And right there, my spirit made the decision. My soul absorbed the choice of my free will. And my body obeyed the order.

I whispered through trembling lips with all of my heart,

"Yes, Lord. I'll let You use me. I love You too much to say no."

And in that moment, I felt it. The peace the Bible talks about. The one that surpasses all understanding. It came over me like a wave, like jumping into the ocean on a sweltering summer day. I felt it hit my skin, my heart, my spirit. It didn't fix anything on the outside, the chaos was still very much there. But inside me?

Peace.
Real peace.
The kind money can't buy.
The kind that holds you together when everything else is falling apart.
The kind that whispers, *"You're safe now."*

My shoulders dropped.
My chest opened up.
I could breathe again.

My joy was restored.
My heart was soft again.
My energy—high.

I felt light. Not because the load disappeared, but because I finally put it in the right hands.

I began walking back to my car, almost skipping. There was a bounce in my step. The kind you get when your spirit finally exhales.

## Answered Immediately

And just as I reached for the door handle—my phone rang.

It was an attorney. He had heard from my previous counsel that I was in a tough spot and needed help. He asked me, "Can you be at my office in an hour?"

My jaw dropped.

**That was the attorney I had prayed for.**

The one with a reputation for fighting for the underdog. The one I'd heard was just as sharp, just as strategic, just as effective as the "top dogs" in the region, but didn't come with the whopping price tag. He was smart, direct, and equipped.

And there it was.
God moved.
Not days later.
Not weeks later.
Moments after my "yes."

I had been waiting for peace to come after the circumstances changed. But the peace came first, and then the help came. Because peace isn't the product of our outcome, it's the product of our *obedience*.

We sat together for two hours, me and the attorney I had prayed for. He had reviewed everything. All the documents. All the chaos. All the legal mess that had landed in my lap.

And then he looked at me and said, **"You know, I have to admit... when I first saw your case, I kind of chuckled. I said to myself, 'I feel sorry for the attorney who takes this one on because it's a mess.'"** Then he paused and smiled.

**"But that attorney is going to be me. I feel like I need to help you."**

My heart softened. It felt like an answered prayer wrapped in unexpected packaging.

But then he got serious.
**"Before we move forward, I need you to mentally prepare for something."**

I leaned in.
**"Okay… what is it?"**

He looked at me gently but directly,
**"I need you to get ready to lose it all."**

I froze.
Those exact words…
They were the same words I had heard from God earlier that day, standing at the foot of the cross during the Stations.
"Get ready to lose it all."

And now, just hours later, this man, who knew nothing about my morning, my prayer, or my pain, was saying the very same thing.

It wasn't a coincidence. It was confirmation. It was as if God whispered again, **"Yes, you heard Me. This is Me. Get ready."**

I took a deep breath. Held back the emotion building in my chest.
And quietly said, **"Okay… okay. I can do that."**

Before I left, he looked down at his calendar and casually said,
**"You know, I didn't even realize today was Good Friday. If I had known it was a holiday, I wouldn't have scheduled this meeting."**

My eyes widened. I hadn't realized it was Good Friday either. Not until he said it.

Another divine wink from God. A gentle reminder that none of this was coincidence, it was all divinely orchestrated.

Just hours earlier, at the foot of the cross during my walk, I heard God whisper, **"Get ready to lose it all."** Now here I was, hearing the same exact words from my attorney, on the very day we remember Jesus losing it all.

Suddenly, the parallel was undeniable: His cross and mine. Both bearing unbearable weight. Both requiring surrender. Both leading to something greater than what could be seen.

As I stepped out of his office, something above the door caught my eye; a plaque. It had a verse on it:

*"This is my command—be strong and courageous! Do not be afraid or discouraged. For the Lord your God is with you wherever you go."* Joshua 1:9

Tears welled up as I walked out the door; it was another God wink. A reminder that I wasn't alone and was exactly where I was supposed to be. That even in the fire, He was with me.

What a mighty, intentional, deeply personal God we serve. One who speaks in signs, in strangers, in timing so divine you can't deny it. One who prepares your heart for the loss, and then walks with you straight into the resurrection.

**Resurrection Day Came**

One year to the day after we went our separate ways, my first children's book was published—a reminder that endings often make room for divine beginnings.

God had given me the energy and courage to keep working on the book through the noise and chaos of that season. At times, I thought I was crazy for even trying. It felt silly to be thinking about a children's book when everything around me was burning to the ground. It was such a bright light in my life during a time that seemed so dark, so I couldn't help but keep going back to it.

I had attempted to self-publish before, but ran into problem after problem. Finally, my illustrator and I hunkered down, right there in the middle of the kitchen at my store.

I'll never forget that day. My staff had called in, so it was just my boyfriend and me running the shop, taking orders, serving customers. In between transactions my illustrator and I worked on finalizing files, reviewing pages, solving formatting issues.

And we did it. *In the middle of the noise,* we got it done. The book finally published.

As the anniversary of the shutdown approached, I could feel the anxiety building in my chest. It felt like remembering the date of someone's death. I didn't want to relive the pain. That date represented loss, betrayal, heartbreak, and I wasn't looking forward to it.

But then, *on that very day*, we hit publish.
And God spoke to me loud and clear:

**"I am making your crooked path straight. You will never remember this date for what happened to you. You will remember it as the day you became a published author."**

I sobbed and hugged my boyfriend and illustrator who cried with me after I shared with them what I had just heard.

And just a few days later, without a single ad or dollar spent on marketing, my little book, *Raspas Con Mi Grandpa*, shot to #1 on Amazon in Hispanic and Latino children's books.

All I had done was send out one press release for Hispanic Heritage Month. It was picked up by the media, and then my phone started ringing, my inbox filled up, and schools all across the state began inviting me to speak. They wanted me to read my book to their students, and empower them through the power of story.

And just like that, God was paving a new path. A new *career*. One I didn't even see coming. He wasn't sending me out broke or empty-handed.

**He was sending me out *blessed*, and the *manna* in the wilderness was pouring in.**

Because that's the kind of God we serve. Faithful. Strategic. Intentional. Good.

Since that moment, my life has blossomed in more ways than I can even explain. I'm walking in an abundant life, one marked by true wealth. The riches that money could never buy:

Friendships that are rooted in faithfulness.
Family who are my biggest cheerleaders.
A thriving career doing what I love.
Projects that align with my calling and heal my soul.
A heart full of joy, peace, hope, and supernatural strength.

I wear *Godfidence* now like it's a garment of clothing. Opportunities continue to brim. Doors keep opening. And life—life is grand.
There is so much to look forward to.

That doesn't mean challenges don't come. Of course, they do. But now, I walk through them with the assurance that my life has been restored, and it just keeps getting better.

I often think back to that moment at the park, standing at the first station of the cross. The visual still makes me emotional. That station of Jesus carrying the cross was ironically and perfectly aligned with my store in the background.

And I knew in my spirit that it was my cross to bear.

The Word says that if we partake in the suffering of Christ, we will also partake in the resurrection, and I am living proof that it is true.

**The Mirror and the Medicine**

It's easy to stay in the place of hurt, to rehearse what they did, how it broke you, how it all could've gone differently if only they had changed.

But real growth doesn't happen there. Real growth comes when you stop pointing outward and start looking **inward.**

Yes, someone else may have delivered the blow, but I had a part to play in my own pain. The eruption in my life didn't happen overnight. It was pressure building over time, from my lack of boundaries, my silence in the face of red flags, my hunger for validation, my self-worth that shrank when money entered the room.

I allowed things to slide that should have been confronted. I confused loyalty with silence, and humility with shrinking. I gave away power and called it partnership, because deep down I didn't believe my voice carried equal weight.

And yet, I don't resent any of it.

Because it happened for me, not to me. That pressure revealed the wounds I was still carrying. And every single one was brought to the surface so it could be healed.

That was the point all along.

I thought the loss was punishment, but it was actually an invitation to come back home to myself, to let God uproot what was false, and to plant something new in the soil of truth.

Now, I can say with full sincerity, I'm grateful it happened. What once felt like betrayal became breakthrough. What once felt like devastation became deliverance.

And in that process, I found something even deeper: **forgiveness.**

Not a forced forgiveness. Not a "be the bigger person" performance. But a real, soul-level release.

Because here's what I know now:
Hurt people hurt people.
Healed people heal people.
Empowered people empower people.

And the words we speak, the choices we make, they all flow from the condition of our hearts. *"Out of the abundance of the heart, the mouth speaks."* Luke 6:45

So no, I don't carry resentment. We were both operating out of our own wounds. We were two unhealed people building a dream on broken foundations. Of course, it cracked.

But now that I've done the work, now that God has refined me through the fire, I walk forward free.

Because forgiveness is the apothecary of blessing. It's the remedy that clears out bitterness and makes room for joy, peace, and abundance.

It's not about letting someone else off the hook, it's about getting yourself off the chain that's dragging you to the bottom of the sea.

And now that I've let go of the past, my hands are open, my heart is light, and my soul is free to receive everything that God has scheduled in my destiny.

**From Tomb to Womb: You Are Planted, Not Buried**

Dear Sister,

You are not buried. You are planted.

And what looks like a grave is really holy ground. What looks like the end is just the beginning of something *divine*.

That setback? It's not your punishment, it's your *positioning*. That rejection is redirection. God didn't forget you. He's preparing you.

I know the weight feels unbearable. I know you're tired. But hear me clearly: This pain is not in vain. You are in the middle of a sacred transformation.

Scripture says,

*"If we suffer with Him, we will also be glorified with Him."* (Romans 8:17)

The cross you carry now is not the end of your story. It's the evidence that resurrection is coming. What feels like death is just a doorway. And on the other side is purpose, power, and a version of you that only God can reveal through the breaking.

What looks like a grave may actually be the beginning of new life.

What you thought was the end? It's not. It's the turning point.

You see, the tomb was never meant to hold you. It was only the womb—the dark, sacred place where God forms warriors in silence. Just like a seed must go underground before it ever breaks ground, you, too, are being transformed in the hidden place.

So when the contractions come,
when it feels like everything is pressing in,
don't resist the labor.

PUSH.

**P** – Pray
**U** – Until
**S** – Supernatural
**H** – Happens.


You're not breaking down, you are breaking open.
You are not being punished, you are being positioned.

You are not the same woman who walked into that fire. You are not who you were when you fell to your knees. You are becoming someone stronger, softer, wiser, and more radiant than ever before.

So, straighten your back. Lift your eyes. Dust the grave dirt off your crown.

And walk out of that tomb like the resurrection you are.

Because this is not just your beginning; **this is your becoming.**

*"They tried to bury you, but didn't know you were a seed."*

**Eliza M. Garza**

**Instagram:** @authorelizamgarza

**Website:** www.elizamgarza.com

# Chapter 11
# The Surrender That Built Me

*by Naomi M. Perales*

*"See, I am doing a new thing! Now it springs up; do you not perceive it?"*
— **Isaiah 43:19 (NIV)**

### The Moment I Didn't Expect

It felt like it came out of nowhere and all of a sudden, but there were signs, subtle nudges I didn't want to see. Signs that something was shifting. I felt it, everything was about to change. And I wasn't ready.

Looking back, I realize life is full of moments we know are coming but feel unprepared for. Like graduating high school, moments that open the door to adulthood, where life begins to move faster and faster. Work, college, Jesus, marriage, family, new friends, new experiences, moving, new jobs, college graduation, new goals. Life's pace keeps going faster, and even when you're not ready for the adventure, it arrives anyway. And all you can do is trust God and hold on.

I was trying to hold on to the new life I had built, the one I had prayed for, worked for, hoped for, dreamt about, and waited for. After years of striving, sacrificing, and slowly finding my way, things had finally started to come together. There was an ease to my days, a peace in my space, a confidence in my routine. I loved the church I was planted in. I had deep friendships. My job felt purposeful. I was settled, not just physically, but emotionally, spiritually, and mentally.

And then, everything began to shift.

The thought of letting my way of life go, of surrendering the life I had worked on for the past eighteen years, felt surreal. I always knew the day would come when we would have to leave, when the call to care for our family would arrive. I just didn't expect it to be here so soon. I wasn't prepared, and truthfully, I didn't want it to be. Would God let me hold onto this comfort I had fought so hard to find for just a little longer?

But deep down, I knew comfort was never the goal. Obedience was.

Still, that didn't stop me from grasping tightly. I was afraid of starting over. Afraid of losing the version of myself that had finally begun to bloom. I wasn't resisting God's voice, I just wasn't ready to release what felt like stability and safety. I was scared to leave the ease behind for the unknown.

But here's what I've learned: When God calls you out of comfort, it's not to strip you of peace, but to anchor you more deeply in purpose because true identity and growth are found in surrender, not in stability.

## Austin: Where I Built My Life

Austin wasn't just where I lived; it was where I built my life. A city full of beauty, history, culture, art, music, food, and endless things to do; including the scenic hill country. I was thriving. I had opportunities to advance within the company. I had been pursuing my education part-time for years, and finally, I completed not one, but three associate degrees and my bachelor's. A lifelong dream of obtaining a bachelor's degree was fulfilled. A promise to my father, kept.

At work, I was learning new things, I was entrusted with new projects, helping colleagues, and had just been asked to coordinate an annual company event. My professional life was growing. My personal life was rich with friendships, church, and purpose.

But while life in Austin was blossoming, my father's and father-in-law's health were declining. Multiple hospitalizations. Countless five-hour drives home. We always knew we would become caretakers for our parents. Well, that day was approaching, and it was coming fast.

I felt that life in Austin was finally coming together, yet underneath, another reality was unfolding. I was rooted, settled. But God had other plans. Gently He was revealing another path, one that called for my obedience, my presence, and my surrender. The next chapter was beginning to unfold. It started silently, unknowingly, not with a big reveal, but with a stirring in my husband's heart, a need and longing to return home, a quick job search, and job application sent.

My husband began looking for a job during the last visit to see our parents. We were not sure how long it would take or if they would even give him an interview. But I could sense it. The shift was becoming reality. It wasn't very long before he received the news about an interview.

Was this really happening?

I was becoming anxious about leaving my home. I tried to concentrate, meditate, recite his word, "Be anxious for nothing, but in everything by prayer and supplication, with thanksgiving, let your requests be made known to God; and the peace of God, which surpasses all understanding, will guard your hearts and minds through Christ Jesus." Philippians 4:6-7 This was hard, and my emotions were all over the place: sad, excited, confused.

Of course, I was happy for my husband, of course I knew it was the right thing to do. Yet, inside my mind was reeling and my heart was full of heartbreak and excitement, grief for what we might leave behind, and hope for what could be ahead.

When the offer arrived, everything shifted. He was elated, quickly responded in acceptance, and ready to move. He could not wait to get to the Valley. I knew this was coming, but my heart was still wrestling. This was happening! Ready or not and yet, I was grateful.

Grateful for the life we had in Austin.

Grateful for the work, experiences, and people we met.

Grateful for my husband's job offer.

Grateful that soon we would be closer to family.

There was a constant tug in my spirit, the push to move forward, the pull to stay. A quiet resistance battled with reluctant obedience. I kept asking, "God, is this really the right time?" like if I knew better than God. I am sure that I amused Him.

**The Decision: Resignation or Redirection**

The day came when I had to turn in my strategy for the annual event, yet knowing what I was giving the VP was my resignation. I stood there frozen, yet everything around me felt like it was spinning. I wasn't ready to leave my home, my church, my friends, or my life in Austin. But love and duty tugged just as hard on my heart.

I had worked so hard to finally find a church home. Friendships had been built. Wonderful friendships forged, that I still have today. Spiritually, I was growing, attending church, spending time in prayer, connecting with others, participating in lunch and learns, and now God was asking me to surrender it all. I felt guilty for feeling sad and conflicted, but this was hard.

I wasn't sure if I would find a church family again. Would I find the kind of Bible-teaching church where people were willing to do life with you?

I was grateful for everything God had done. But at the same time, I was afraid of what was ahead.

I woke up earlier than usual. I needed time to pray, again. I had already been praying every morning and every night, but this morning felt heavier. I arrived at work early, parked my car, and sat still, trying to calm the storm inside me. My heart was racing. My hands were sweaty. My thoughts kept spiraling into every possible scenario. *What if she's disappointed? What if this ruins our relationship? What if I'm making a mistake?*

I took a deep breath and whispered, *"God, I don't know what's coming next, but please go before me."* I walked in slowly, my stomach in knots, silently hoping she would understand, hoping I would, too.

**The VP's Surprise**

I took one more deep breath in and let it out slowly in hopes that it would calm my nerves. I had carefully rehearsed my words. But I wasn't prepared for what happened next.

As I sat at the chair in front of the VP, it took me a few deep breaths and a little prayer for God to give me the words. Then I proceeded to regretfully decline the opportunity to coordinate and oversee the company's annual event and quickly followed by giving my resignation instead. I informed her about our family's situation and the need to leave Austin in the next thirty days.

I looked at the VP in anticipation of disappointment or even confusion, but instead of accepting my resignation, I heard questions. Do you have an updated resume? What is your education history? And then the words, "We certainly cannot afford to lose someone like you who understands this business. It's difficult to hire someone that has your knowledge and experience. I will make a call to the director at the office in the Rio Grande Valley to see if there are any available positions. Come back tomorrow and let's talk."

Wait what? Hold on. My mind was swirling, was this really happening? I wondered, could I really get to stay with the company? Could God really be opening another door and what would be on the other side of that door? Butterflies in my stomach and awe in my heart cannot even begin to adequately describe what I was feeling at this moment. Yet, I also felt grateful. Grateful I did not disappoint. Grateful that I was valued. Grateful for this unexpected surprise that was about to, hopefully, open a new door. Grateful for God's love and nurturing guidance as this story continued to unfold.

**The Door That Once Was Closed**

The very next day, I returned to the VP's office. There were three job options. Two were safe. Easy. But the third? It scared me. It would stretch me and it would be very uncomfortable. What was even more thought-provoking was that the third position, the one that scared me, was the same one I had inquired about almost exactly a year earlier, but at that time, it hadn't been available.

Back then, the door was closed. Now, God had swung it wide open.

We talked about the positions, and the conversation concluded with the VP making a call, letting the director know which job I would be applying for. The VP would not take no for an answer and said, "You will be great at this job!" I told the VP, "I don't like getting involved in politics." I was in disbelief that I had even agreed, but I knew in my spirit it was the right one. Even repeating the title brought some sense of peace. That peace was a source of comfort. God was right there with me, guiding us through this difficult, yet necessary conversation. But this new job would call me into rooms with decision-makers, leaders, and high-ranking officials. It terrified me. I wasn't used to being the face of anything. I didn't want the spotlight. I just wanted to do good work and go home. I appreciated the confidence in me and my abilities, but I did not see myself in the same way and certainly not at that time. It is a blessing when God puts you in the space of great people that appreciate and value you, see what you do, and see who you can become.

This was really happening! The doors in Austin were closing. The doors in the Rio Grande Valley were opening. This was more than a move, it was divine redirection.

I was perplexed and yet in awe at God's timing. God is a God of order. He was curating my story and it was obvious that I did not have a say in the "when". Yet, looking back, I see that he allowed me to see where. But I did not recognize His divine insight. I was in awe of how things were being orchestrated, how things were beginning to align. How a no then, became a yes at this moment in time.

Swirling in my mind were also thoughts of the new, the unknown, and I felt butterflies in my stomach and a little light headed. Was this really happening to me? I felt fear, a little anger, and yet excitement, but anxiety at the same time. Layer upon layer was unfolding and this new redirection was becoming more obvious, God was asking something different of me. A redirection into an uncharted territory where fear and anxiety were at the helm. I knew very little of the job, but I knew this was a 2 Corinthians 12:9-10 moment, *"But he said to me, "My grace is sufficient for you, for my power is made perfect in weakness." Therefore, I will boast all the more gladly about my weaknesses, so that Christ's power may rest on me. That is why, for Christ's sake, I delight in weaknesses, in insults, in hardships, in persecutions, in difficulties. For when I am weak, then I am strong."*

I was stepping into a role, one that God helped me attain, that came with a job description, but no clear roadmap. I would have no training. There were things on the job description I had never attempted to do; this was a new blank slate and I was expected to build the roadmap as I walked it out. There was no formula, no checklist, just faith.

Stepping into the unknown was a mirror to what was happening spiritually; I was no longer just learning about faith, I was being asked to live it. I could not rely on traditional systems, instead I had to rely on God in real time, live, up-front and personal.

Before, I knew where I rested in my faith. It took me a while, but I found a new church, prayed, and stayed spiritually fed. But now, I had to live in faith. I had to rely on God in real time. Not just believe He was with me, but move like He was. Because this was hard, and I didn't know how I was going to get it all done.

A revelation emerged gently, one more added layer. The difference between believing in God's promises and depending on them: the old me found comfort in preparation, but the new me had to lean fully on the Provider.

**The Unraveling of Comfort**

Relocating wasn't just physical—it was emotional, spiritual, and deeply personal. God was stripping fear from me, one layer at a time.

After eighteen years away, the Rio Grande Valley didn't feel like home anymore. Everything was different. The food. The culture. The pace. Even simple tasks felt overwhelming.

Raised by parents and grandparents who modeled excellence, discipline, and pride in their work, I believed deeply that your work reflects your character. You show up. You follow through. You care. You give back.

But here, I was often met with the "mañana *(tomorrow)* mindset." It was so foreign to me, not bad, just unfamiliar.

In Austin, everything revolved around attaining the goal and meeting the deadline, urgency was the rhythm of the workplace. But in the Rio Grande Valley, I quickly learned that deadlines were more like suggestions, sometimes extended and sometimes kept, and the word urgent was rarely used.

I had been working hard on a project all week, aiming to meet a Friday deadline. I walked into a brainstorming meeting ready to work on finalizing the details, still operating at the same pace and pressure I was used to in Austin. I was stressed, laser-focused, and determined to meet the deadline.

Then, in the middle of the discussion, one of my colleagues quietly leaned in with a smile and said, "Slow down. You're not in Austin anymore."

I blinked, confused, and wondered, "Wait, are you serious?" As I looked at him in bewilderment, he looked back at me with a smile and I remember letting out a quiet small giggle, not because it was funny, but because in that moment, I realized how tightly I was still holding on to my old rhythm and my old habits. It was the first time I really felt the cultural shift, and the invitation to breathe, to look at things from a different perspective.

It took me a while to accept the shift. But looking back I see clearly, my colleague was trying to help, but the way God used that phrase stopped me in my tracks. He reached me in a way I was not expecting. It was not just advice; it was a pause, a shift, a divine interruption—a moment of grace. That giggle? It was my body catching up to what my soul already knew: I needed to let go.

### The Wrestling with God

The new role was not one I would've chosen. I never imagined myself doing this kind of work. But others saw qualities in me, gifts I had not yet discovered. They believed in me, and I clung to that belief like a lifeline, trusting that God had a plan even when I felt out of place.

My responsibilities kept growing beyond my job description—special projects, new challenges, constant stretching—I felt the tension between who I was and who I was becoming. It was uncomfortable, but it was holy. God was using the stretch to shape me, teach me, and give me a new perspective about myself.

I questioned God often:

*"Are You sure this is where you need me to be? This doesn't feel like me. I'm not bold. I'm not political. I feel out of place. I'm not polished. I feel misplaced. I feel like I am pretending. Am I even equipped to do this?"*

The doubts were loud and relentless:

"Am I the right person for this?"

"What if I'm not enough?"

"What if I mess this up?"

"What if I don't belong here?"

"What if I fail?

"What if I can't connect, can't deliver, can't build the relationships this role demands?"

"Do I even look like a leader?"

Slowly—sometimes painfully so—I began to see that what I lacked in confidence and self-image, God covered with mercy, grace, and favor. He never asked me to change who I was or to be perfect; He simply asked me to trust Him, surrender, and be willing. He surrounded me with people who spoke life into my doubt. Through their wisdom, their challenges, and their unwavering belief in me, I began to grow, not into a different person, but into the person God was calling me to be.

**The Slow Refining Process**

My breakthrough didn't come all at once. It came like gold being refined, slowly, gently, one fire at a time. And now, I see that was the blessing.

> *"...that the genuineness of your faith, being much more precious than gold that perishes, though it is tested by fire, may be found to praise, honor, and glory at the revelation of Jesus Christ"* (1 Peter 1:7)

I'm grateful God didn't rush the process. If the refining had come fast and furious, I don't know if I would have been able to acclimate or grow the way I did. The slowness was mercy. It was God's patience, His love, and His grace in action. He knew I needed time, not just to build new skills, but to believe in myself, to rebuild confidence I didn't know I had lost.

And in that slow refining, He brought people into my life who became part of the blessing. Their presence, support, and guidance reminded me that even in the stretching, God was surrounding me with everything I needed.

Gratitude became my anchor, and through it, I found steady ground.

It didn't fix everything overnight, but it changed how I saw everything. Little by little, gratitude shifted my perspective. It opened my heart. It softened the stress. It reminded me that even in the unfamiliar, God's fingerprints were everywhere. And that's when I started to see the hidden gifts, right in the middle of the stretch.

> *"...in everything give thanks; for this is the will of God in Christ Jesus for you."*
> Thessalonians 5:18 NKJV

**The Power of Gratitude**

Gratitude shifts everything.

Appreciation to our divine Lord and Savior doesn't just change our attitude—it recalibrates our entire being. It tunes our hearts to heaven's frequency, allowing joy and peace to flow through body, soul, and spirit.

Gratitude opens the door to intimacy with God. It's the quiet whisper of thanks that acknowledges His presence, His provision, and His grace—even when life feels uncertain. It's the sacred connection to our true source of love, a connection deeper and more powerful than anything this world can offer.

In gratitude, we don't just feel better—we live better. We see clearer. We love deeper. And we walk in peace that surpasses understanding, because we know we're held by the One who never lets go.

> *"...and the peace of God, which surpasses all understanding, will guard your hearts and minds through Christ Jesus"*
> Philippians 4:7

Gratitude shifted everything. It gave me creativity when I felt stuck, problem-solving ability when I felt overwhelmed, and perspective when I felt lost. Instead of asking, "Why is this happening?" I began asking, "Lord, what do I need to learn?"

As I was preparing to lead a meeting surrounded by business professionals, community leaders, and field experts, coupled with the expectation to speak with authority, my heart raced, my mind spiraled, and fear whispered, "You don't belong here. You're not ready. What could you possibly offer?"

But in that moment, I closed my eyes, took a deep breath (in and out), paused and chose gratitude. I thanked God for the opportunity, for the growth, for the people who believed in me, for the people before me, for the work I "get to" do. I whispered, "Thank You for Lord for being with me and trusting me with this, even when I struggle to trust and believe in myself." And something shifted. Peace settled in, not because the fear vanished or because I was doing this the 'right way,' but because I remembered I wasn't alone. Gratitude became my anchor.

That moment broke through the anxiety and fear. It didn't just calm my nerves—it awakened joy. A quiet, steady joy rooted in knowing that God equips those He calls. Gratitude gave me reassurance and a quick reset. It reminded me that breakthrough doesn't always come through strength—it often comes through surrender.

Gratitude didn't just lift my spirit, it gave me life. It reminded me that joy isn't found in ease, but in presence. God used gratitude to breathe hope into my heart, and in that blend of contentment and surrender, I found breakthrough. I didn't just survive, I began to thrive.

**The People God Sent to Speak Life**

Because when we surrender and thank God for the people He sends, we begin to see the gold He's refining in us. When I couldn't see or believe in myself, God sent precious people who saw me.

In the fire of refinement, slow, stretching, and sacred, He didn't leave me alone. He surrounded me with people who carried His heart, His words, and His encouragement. Their presence was my provision. Their voices were my lifelines.

My pastor and his wife, along with church friends, prayed over me and declared destiny when I felt directionless.

My parents reminded me, "Mija, you can do anything," when I doubted everything.

My sisters, nieces, and cousins cheered me on, "You'll be great at this," when I wondered if I was the right person for the job.

Leaders, mentors, supervisors, and colleagues saw gifts in me before I could name them myself.

And then there were the women—I can't even begin to thank all of them or name them all, my mother, aunts, sisters, cousins, friends, colleagues, acquaintances, and even strangers—each one sent with a word, a hug, a prayer, a truth that pierced through the fear and the lies.

Their words didn't just comfort me, they allowed for shifts to begin taking place deep inside. Slowly I felt peace settle in and I felt joy rise. Each conversation, each provision of love and hope, each moment they relayed direction, confidence, and assurance.

It reminded me that God's provision isn't always a solution, it's often a person.

And in that gratitude, I found life, not just encouragement and survival, but renewal and unimaginable transformation.

**The Unexpected Fruit**

Had you told me when I began this new adventure that I would be here with the people I have met and loved, with this job, with the experiences I have had, I would've never believed it.

I was uncertain, stretched, and questioning everything. But in surrendering to God's plan, not my own, I found an adventure I never could have imagined which continues as I write these words.

I spend time with friends and family in ways unimaginable with joy and fulfillment.

I spent precious time with my father before he went to be with the Lord.

My niece and nephew came to Christ, and I watched their hearts awaken to faith.

I serve on boards that impact my community in ways that matter.

I stepped into leadership roles I never thought I was qualified for, yet somehow, I was prepared.

I mentor students, future leaders, and entrepreneurs - planting seeds I may never see bloom, but trusting they will.

This was never about a job. It was never just about a title or a task. He uses us, not because we're perfect, but because we're willing. It was about divine realignment, God placing me exactly where I needed to be, not just for my growth, but for the growth of others.

Gratitude became my lens. It helped me see the fruit I didn't expect:

Peace in the stretching.

Joy in the serving.

Love in the leading.

Hope in the mentoring.

And through it all, I have come to learn that surrender isn't just about letting go, it's where God begins His greatest work, leading us, transforming hearts, multiplying impact, reshaping us, expanding our reach, and breathing life and beauty to the places I thought were beyond hope.

**The Wisdom I Carry Now**

Surrender is not weakness; it is trust, and an act of faith that transforms everything. Gratitude is not an emotion, but a daily discipline that helps us see the sacred in the ordinary. This season continues to teach me that surrender is not the end, but it is the beginning of a more meaningful story.

With each pivot, I walked away from comfort and into uncertainty. And every time, God met me there, not with answers, but with love and grace. Not with guarantees but with purpose. In learning to hear and trust His voice, even when it led me into the unknown, He gave me quiet strength and peace. I'm learning that identity isn't built in achievement, it is revealed in the quiet moments of surrender and is becoming the foundation for the woman He is shaping me to be.

I don't always get it right. I stumble, I question, I fall short. I miss the mark and don't always walk this Christian life perfectly. But God never asked for perfection, He asked for willingness to let go and let God. A willingness to listen, to follow, and to be used for His glory.

It's about listening, seeing the signs, responding, and choosing to follow the Holy Spirit as He gently guides me through God's perfectly curated adventure for my life. So I pray daily, "Lord, who do You need me to serve today? Use me Lord and help do this for Your honor and glory. Let my life reflect Your love, kindness, grace, and purpose."

Choosing to see God in everything has reshaped my life, layer by layer. Gratitude is felt deeply. Surrender is freeing and a gateway to change, healing, and transformation. Trust, although the most difficult, has become an unexpected yet quiet strength. Obedience is not about having the answers, it is simply about having faith. Faith that walks even when the path is unclear. Faith that believes even when hope feels distant.

This journey has not been perfect, but it has been sacred. And in every imperfect step, I have found glimpses of God's perfect love. If you're in a season of uncertainty, know this: surrender is not your defeat; it is your beginning. Gratitude will anchor you. Trust will carry you. And faith will light your way. Keep walking and learn to recognize that you are being shaped, refined, and are deeply loved.

**A Prayer and a Blessing for You**

Heavenly Father,

Thank You for the gift of this moment. I lift up my sister to You, Lord.

Thank You for seeing her right where she is. She's tired. She's wrestling. She's holding tightly to what once felt safe. She's anxious and afraid. But You, Father, know the weight she carries, the dreams she guards, and the comfort she is hesitant to release. You see her in the quiet moments where surrender feels heavy and change feels overwhelming. You understand the ache of letting go and the fear of starting over.

Remind her, Lord, that this breaking is not punishment; it is preparation. You are not tearing her down; You are building her up.

Thank You for standing with her as she stands at the edge of something new. She is uncertain and cautious, but willing. She senses the shift, and though it's unfamiliar, she trusts You. She's lived in comfort, but now You are calling her deeper.

Give her courage to step forward, boldness to obey, and joy in the becoming. Help her grow in faith, belief, and knowledge. Let her rest in Your promises:

- To be still and know that You are God (Psalm 46:10),
- To trust in You with all her heart and lean not on her own understanding (Proverbs 3:5–6),
- And to believe that You have plans to prosper her, not to harm her, plans to give her hope and a future (Jeremiah 29:11).

In the name of Jesus, we ask that You give her peace, break every stronghold that keeps her from stepping into her purpose. Lord, do it gently. Refine her. Rebuild her. Make her stronger than she's ever been. Remind her that when her strength runs out, Yours never will. Let her know her identity is not found in her location, her role, or her routine, but in You alone.

May she feel Your strength with every step, Your peace in every storm, and Your love in every moment. Bless her, Father, in the surrender, in the shift, in the letting go, in the trusting, and in the rebuilding.

Let her know she is not defined by what she does, what she wears, or where she lives, but by who You say she is.

- She is Yours.
- She is the daughter of a mighty King.
- She is fearfully and wonderfully made.

- She is held.
- She is protected.
- She is becoming.

Wrap her in Your love, protect her and guard her heart. Hold her close in the transition, in the breaking, through the forgiveness, in the surrender, through the fear, in the healing, through the anxiety, in the strengthening of her belief, through the resistance, in building up her faith, and giving her clarity and courage to recognize the doors that are opening. Thank You for walking with her every step of the way.

If it be Your will, may we see her shine, in love, in grace, and in purpose, trusting You will see it through to completion for Your honor and glory.

I thank You, Father, for this beautiful sister, the amazing adventure You have prepared for her, and the impact of her surrender and obedience.

We give you thanks, bless your holy name, and praise You.

We pray all these things in the blessed and mighty name of our Lord and Savior, Jesus Christ, Amen.

**Do You Have a Relationship with Jesus?**

If you don't know Jesus, but would like to begin your journey, accepting Him into your life begins with a simple, sincere step of faith. You start by acknowledging your need for Him, believing that He died for your sins and rose again to give you a new life. Then, invite Him into your heart. Ask Him to forgive you, guide you, and be your Savior. You don't need perfect words, just an open heart. Jesus meets you right where you are, with love, grace, and the promise of a transformed life.

Suggested prayer:

"Lord Jesus, I know I need You. I believe You died for my sins and rose again to give me new life. Please forgive me, come into my heart, make me new, and be my Savior. I surrender my life to You. Help me to follow You, trust You, and grow in Your love. Thank You for saving me. In Jesus' name, I pray, Amen."

**Anchor Scriptures:**

1 Peter 1:7, 1 Peter 5:6-7, 2 Corinthians 5:17, 2 Corinthians 12:9-10

Ephesians 3:20-21, Galatians 2:20, Galatians 5:18, Hebrews 11:8, Hebrews 11:32-34, Isaiah 40:28-29, Isaiah 41:10, Isaiah 43:1, James 4:7, Jeremiah 29:11, John 3:16-17, John 14:1, John 14:6, John 14:16-17, Matthew 6:33-34, Philippians 1:6, Philippians 4:6-7, Proverbs 3:5-6, Psalm 37:5, Psalm 46:10, Psalm 61:3-4, Psalm 139:14, Psalm 37:5

Romans 8:14, Romans 8:16-17, Thessalonians 5:18

### Naomi M. Perales

**Instagram:** @naomiperalesmk

# Section Three

# The Rising

*"Arise, shine, for your light has come, and the glory of the Lord rises upon you."*
**—Isaiah 60:1**

There comes a day when tears dry, chains break, and the soul begins to breathe again. This is The Rising. It is not an instant moment but a tender unfolding, like dawn breaking after the longest night.

The Rising is where women learn to walk in freedom, to embrace their identity as beloved daughters, to live as though healing is not just possible but promised. In these chapters, you will hear stories of women finding joy again, reclaiming their worth, and daring to believe that God's love is stronger than any wound.

Rising is not about erasing the past. It's about carrying it as a testimony of God's goodness. It's about lifting your head, squaring your shoulders, and saying, *"What tried to bury me has only made me bloom."*

May their stories remind you that your rising is coming too, and when it does, it will be beautiful, undeniable, and unstoppable.

# Chapter 12

# The Extraordinary in the Ordinary: A Tribute to the Women Who Raised Me in Faith

*by Dr. Rutchie Contreras, PT, DPT*

*"Whatever you do, work at it with all your heart, as working for the Lord, not for human masters."*
— **Colossians 3:23**

### Where Prayer Was Planted

My earliest memories of God and Faith had to do with the influence of my grandmother, Dolores A. Ileto. She instilled in me a deep sense of the wonder of God and His power to protect me and to guide me. I remember her calling us to pray the rosary as a family, every day at 6 pm sharp. No one was allowed to miss a single day of prayer. No excuses were accepted either, much to my dismay since this was the exact time of my favorite Filipino telenovela on TV. I tried to convince her to reschedule rosary time, but she would always say 6 p.m. was Mother Mary's time, and for me to ignore the voice of the "devil" in my head because it was "Satan" who was instructing me to tell her this.

Of course, that was enough for my younger self to freak out and stop questioning her. She had a prayer for every occasion, every need, and every trial. She had us pray to different Saints depending on the outcome we wanted. For example, St. Anthony if you lose an important object, Our

Lady of Perpetual Help for health, and St. Jude for dire causes, etc., you get the picture.

Another significant person who has had a profound influence on my faith and belief in God is my mother, Ruby Ileto Nolasco. I still have vivid memories of her moving forward on her knees, while praying the rosary in the center aisle of the church, all the way from the back of the church to the front. I remember her removing bloody bandages from her knees because of course, the floor was not clean, it was full of tiny rocks and dirt that people had on their shoes while they were walking on the church floor. I remember wondering to myself what she could possibly be asking for, but I never did ask her. I just looked at her wounded knees then I looked away. My mom is the person our entire family goes to when we needed prayers.

I remember calling her when I had a particular request and I am not exaggerating when I say, when I ask her to pray, my prayers are granted. This is true for all other family members who ask her to pray for them. She has always told me that when a prayer is for me or my sister, she would pray the rosary kneeling with both arms outstretched the entire time. She would also have a prayer she would say on the hour. She told me the time had to be exactly every sixty minutes for the prayer to be effective and that sometimes, the "devil" would prevent her from fulfilling this requirement so she would have to start all over. She says this is the hardest prayer for her to do and that she only does this for me and my sister, Rusier.

My mother's faith was fierce and full of fire. It covered us, shaped us, and protected us in ways I am still discovering. But as I reflected on where this legacy began, my heart returned to the woman who came before her, the one who first taught our family how to pray, how to serve, and how to persevere with grace.

## Nanny: The Quiet Giant Behind It All

My grandmother was affectionately called 'Loleng'; to me, she was 'Nanny. I knew her as a quiet woman, always sitting in the living room sofa, playing her favorite card game, solitaire. She would play it for hours on end, pretty much all day. She even taught it to me and I would also play it myself in my free time. It was a very therapeutic way to clear your thoughts. She would wait for me to come home from the university so I could bring her favorite snack, sampaloc—a sour and salty tamarind candy. If I forgot to bring it, she would gently remind me of my forsaken duty. She was my "alarm clock" during my college years, she told me that my brain would absorb the most information in the early morning so that was when I should study. She wouldn't sleep all night so she could keep an eye on the clock and then at around 2 am, she would wake me up so I could review my notes.

My mom told me much later that Nanny would complain about seeing my bedroom light turn off thirty minutes after she had woken me up and that all her efforts seemed in vain, but they really weren't. I just needed those thirty minutes to stick the information into my long-term memory.

It wasn't until after she passed that I realized how great her legacy was. I remember being so devastated when this happened. We brought her home to Bulacan, the province of her spouse, Dr. Jose V. Ileto, my grandfather. Much to my surprise, there was a procession about a mile long to lay her to rest in our family mausoleum. They closed the entire high school in our town so the students could honor her memory and her legacy. The whole town mourned the loss of a great woman, my very simple, very humble grandmother.

My grandmother was born September 17, 1901. She studied to be a nurse, which was one of the few professions acceptable to women in that era, around the time of World War II. She met and married my grandfather who was a physician. They lived in San Ildefonso, Bulacan where they raised their family of 4 children. My grandmother was a firm believer of the value of education and was very passionate about sharing the gift of education to people of different backgrounds. She realized that there was a need in the town at that time to educate the children of the people who worked in our family's rice fields. She worked diligently for what seemed like ages until, finally, in 1946, all her tireless efforts and her dream came to fruition. In 1946, the Buenavista High School was founded. It still stands to this day and has educated thousands of students who went on to university and have earned a college degree and a way to a better life. My mom told me that all this was accomplished by my grandmother with a lot of prayer, countless masses and endless rosaries together with her hard work and perseverance. God has answered other people's prayers for a better future through her. It was a great feat for a woman during a time when women were neither seen nor heard, much less taken seriously enough to lead a large institution.

While my grandmother laid the foundation of faith and service for our family, it was my mother who carried that torch with unwavering devotion. Where my grandmother built institutions, my mother built people. Her compassion, instinct, and generosity made an impact not just on our family, but on every person lucky enough to cross her path.

**My Mother, Heaven's Helping Hand**

My mother, Ruby Nolasco, is a very petite lady. If you look at her, you see a beautiful, elegant, tiny lady who appears entirely innocent and harmless. Little does everyone know, she is a veritable powerhouse, a woman full of personality, grace, and charm. She has regaled me with tales of how she was as a child, and how her friends and family are important to her. She will go to great lengths to help her loved ones, especially when she sees them struggling. They do not even have to ask her for help. She hears their unspoken plea and offers aid without being asked and without asking for anything in return. I have so many memories of her helping so many of our family members and offering free food and lodging so their children can finish school. She was a music teacher in a public school in the Philippines, and she would notice immediately when her students were not performing well in the classroom. She would know right away when her students had not eaten for the day. She would take them to the school cafeteria and pay for their meal. This was not something she did only once; it was something she did daily. The welfare of her students was that important to her.

     My mom cannot pass by any homeless person on the street. While other people stay away from them or choose to overlook them, my mom finds it impossible to ignore them. She always carries a small purse with enough small bills so she always has something to give to those asking for alms. She goes so far as to ask for an apology from God if she does not have money to give to a stranger who is begging on the street, and I can see the tremendous guilt she has when she has to walk away from someone in need because of the extremely rare instance that she forgets to bring her purse with her. She notices every single person in the street who is homeless or hungry. I know this for a fact because she points every single one of them out to me when we are driving or walking. If she does not have money on her, she asks me to look in my purse if I have any change to give them. It is because of her that I make sure I always have something to give someone in need. It is because of her, I notice homeless people and people begging on the street. It is because of her that I stop my car in the middle of traffic just to give alms to those who are asking for it in the middle of a hot scorching day. My mom is an ordinary woman who chooses to be extraordinary to each person she has aided. She has touched several lives through her generous heart and has shown God's hand through her efforts to help others.

**Love Rooted in Faith**

I remember when I met Omar, I did not know he was going to be my future husband. My mom told me that even as an unmarried couple, we should go to church together. I thought this was unusual because I thought that going to church should only be for married couples and their kids. I took him anyway and I guess he wanted to impress me so he went with me every Sunday. At first, I thought he was just going along with my faith because me and my family were very passionate about our religion and we talked about praying all the time, especially my mom. He surprised me years later when we were going through tough times and he told me he went on his own to the St. Jude shrine to pray for us. He also told me that he went to the shrine to light a candle periodically to pray for any intentions he had. I was so impressed by this and it made me love him even more. I was so happy that we share this faith together.

I have now turned into my mother when it comes to my son, Andrei. The first thing I tell him when he confides in me about a trial is, 'Don't forget to pray.' When he goes out the door, my mom's words come out of my mouth "Don't forget to do the sign of the cross." Now, when I ask him if he has seen something that I have misplaced, the first thing he says is "Did you pray to St. Anthony yet?" It really surprised me the first time he told me that. I was also filled with a sense of fulfillment that I have somehow continued with my mom's and my grandmother's faith legacy through him. Another happy surprise is that he now comes to me when he has a problem and asks me to pray for him just like I do with my mom.

**A Family Rewritten by Grace**

For sixteen years, my immediate family only consisted of three members: me, Omar and Andrei. All of a sudden, God placed two wonderful boys in our path They were brothers who were Andrei's friends from school. Andrei was the one who insisted I let them sleep over one night. That one night turned into one week and then two weeks. I thought this was not appropriate and was concerned that their parents were going to miss them but Andrei fought for them to stay longer even when I was questioning why they weren't with their own family and why they were staying away from their mom I sincerely thought they were rebelling against their parents, and as a mother, I didn't think it was right for them to do that to her. When we finally found out the truth about their need for a place to call home, we immediately took the appropriate steps to have them legally remain with us indefinitely. Omar and I both consulted our mothers who did not hesitate when we told them about our chance to help out. They both said "you have to help them." Now, our family consists of me, Omar, Andrei, Julian and Erick. We are now a family of five.

Later on, Erick asked me how we could just take in complete strangers without being scared. I told him that as soon as we found out that he and Julian needed us, Omar and I prayed, my mom prayed and so did my mother-in-law. The path was cleared by God and the rest, as they say, is history. I also told Erick that I prayed to God that they would not kill us in our sleep, to which, Erick and I both started laughing. Andrei went from being an only child to being a middle child and he absolutely loves it. He is so content with his current situation. He now has his own group who he feels he belongs to, who always has his back. People constantly ask me and Omar how we did it to take in strangers into our home.

The answer is simple: my mom always did it and I had seen it and experienced it growing up. My mom always took in family members who were strangers to me at that time to provide them with shelter and food when they were in need. My husband's mom did the same thing. Omar told me that his mom, Rosa, did the same thing. His childhood home was always filled with extra family members he hardly knew because they were in need and his mom was always the first one to help. Looking back, I realize that if I had not been looking at two ordinary boys, Julian and Erick through God's eyes, I might have missed that they needed us, and we would have gone on living separate lives. I firmly believe that it was God and the Holy Spirit who whispered in my ear and who spoke through Andrei revealing that something was amiss and that Julian and Erick needed our family. I am so happy that we heard His message loud and clear.

Looking back, I can see now that the seeds of compassion, generosity, and faith were planted in me long ago by the two women who shaped my heart. Their example didn't just teach me how to respond in moments of need, it formed the very lens through which I see the world. And as I reflect on how our family grew in the most unexpected and sacred way, I'm reminded of what they taught me, not just with words, but with their lives. This is what I've learned from them.

**Lessons That Live in Me**

My faith has been formed, tested, and strengthened by the quiet power of two women, my mom and my "Nanny." They didn't preach from pulpits or hold titles, but their lives were daily sermons of trust, love, and surrender to God. This is what I have learned from them.

He doesn't always give us what we want. We may not see the reason why at the beginning but eventually, His greater plan will be revealed. I tell my mom all my troubles and my aspirations. I also tell her when those aspirations do not come true. Her answer is the same every time. It's because God doesn't want it for me. My mom has always been right about this I used to question why I didn't reach a goal, but every time it happened, I eventually saw that it would have taken me down a road that led to unhappiness. I have learned to stop asking why and put my complete faith in God. He has never led me down the wrong path.

Even the storms in our life are there to make way for the rainbows that come after. My grandmother had to go through hardships in order to make her dream of starting a High School in her town come true. She weathered the storms and because of this, Buenavista High School was founded. I remember when I was younger, my mom would always say, "remember, when one problem comes along, more and more will come until you feel like you cannot handle it anymore." She used to tell me this all the time, and I always wondered if she was trying to inspire me with her words, because I certainly did not feel inspired. I wondered what kind of a pep talk she was trying to give me, because it sure as heck did not sound like any kind of pep talk I have ever heard. As I grew older, I began to realize she just wanted to prepare me for life. Life is not easy. As a matter of fact, life is difficult. It is full of twists and turns and ups and downs and she was right, one problem would come, then another and then another until it felt like I would never resurface. But I always did. I learned not to drown when problems arise. I learned that challenges will come and it is up to me to not let it drag me under. It is only temporary and as long as I have unwavering faith, I do what is right, and I pray, everything will be fine.

    My role models always told me that our bodies are the temple of the Holy Spirit and that we can transmit God's love by not turning our backs to those who are in need. We must protect God's temple not only in what we do but in who we let into our minds and hearts. We must surround ourselves with people who enrich our lives, because they also enrich God's temple. I remember my mom always taught me to choose my friends very well. She tells me that she prays for me every day, that I may be surrounded by good people all the time who are upright and virtuous. People who will enhance my life and be an inspiration to me. I have always kept this in mind and have managed to keep wonderful people around me. People who inspire me to be a better person every day. People who are vessels through which God sends me his love.

**The Extraordinary in You**

My two role models have also taught me that there is greatness in being ordinary. Some people have earth-shattering, life-changing moments where they feel the hand of God in their darkest hour. This is not the case for everyone. For most people, God shows his hand in the simplest, most subtle, you can even call it basic way. It could even be in the form of a stranger who says hello to you and gives you a smile when you a stressed out and have a lot of things on your mind and makes you smile back and forget your troubles even if it is only for a few seconds.

God could be working through a friend or sister who calls you out of the blue because you crossed their mind, only for you to realize you desperately needed someone to talk to at that exact moment. God could also be working through you when you chit chat with and laugh with the exhausted cashier at the supermarket. She may be going through a hard time, and you helped her forget her troubles for a moment. To that cashier, you are extraordinary.

My two role models have also taught me to rejoice in my ordinary self because God sees me as extraordinary.

I pray that you, as a reader, see how deeply you matter in the eyes of God. If you ever find yourself wondering if your quiet efforts matter, if your ordinary life makes a difference, let this be your reminder, yes, it does.

May you never underestimate the power of a kind word, a helping hand, or a whispered prayer. May you recognize the divine hidden in your daily routines, and may you have the eyes to see others through God's loving gaze. May your life continue to reflect the quiet strength, unwavering faith, and compassionate heart of the women who raised you.

And when the world calls you ordinary, may heaven smile, because God does extraordinary things through hearts like yours.

**Dr. Rutchie Contreras, PT, DPT**

**Instagram:** @rutchie_contreras

# Chapter 13

# Signs From Heaven: From the Father Above and the Father I Loved

*by Carolina Chams*

*"For God does speak—now one way, now another—though no one perceives it."*
— **Job 33:14 (NIV)**

**1. Invisible Hands at the Wheel**

It was 2008. I was approaching a four-way intersection, ready to turn left. The light had just turned yellow, and I was already moving into the crossing. From the opposite side, a bus came speeding toward me, so fast it seemed to slice through the air.

In that instant, something inside me, an impulse stronger than reason, told me: *"Go."* I obeyed. But as I made the turn, I realized the bus wasn't slowing down. It was accelerating, straight at me.

Everything went silent. Time seemed to stretch. I closed my eyes, gripped the wheel, and braced for the impact I felt was inevitable.

But it never came.

When I opened my eyes, my car was perfectly parked on the sidewalk in front of a restaurant. No crash. No scratches. No memory of steering out of harm's way.

I knew in my soul: it had been my dad. He had died in 2001, but in life, he had a driving skill that bordered on impossible, navigating traffic like a chessboard. My mom used to be terrified by his maneuvers, but he always made it home in one piece.

That moment had his signature. I felt God had allowed him to guide my hands, or maybe take the wheel entirely. I didn't try to rationalize it. I just sat there, trembling, certain I'd been protected.

## 2. Shooting Star

In 2001, when my dad died, it felt like the ground opened beneath my feet. It wasn't just sadness; it was rage, helplessness, disbelief.

I was in Austin, finishing my last semester of college, when I got the call: he was gravely ill, in his final hours. Without thinking, I booked a flight to Barranquilla, with a layover in Miami.

During that layover, before I could even see his face, the phone rang:
*"He's gone."*

The first thought that hit me was, *He didn't wait for me.*

I felt robbed of the chance to say goodbye, to tell him all the things I wanted him to know. Instead of arriving at his side, I arrived at his funeral. That absence burned inside me.

Nights were unbearable. I couldn't sleep. The heaviness of grief and anger pressed on my chest. I was angry at him and at God. All I wanted was to know, somehow, that he was still here.

Weeks later, back in Austin, one night I stepped outside to breathe. I wandered aimlessly until I dropped onto the grass, staring up at a sky so full of stars it seemed to lean toward me. In a faint voice I said: *"Just show me you're still here."*

Within seconds, a shooting star blazed across the sky, quick and brilliant, like a flash of love sent directly to me.

I didn't doubt it. I didn't look for logic. I just let the tears fall and wrote it in my journal: *Today I felt your presence through a shooting star.*

I learned that when you ask from certainty—not desperation—God answers. And often, He uses our loved ones to send the message.

**3. God Wink**

Years later, in 2009, during my civil wedding in Mexico, I experienced another magical moment. We were dancing to our song, *Coincidir*, outdoors at the marina where we celebrated. All the guests were dressed in white.

And out of nowhere, a white dove flew over our dance.

My mom rushed toward me and shouted: *"It's your dad!"*

Seeing a white dove flying at night symbolizes of peace, innocence, purity, and new beginnings, even in the dark. For me, it was his silent blessing.

Six months later, during our church wedding in Barranquilla, Monsignor Tamayo—the same priest who had baptized me and married my parents—asked Jorge's parents and my mom to come forward and place their hands over ours as a sign of support before God. My dad wasn't there physically, but something magical happened: Monsignor placed his own hand to represent him.

When I looked into his eyes, he winked, just like my dad used to do.

I couldn't hold back the tears. I turned to my mom and whispered: *"Dad is here... I just felt him."*

That wink was everything. Not just a gesture, it was the confirmation that he was walking me down the aisle, too.

## 4. The Bear of Strength

My marriage lasted eleven years. It ended during a move from Mexico to the United States, just months before the pandemic.

With three children under the age of eight, in a new country I was barely beginning to call home, it felt like the ground had been ripped from beneath me. I didn't have a strong support network, only my mom, who lived in Minnesota. I had arrived in McAllen, Texas for what was supposed to be a one-year stay, but now it seemed permanent. We moved to Minnesota when they announced everything would shut down for COVID-19.

Amid the pain, I began to receive messages from God. Each day, the signs became more constant, clearer, and more sacred. I started writing without a plan—words, phrases, and messages flowed into my mind as if someone were dictating them to me. Those "downloads" became several projects that would form my coaching methodology and life's purpose.

On my 40th birthday in May 2020, a black bear appeared right in front of my door. I had never seen a bear, let alone so close. We stared at each other, and I swear it winked. My dad.

I looked up the spiritual meaning: power, strength, resilience. I felt he had come specially to give me a birthday message, saying:

*"This is you now. This is how I want to see you: strong, unstoppable, and able to survive anything."*

A Divine messenger, reminding me that communication with God goes beyond prayer and religion, it's a relationship built from the spirit, anytime, anywhere, and in any form. That day, it came through a black bear on my birthday.

## 5. White Feathers

After returning to South Texas and working for two years as the director of a hotel, I decided to resign and bet everything on my life's calling: becoming an author, coach, and motivational speaker. On paper, quitting made no sense. I had a good salary, flexibility, benefits, and could even bring my kids with me in emergencies.

But I couldn't ignore that inner voice any longer. I felt the same clarity you feel when you know a cycle has ended. It was time to go. And in that calling, my dad was there too—like a force pushing me forward, as if saying: *"It's time to take the wheel, daughter. Don't be afraid to change routes."*

I obeyed. Before making the decision, I asked for a sign. Since my divorce, I had been receiving white feathers from my angels. Whenever I found one, I knew I was on the right path. In the days before resigning, the feathers multiplied down the hotel hallways, in the gardens, even on my car window.

I knew it was the right choice and that everything would be okay. So, I took the leap and embraced the adventure of entrepreneurship. Today I'm a certified coach by the Napoleon Hill Institute, an international speaker, TEDx speaker, and best-selling author. This has been possible because I made God my CEO, and because I know I always have an invisible co-pilot who never leaves my side.

## 6. The Dove

It was June 11, 2025, and my home was buzzing with energy. My sisters from the M3 mastermind group had come over for a special exercise after an event led by Eliza, where she spoke about releasing the ego's mask. We had decided to write a letter, read it aloud, and burn it as a symbol of letting go of our old selves and our ego. Present were Eliza, Magdalena, Esther with her boyfriend, and Giselle.

When my turn came, I held my letter in my hands. Every word I had written carried pieces of my story, my burdens, and my old identity. I read it all, feeling guilt, fear, and wounds fall away from me.

Just as I finished, something unexpected happened. Eliza, eyes wide, interrupted:
*"Caro... a dove."*

She was the only one who saw it, but her description still gives me chills: a white dove appeared right behind me, as if it had come out of my back. It flew over me, then over each person present... and disappeared.

I didn't see it, but I didn't need to. I felt it. I knew it was God confirming my rebirth, and my dad celebrating it with me, surrounding me with his blessing. It was as if they both said:
*"You're ready now. Walk lightly."*

That moment reaffirmed what I now know about God: He is always here. He whispers, guides, waits. And so does my dad. Together they have filled my life with winks, feathers, shooting stars, and invisible hands.

## 7. Ask for a Sign

If you wait for a sign, don't ask from fear. Fear clouds your vision and makes you doubt what you receive. Ask from certainty, the kind that feels as certain as the sun rising tomorrow.

When you ask, be clear. Talk to God, the Universe, or your angels as if you were speaking to a friend. Tell them exactly what you want to see as confirmation:

- *"If this job is right for me, let me see a red cardinal"*

- *"If I'm meant to take this leap, send me a white feather"*

- *"If my loved one is with me, show me a butterfly that gets close enough for me to notice."*

Then, **let it go**. Don't hunt for the sign. Don't obsess over it. Live your life and trust that, if it's meant to come, it will, often when you least expect it.

Be open to *how* it arrives and what form it takes. The cardinal might be on a coffee mug. The feather could be in a parking lot or even in the background of a random Instagram post. Sometimes your sign won't come in the literal way you imagined, but the feeling will be unmistakable, like God leaning in and saying, *"This is for you."*

When the sign arrives, stop. Receive it. Let it sink in. Give thanks out loud. Gratitude seals the moment into your soul, making you more attuned to future signs.

If my children read this someday, I want them to know: you never walk alone. Ask. Trust. Open your eyes wide. Because when heaven is on your team, there's always a move that changes the game in your favor.

And when you see your own shooting star, find a white feather, or receive an unexpected wink, smile and whisper: *"You're here. You always were."*

God and my dad speak to me through details others might dismiss as coincidence: a butterfly tapping at my window, a song carrying the exact words my soul needed, a white feather where no feather should be, a sunset that stops the world in its tracks.

For me, each is more than a sign. It's a love letter from the unseen.

And once you learn the language, you'll realize that heaven never stops speaking.

## Carolina Chams

**Instagram:** @carochams

# Chapter 14

# The Beauty of God's Grace

*by Jaimie Luna*

*"Do not be anxious about anything, but in every situation, by prayer and petition, with thanksgiving, present your requests to God..."*
— **Philippians 4:6–7 (NIV)**

**Your Story Matters**

For as long as I can remember, I didn't think I had anything worthy to say. Like my story was too quiet, too complicated, and wasn't impressive or interesting enough to be heard. But looking back at my life, I have come to realize that God had a story in mind for my life. In God's word, it says, *"Before I formed you in the womb I knew you, and before you were born I consecrated you; I appointed you a prophet to the nations"* (Jeremiah 1:5).

Because I choose to believe what God says about me and not the enemy, I know now that my story does matter. Because if God could move in my life the way He has, I know He can do it for you too.

**The Quiet Struggles**

I gave my life to Jesus in the second grade. One day my best friend invited me to Vacation Bible School, and something stirred in my heart that stayed with me forever. I didn't understand a lot about God, but I knew He was real and I knew that He was with me through every season of my life:

the good, the bad, and all the messy, misunderstood parts in between.

I grew up in Houston, in a two-story white frame house on a corner lot. Each room had a different colored carpet: blue, red, and pink, a detail left behind by the Chinese couple who lived there before us. On the outside, our home looked like one of the best on the block, but on the inside, there were quiet struggles that shaped how I saw myself and how I would live my life for a very long time.

My parents had me at a very young age, and they worked hard to provide for us. For that, I am truly grateful. I know they did their best to raise us the best way they knew how but I believe they were carrying their own wounds. They carried wounds that were hard to deal with, and maybe they just weren't given the right tools to overcome them in victory.

My father was a proud man that always had a strong and powerful voice. One that was very intimidating when it got loudest. My dad had a deep knowledge of Scripture to the point where he could quote verses and talk about the Bible in such an articulate and intelligent way. But like many of us, he wrestled with the desires of the flesh and living in the power of the Holy Spirit. He was a hard worker who provided for his family, but there were nights I remember him getting home late after drinking, which caused many arguments between him and my mom. It also caused a lot of worry and anxiety in my own life.

Now, as an adult, I can see more clearly. I've come to understand that my father wasn't trying to hurt anyone. His childhood was full of hardship, poverty, and tough love, along with the pressure to help his mom provide for the family at a very young age when his father was not present. Those deep wounds didn't disappear just because he became a dad. No one taught him how to deal with deep emotions or deal with the weight he was carrying. I believe he did the best he could with what he had at the time. He could not give to us what he did not have himself. But at the time, I did not realize this because my perspective was different. When God comes into your life, He gives you a whole new lens to see from that actually allows you to see the whole picture with eyes of faith compared to the limited vantage point the enemy wants to keep you in when you only see through your own eyes.

**Always Trying to Blend In**

Even still, I felt the weight of it as a little girl. I can remember always feeling like I was walking on eggshells, trying not to say the wrong thing because it might get him upset. I became my mother's quiet helper, carrying emotional burdens I didn't yet know how to process. I didn't want to add to her stress, so I kept everything to myself because it was easier that way. I learned early on that keeping it all in and staying busy helped me regulate my emotions. I made it a point to get involved at school—orchestra, drill team, student council, Girl Scouts— just trying to feel a sense of belonging. I smiled, I performed, I achieved. But deep inside, I often felt rejected and anxious all the time. It didn't matter what I did because the feelings of rejection always seemed to get the best of me.

 I remember my Elementary years being so hard because I was so shy and timid. Do you remember ever feeling like you just wanted to crawl in a hole and never come out? That was me!!! I had the kind of anxiety that was so gut wrenching you felt it deep to the core of your being. I remember hating to walk into class late because that meant everyone's eyes were on me. I always felt like I was trying to just blend in so that no one would really notice me. There was one time that my mom dropped me off late and I accidentally closed the car door on my finger so I got off the car and hid behind a bush in front of the school and my mom noticed that something was wrong but I did not want to tell her because I was just that type of girl, the one who held everything in, even pain, and didn't want to tell a single soul what I was going through. I was hoping the pain would go away and I wouldn't have to be a bother to anyone but it didn't. It actually kept throbbing more and more as I stood there behind the bush that day. My mom finally got off the car to see what was wrong with me and I ended up having to go see the doctor because my whole thumb nail had come off.

That's how hard I had slammed the door on it. Because I was so painfully shy, I would find great comfort in writing in diaries at such a young age. I felt this was the only way I could express myself and get all the feelings out that I was going through. My journals became my safe place, filled with drawings, prayers, and pages I wrote as letters to God because I knew that even though I couldn't see Him, He was always there. I didn't fully understand why I was going through what I did, but I knew He was with me and that gave me such peace in my heart. A peace that doesn't come from this world, but only through the Grace of God.

*"You will keep him in perfect peace, Whose mind is stayed on You, Because he trusts in You,"* (Isaiah 26:3)

### The Power of a Parent's Prayer

In middle school, I struggled with the way I looked because of my weight. Food was one way that I learned how to cope and deal with my feelings and emotions. I remember eating and then trying to make myself throw up so I wouldn't gain more weight. I already felt bad about myself and now I had to deal with my outward appearance. One day I remember waking up, and one of my leg's didn't want to move. It was very strange and I did feel scared. I went to school that day and I continued to feel my leg get tingly and stiff throughout the day so I went to the nurse and my mom came to pick me up so that she could take me to the doctor. As I was walking with my mom I had a seizure in the middle of the school hallway. My mom later told me that I just fell to the floor and she screamed so loud for help that everyone came out to see what was going on. The next thing I knew I was in the hospital. The doctors would later tell my parents that I was going through adolescence and my body was under a lot of stress because all the other test came back normal. I had a few more episodes of seizures so the doctor put me on medication. This traumatic experience really made my dad turn to God for help. I remember him telling me that he asked God to heal me and if He did, he would change his ways and would serve Him. I really felt that God heard my parent's prayer request and He healed me from epilepsy; I stopped taking medication after a few months and never had another seizure again. Looking back on that journey, I don't think I fully realized how God had healed me until I was much older. I will be forever grateful. Only God could have done something like that.

> *"And whatever things you ask in prayer, believing, you will receive."* (Matthew 21:22)

**Heartbreak and more Challenges**

In high school, I experienced my first heartbreak. My boyfriend cheated on me with a very close friend of mine at the time and she was also on my dance team. I was devastated. I cried to my mom—one of the few times I let my guard down like that. She was there for me. Her presence was everything to me. She always had such a quiet strength about her that I will never forget. No matter what she was going through, she got up every day, went to work full time and she never let it stop her from being the best Mom that we could ever ask for. She is the strongest person I know.

The pain that I went through, as much as it hurt, became the push I needed to leave Houston and start fresh in the Rio Grande Valley since my dad always wanted to move back to his home town. The move came with its own challenges, as I would miss all my childhood friends and my life as I once knew it. Thankfully, I was able to join the dance team at my new school and by the grace of God, I made new friends because I always considered myself an introvert. On the outside, I was fine. But inside, I still carried that sense of rejection, like I didn't quite fit in anywhere. That's something I've had to deal with all my life.

I remember suffering from my first mental breakdown at the age of seventeen. When my family and I moved to South Texas, we lived with my grandmother as my parents looked for a house to provide for us. But for those that know, it is very hard to live with more than one family in a household. My uncle, aunt and my cousins also lived there with us at the time. You never really have privacy and my dad was very strict with us growing up so having to deal with his mood swings in someone else's house gave me so much anxiety because we were always on edge. Never really having that sense of peace that I longed to have as a family. One night, I remember having so much anxiety that I could not sleep. I would toss and turn and I just didn't feel right. My heart was racing and my nerves were all over the place, my eyes twitched, and I couldn't stop shaking. I thought I was having another seizure so I told my sister how I felt and she quickly told my mom and she called 9-1-1.

I remember my uncle trying to calm me down and asked me if I knew Jesus and I told him, yes, I did. It was then, that the paramedics came into the room to check me and they told my mom that I was not having a seizure but that I was having a mental breakdown. I didn't even know what that was at the time. All I know is what I felt was real and I could not process all the emotions I was feeling. I remember always asking God, "Why me, Lord? Why is all this happening to me? I wish it would all just go away!" There were times that I did not even want to live anymore. I just wanted to go to Heaven, my permanent home and not feel any pain or hurt anymore. Even though I was going through so much God never left me.

> *"Where can I go from your spirit? Or where can I flee from Your presence? If I ascend into heaven, You are there; If I make my bed in hell, behold, You are there. If I take the*

*wings of the morning, And dwell in the uttermost parts of the sea, Even there Your hand shall lead me, And Your right hand shall hold me."* (Psalm 139: 7-10)

**Fear, Failure, and God's Unmerited Favor**

College brought another wave of struggle. I didn't know exactly what I wanted to do but I knew I wanted to use the gifts and talents the Lord gave me. I was not always the smart one or the fastest, but I was very creative! I always found myself doodling on paper or journals and I always had a love for drawing and writing ever since I was a little girl so I knew I wanted to do something that I could use my creativity. I always doubted myself, and I remember changing majors a lot because I was afraid to fail in anything I did. One day I was having a conversation with my aunt about my future, and she told me that I was very nurturing and that I would make a good teacher! Because of her encouraging words, I decided to just go for it and face my fears to become an art teacher! She really helped me to believe that I was good at something, and her words made all the difference. Always try to help others with words of encouragement because it might just be the words they need to hear to move forward in the plan God has for them!

Anxiety and fear took over my mind and my heart at a much deeper level. I would register for classes and then skip final presentations because fear had such a hold on me. I failed classes, not because I didn't care but because I had so much anxiety and I struggled with public speaking so much that I would rather drop a class right at the end if it required me to stand up in front of class and give a presentation. Because of this destructive cycle, it took me many years to finish my degree not because I wasn't capable but because I let fear get the best of me. I worked multiple jobs while I was attending school because it was easier to stay in my comfort zone. I was afraid of the future because I didn't believe in myself, but that was the problem. I had been looking in the wrong place. I didn't need my own strength or confidence; I needed God's. This is something I am still working on to this day. All my instructors would fail me for not giving that last speech all except for one.

I remember it was my turn to go up to the front and present my final presentation for the semester. I had already spent the whole night rehearsing my speech in front of my room mates and I really felt I was ready this time and I was actually going to do it! But as I stood there looking at everyone, I looked back at my professor and told her I couldn't do it. I walked out of class and guess what happened? She came out right after me and asked what was wrong? I told her I just couldn't do it and I began to explain to her my anxieties that held me back for so long. She told me, "You know I can fail you right now, but I'm not.

Instead, I am going to give you one more chance because I know you have potential and you can do this." I could not believe it! I was beyond grateful! I practiced, prayed, and asked God to help me, knowing I couldn't do it alone. I needed his strength more than ever. I went back to class that week and felt worried but all of a sudden, I felt like this wave of confidence that I asked my speech professor if I could go first to present and she said yes. I went up there and I did the thing!!! Thank you, Jesus!!! To make a long story short, my professor not only passed me, but she gave me an "A" for the class. Again, only God!!!!!

> *"My grace is sufficient for you, for My strength is made perfect in weakness. Therefore, most gladly I will rather boast in my infirmities, that the power of Christ may rest upon me"*
> (2 Corinthians 12:9)

God was so faithful that He gave me the opportunity to finally finish but it definitely did not come easy for me. I felt so overwhelmed and defeated right before my last semester of college that I dropped all my classes. I believe this was the worst that I had ever gotten. I let the enemy convince me that

I didn't have what it took to complete what God had started in me. I remembered that I isolated myself in my room, listening to every lie in my head: *"You're not enough. You'll never finish. Just stay where it's safe,"* and still to this day, it brings tears to my eyes because I remember everything I felt during that time, and it was the hardest thing to overcome. I believe it was because God was up to something big in my life and when God is doing something in your life so lifechanging, you better believe the enemy will do his best to distract you from God's purpose for you. That is why it is so important that you stand your ground no matter the circumstances and never give up no matter how hard it gets because the Lord will fight your battles if you will trust Him with your dreams and your goals.

> *"But as for you, you meant evil against me; but God meant it for good, in order to bring it about as it is this day, to save many people alive."* (Genesis 50:20)

My dad, whom I didn't have a close relationship growing up noticed something was off. He sat me down and said, "I don't know what's going on, but I BELIEVE IN YOU". And if anyone can do this, it's you." Those words were life changing for me at the time. It is amazing to me how our words can bring life or death to a person. I had never heard him say that before. It was like God Himself reached into the broken places of our relationship and spoke healing through the very same person I had struggled to understand as a child. I truly believe God can use anyone, especially those you would least expect. Never underestimate the people God brings into your life.

I prayed and sought God like I had never done before. I asked God to make a way. I went back to the university and asked to re-register for my classes. The woman at the counter looked doubtful and knew the school policies and procedures wouldn't allow this. But after a conversation with her supervisor, she came back and said, "We're going to let you back in just this once."

Now that was the hand of God because I knew without a shadow of a doubt that it wouldn't have been possible without His intervention. I was so thankful and relieved of what He had done for me.

> *"With men this is impossible, but with God all things are possible."* (Matthew 19:26)

**God is Good and He is Faithful**

The day finally came for graduation. I was so happy and still in disbelief that I actually accomplished what I had set out to do.

Despite all my fears and failures and so many sleepless nights full of anxiety, God was still working behind the scenes on my behalf and I finally accomplished my goal of becoming an Art Teacher. Three years later, I was humbled and honored to have been named **Teacher of the Year** at my school and to my greatest surprise, **District Teacher of the Year**!!! Me, the scared little girl who once believed she'd never make it through college. All I could think was: *Look at what God has done! I could have never imagined that this would even be possible for me. The one who wanted to quit. Had I done that I would have never experienced all of God's goodness and what He could achieve through me. I don't share this part to boast about myself in any way because none of this would be possible without the Lord. I share this to let everyone know the faithfulness of God that He will not only bless you but He will bless you in abundance! More than you could ever imagine if you will just surrender and trust Him.*

> *"Humble yourselves, therefore, under the mighty hand of God so that at the proper time he may exalt you, casting all your anxieties on him, because he cares for you."*
> (1 Peter 5:6-7)

*There are students that I still run into that are already in college or married and that I don't always feel that I left any impact in their lives but I recently saw one of my students working at a store near my house and I didn't recognize him right away but as he was ringing up my items that I had bought all of a sudden I saw quiet tears coming down his eyes. I asked him if he was ok and he said yes. But as I looked up at him, I started to recognize him. I asked him if he attended the first school that I worked at and he said yes! I knew it, he was one of my former students and he was all grown up now. I could not remember his name but I did remember his face. He had told me that he got teary eyed because he remembered me and it brought back good memories of how I helped him through a tough time that he was going through as a young boy. He had never told me this before so I was unaware but I was so thankful to hear him share that with me. You just never know who you will impact in your journey. This young man made my day and made me realize that everything I endured, all the hard work, anxiety and fear was all worth it because I was able to help him when he needed it most. I would have never been able to experience that moment and many others like that if I had given up and not had the courage to complete what God set out for me to do.*

"*Being confident of this very thing, that He who has begun a good work in you will complete it until the day of Jesus Christ.*" (Philippians 1:6)

**A Late Bloomer Is Not Always Late**

I have always been a late bloomer in life with pretty much everything but I know that God had a reason for that too. I received my bachelor's degree at the age of thirty. I got married at 35 and I always share the funny story that five years later, my husband and I went on a cruise and came home with a souvenir. You guessed it, at the age of 40, God gave us a little firecracker—a very bright, funny, creative and precious boy who reminds me every day that God's timing is perfect! I found out I was pregnant a day before Mother's Day and we couldn't believe it!!! I was a TIA and a teacher but now I was going to be a Mama and I was just in awe of God! It took me a while to wrap my mind around the fact that I was going to be a Mother to a baby of my very own. God is never late but always on time, His time that is.

*"He has made everything beautiful in its time."*
(Ecclesiastes 3:11)

Now that I am a parent, I try so hard to be intentional with my words. I try my best to tell my son as much as I can that he's loved, seen, and that his voice matters. I affirm him not just with actions, but with God's truth. I know the power of words, because I know what it felt like to hear hurtful words, and I know how it can affect your entire life if you let it. I know my parents did their best with what they had to give and I appreciate them more now that I am a mother. I realized that it is not easy being a parent and that we can all make mistakes because we all fall short of God's glory, including myself. My only hope is that my son will also find it in his heart to forgive me of all my short comings, the ones that I am aware of and the ones that I am not. We all strive to be good parents, but sometimes life and circumstances get in the way of our better judgement. I hope that I will also teach him to love others the way God sees them and to forgive even when they don't deserve it. I love my son so much, and I am deeply grateful and honored to be his mama. Never in a million years did I think I would become a mom, but God!

He is the reason why I wanted to contribute to this amazing book so that he could see the goodness and faithfulness of our Lord and Savior.

God knew what He was doing when He brought him into my life at the time that he did. My son has changed me for the better and has helped me to be much more braver than I ever thought I could be. I also want to leave a legacy of what God has done for me in hopes that it will inspire not only my son but all my nephews and nieces and all those that I love to trust God with their lives too. Knowing and believing that

God has great plans for their lives even when they can't always feel it or see it.

> *"For I know the thoughts that I think toward you, says the Lord, thoughts of peace and not of evil, to give you a future and a hope. Then you will call upon Me and go and pray to Me, and I will listen to you. And you will seek Me and find Me, when you search for Me with all your heart."*
> (Jeremiah 29:11-13)

**Choosing to Forgive**

Through the grace of God, I believe I have overcome many things in my life but I'm still healing and growing stronger in the Lord everyday through prayer and reading God's word. My relationship with my dad was a very difficult one growing up but through the years has gotten so much better now because I chose to forgive him for the past. It was not easy and it took many years to learn that forgiveness takes time and patience but it is necessary in order for you to have peace and for God to be able to move in your life. How can we not forgive if God has chosen to forgive us of our sins time and time again.

> *"For if you forgive men their trespasses, your heavenly Father will also forgive you. But if you do not forgive men their trespasses, neither will your Father forgive your trespasses."*
> (Matthew 6:14-15)

I've seen God work in his life through illness, from a stroke to sepsis, and yet he is still here with us. I prayed for MANY years for him to go to church and let God change his heart and God did answer that prayer too. After he got sick, I started to see a change in him and he was more active and present in our family's lives. I also had the privilege of seeing my dad and my mom get baptized together and they are now attending the same church I attend. I stand next to him and my mom on any given Sunday and I am still in awe of what God has done and continues to do when we trust Him. Our family is not perfect and there are still some things that need to change but we serve a God who is faithful and when we put our faith in Him, He continues to transform our lives from the inside out. Focus on the things that are good, the things God has already done for you, and leave the rest up to Him. I am so thankful for my mom and dad no matter what we have gone through as a family because I wouldn't be who I am today without them. Even through heartbreak, fear and anxiety, there was still always genuine love and a sense of strength, grit and resilience that I wouldn't have had without the first parts of my story. Most importantly, I grew closer to the Lord because of it and I learned to depend on God and not man.

> *"And we know that all things work together for good to those who love God, to those who are the called according to His purpose."*
> (Romans 8:28)

## Learning to trust God with your story

I'm still healing and growing every day because I do not want to hide anymore. I'm learning to trust God with my story, not just the shiny parts but the parts that are vulnerable and hard to share for fear of judgment or rejection. But in God's word, it tells us *"For God has not given us the spirit of fear, but of power and of love and of a sound mind."* (2 Timothy 1:7). I choose to believe God and His truth because the enemy is a liar and he only wants to do one thing and that is to destroy our testimony.

> *"The thief does not come except to steal, and to kill, and to destroy. I have come that they may have life, and that they may have it more abundantly."* (John 10:10)

Don't let him win this time. I have wasted so much time believing the lies that I don't want to waste another minute because I want to live the best life that God has for me. Life is too short not to be living your best life in Christ.

And if you're reading this, feeling anxious, afraid, or like your dreams are too far gone or out of reach, let me tell you: *You are not too late and God sees you and he wants to meet you right where you are.*

God has a way of redeeming every moment. Every failure. Every delay. He turns brokenness into beauty. Silence into testimony. Pain into purpose. Don't waste your pain but share it to help someone else tell their own story one day. God has given everyone a story because He created you and He knows your beginning and your end and everything in between. What is yours? What is God asking you to do so that you can walk boldly in your calling? As my dad once told me and I will never forget it because it has helped me in so many ways, "Do it afraid." That's the only way you will learn to overcome hard things by doing it afraid and realizing that you can do them if you will trust that God is with you. This verse has been my favorite verse that I hold so close to my heart because it has given me so much peace in my life.

> *"Be Anxious for nothing but in everything by prayer and supplication, with thanksgiving, let your request be made known and the peace of God that surpasses all understanding will guard your hearts and minds through Christ Jesus our Lord."* (Philippians 4:6-7)

Dear friend, I believe in you and your story! Live to tell it and see what God can do through your courage and obedience. He has given us all an assignment on this earth. The question is, are you going to do your best to walk in faith and accomplish all that He has for you or are you going to shrink back and just live to survive in your current circumstances. Be encouraged today and believe that God created you for so much more! Choose to believe that He doesn't always call the qualified but He always qualifies the called! He has given you everything you need for your assignment. All you have to do is ask Him what He wants you to do and be willing to be obedient.

*"As His divine power has given to us all things that pertain to life and godliness, through the knowledge of Him who called us by glory and virtue."* (2 Peter 1:3)

**A Prayer for You, my Friend**

Dear Lord,

I ask that you be with your beautiful daughter today. The one that is tired and overwhelmed and who is reading this right now in the season that she is in. I pray that you would wrap your loving arms around her and she would feel your presence in such a way that is undeniable. I pray that you would fill her life with great hope and purpose that you have planned for her even before she was born. Let her know that she was created in your image to do great things and that even though she may not see it right now, you are working all things for her good. *"And we know that all things work together for good to those who love God, to those who are the called according to His purpose."* Romans 8:28 There is nothing that she has gone through that is ever wasted because you will use everything to reveal her true calling on her life as she learns to trust you. Help her to live with intention, purpose and passion from this day forward, knowing that she is never alone.

Let this be her wakeup call that now is the time to rise up and step into who it is that God has called her to be. Help her to live in the expectancy that God will bring miracles and blessings into her life as she learns to surrender the past that she can't change and forgive those that have hurt her deeply. Help her to release that burden to you so that you can replace that emptiness in her heart with your perfect peace that she has been longing for. Help her to move forward in your unfailing love, mercy and grace all the days of her life because the world needs to see more of her and everything God created her to be. Know that I, along with all my sisters in Christ, am cheering and rooting for you, friend! You got this!!

*"Fear not, for I am with you; Be not dismayed, for I am your God. I will strengthen you, Yes, I will help you, I will uphold you with My righteous right hand."* (Isaiah 41:10)

**Jaimie Luna**

**Instagram:** @mrs.jaimie29

# Chapter 15

# Legacy in My Blood

*by Chelsea Victoria Gonzalez*

*"One generation commends your works to another; they tell of your mighty acts."*
— **Psalm 145:4 (NIV)**

They say blood remembers. It carries laughter, pain, grit, and love. I didn't understand that until I became a mother and realized that everything strong in me came from a woman born in a different world, my grandmother, Maria de Los Angeles Rios Uribe.

She was born in 1931, in Linares, Nuevo León, Mexico. One of ten siblings, seven girls and three boys, raised on a farm by campesino parents and grandparents. Life was tough, pero la familia era fuerte (but the family was strong). They worked the land with their hands and held each other up with their hearts. There wasn't money, but there was love, pan casero (homemade bread), and unity. They survived together. That's how she was raised, and that's how she raised us.

At just sixteen, Grandma Maria became a schoolteacher, *la maestra*. Smart, driven, and full of ganas. She brought her whole family from the rancho to the city so they could have better opportunities. That's who she was: always looking out for everyone. Always ahead of her time.

Then came the love of her life, Juan Uribe. They met at a dance, the kind where dresses twirled, laughter filled the air, and sparks flew across the dance floor. They fell in love.

Deeply. Honestly. He was a carpenter and a construction worker, calm, patient, and good. He built their house with his own hands. She left her teaching job, followed her heart, and started a new life with him in McAllen, Texas.

There, they had six children, Juan, Mirna, Victor, Belinda, Rosina, and David. All different. All loved. She was the disciplinarian, and he was the soft-spoken balance. They were a team. But then life shifted.

One day, as Juan was finishing touches at a construction site, he fell off a ladder. A broken leg turned tragic in the hospital. Too much anesthesia. Not enough answers. He didn't make it. In 1970, Grandma became a widow at 38 with six young kids, some just toddlers.

She didn't get to grieve the way people should. There was no time. Discrimination was heavy in those days. A single mother. A Mexican woman. Trying to survive in America. It was hard to get work, hard to get by but she did it. Somehow.

She went back to school to learn English, reading it, writing it, speaking it. She took a job at a warehouse, starting on the line and working her way up to supervisor, managing over one hundred employees. Respect wasn't given, it was earned. And she earned every ounce. Even when her body ached from hours on her feet, she never showed weakness. Her strength was quiet, steady, and consistent. She was the kind of woman who didn't need applause to keep going.

But life wasn't done testing her. Years later, she lost her son Victor at seventeen, a drowning accident at South Padre Island. She wasn't there. And it shattered her. Shattered all of us. But still she stood. She kept going. For the rest of the kids. For the future. For the hope that something good could still be built from the ashes of her pain.

Her oldest, Juan Uribe Jr., stepped up. He became a second father to his siblings, graduated from Texas A&M, and became an engineer for NASA in Houston. Grandma's eyes sparkled with pride every time she spoke of him. Her other children went on to build good lives too, educated, strong, married, parents of their own. Each of them carries her fire, her faith, her fierce love. Each of them a testament to her sacrifice and her relentless belief in a better future.

And then there's us, the grandchildren. We grew up at Grandma's house. Sleeping over, getting disciplined with just one look, *ya tú sabes*, the kind of stare that straightened you out without a word. We learned to make tamales, eat nopales and papaya, and sit with her and her *comadres* in rocking chairs while they chismeaban and laughed like girls again.

She always had family around—tías, cousins, people she helped immigrate from Reynosa and Monterrey. She gave them papers, jobs, shelter, and love. She was the center of every gathering. The loudest laugh. The warmest plate of mole. The softest heart, but only if you earned it. Her home was more than four walls. It was a sanctuary. A place where you were fed, prayed over, and reminded of who you are.

Now, as a mother myself, I look back at all she endured, widowhood, poverty, discrimination, loss, and I draw my strength from her. If she could survive all that, raise good children, help her family, and still love with her whole heart, then I can too.

Her story is about that legacy. It's about the kind of woman who bends, but doesn't break. Who mothers, not just with her hands, but with her prayers. Who plants seeds of faith in a world that didn't make space for women to fall apart and somehow bloomed anyway.

Her story left a permanent imprint on my heart. Becoming a mother helped me understand the depth of her sacrifice and the weight of her love. She didn't just raise a family, she built a foundation that still holds all of us. She believed she could, and she did. Alone but never without God. And now, because of her, I believe I can too.

Motherhood opened me up. It stripped away distractions, ego, and self-centeredness, until all I had left was me and God. I stopped feeling sorry for myself. I stopped complaining. Because I understood: She did it with less. She did it through pain. And she did it with grace.

She made me reflect. Not just on her life, but on where I come from and what I'm leaving behind. I began asking my family more questions. I wanted to understand more about how they survived, how they kept their faith. I started to realize that their strength isn't just a story, it's my inheritance.

There's something about the first year of motherhood that humbles you. No matter how prepared you think you are, it will shake you. It will test you. And it will grow you. I remember holding my daughter, sleep-deprived and sore from a difficult delivery, and thinking, *how did Grandma do this six times?* Without help. Without Google. Without rest. I started to cry, not out of fear, but out of awe. I finally saw her. Not just as Grandma, but as a woman. A warrior. A survivor.

I now carry the generational blessing of presence. I make time for my cousins' kids. I plan outings. I say, "Let's all go to church together," or "Let's meet at the market." It's not about the event, it's about staying connected. My grandmother's home was the heart of our family. I want my children to feel that same heartbeat.

I want my daughter to know that resilience runs in her blood. That she comes from people who endured, who believed, who rose. That she carries the light. Because legacy isn't just what we leave behind, it's what we *live* right now.

And even now, I can hear Grandma's words in my spirit: "Life keeps going, so you have to keep going. All we have is our family, so keep your faith."

If you're reading this, and you're in a season where it feels like too much please know, you're not alone. You come from women who made a way when there wasn't one. You come from strength. You come from love. You come from God.

Sometimes the strongest thing you can do is simply keep showing up. To your children. To your calling. To your healing. Even when it's hard. Even when you're tired. Even when you don't feel like enough.

But you are, because they were.

With love, faith, and presence you will rise, just like they did.

**Gracias, Grandma.** For every lesson, every look, every laugh. For the stories. For the recipes. For the sacrifice. For showing us what it means to never give up.

*Te amo para siempre.*

With all my heart,
Your granddaughter,

**Chelsea Victoria Gonzalez**

**Chelsea Gonzalez**

**Instagram:** @mschelseabella

# Chapter 16

# Jesus and Ganas

*by Dr. Esmeralda Adame*

*"You intended to harm me, but God intended it for good to accomplish what is now being done, the saving of many lives."*
— **Genesis 50:20 (NIV)**

**Pulled From the Water**

You never forget the moment your life flashes before your eyes. Not just in memory, but in surrender. I was sixteen. Drowning. My body gave out before my faith did. In that final second, I whispered, "Okay, God. If this is it, then let it be for something." And just like that, the lifeguard came to my rescue, reached for me, and pulled me out to safety. It wasn't just a rescue, it was a reminder. That God had been there all along.

I did see my life flash before my eyes and something very vivid in my mind still is that I didn't want to ruin my sister's wedding that was just a few months ahead. But I did not know how to swim, I felt I was about to pass out, and all I said was God if it's your will I'm ready. However, it wasn't my time, or He left me here to fulfill my purpose.

I approached life with a different lens even at that young age.

What truly carried me all these years was Jesus. Through it all, I knew He was always there. He never left me. And that knowing, that deep assurance, was the anchor to my soul. The most incredible thing was realizing that I didn't choose God, God chose me. The fact that He knows my name, this is just unbelievable, and it makes me feel chosen and loved.

I believe that's why the attacks on my life have always been fierce, because the calling on my life is just as powerful and is meant to impact thousands.

The enemy has attacked every area of my life and has fought my future because he knows that God will use my testimony to influence generations.

But that wasn't the beginning.

**Roots, Wounds, and Silence**

The beginning was a little girl with pigtails, living in a crowded house, where love was present but so was poverty. The kind of poverty you don't realize you're in until you leave it. We were twelve in total. My parents worked tirelessly to put food on the table. We didn't have much, but we had faith. I grew up hearing stories of God's power about how He healed and how He saved.

We were a big family and much more when you counted the extended family. Childhood memories, the good ones, I keep close to my heart. I remember vividly walking to church on Sundays and during the week. The ranch as we called it, was a small town with a Pentecostal church where my mother would take us. My father never attended, however but he never kept my mother from taking us and he always made sure we had an offering.

I grew up listening to God's miracles and the wonderful things He did. The Sunday school stories of how He created heaven and earth and how He gave sight to the blind, how He cured the crippled and so many amazing deeds. It was so ingrained in me that even though I had not seen one with my own eyes, I was a believer.

However, at just three or four years old, I experienced it firsthand when I was miraculously healed from an unknown leg condition. God heard my mother's daily prayers and tremendous faith. That was my first encounter with Jesus. The first time He performed a miracle on me.

But knowing Jesus and walking with Him are two different things.

When I was about five years old, something happened that should never happen to a child. But I didn't know it was wrong. I didn't have a name for it. So, I buried it deep, the way I was taught. In our culture, you don't talk about it. You stay busy, focus on the positive, protect the family, even the abuser. So that's what I did. I stayed busy with school, family, and church.

In a Mexican household, if you have time to think, you have time to clean. We don't always process; we survive. We keep going.

The first time it happened we had a full house, besides our family there were others visiting. I can still remember the noises, my mom cooking in the kitchen, kids running around, adults talking. Then it happened, he lured me outside into a truck. And then took my innocence just like that. Not knowing the harm and scars that this would cause.

After a while I remember my mother asking for me and then asking where I was, my sisters were around. And when I told her where and who I was with I was scolded, was told to let her know where I'm going next time and was brushed off. I never shared what actually happened since as a child I was afraid of being scolded again.

And that's how that memory was hidden away and never talked about again. The abuse continued multiple times. Later, it came from another family member as well. As an innocent child at that age, I had no idea what that was nor was I aware that I needed to speak up or that I should have told my parents. Too young to understand, no idea how to deal with the trauma, no clue on how to process the awful experience.

**Encounter and Surrender**

Still, it wasn't until I was fourteen that everything shifted. That's when I truly had my first encounter with Jesus and I felt His embrace. Not just the God from the Sunday school stories, but the One who chose me, the one that had been there all along. It was then when I surrendered and asked God to take it all.

Jesus has always been my anchor no matter how far I go, what I go through or how bad the devil attacks. Jesus chose me, and since that true encounter with Him, I knew that He would make a way, take my pain, and my story. He would guide me and use me for His kingdom.

Up until then, life had been a mix of school days and youth group nights. I believed in God, yes, but it was that encounter at the Weslaco Apostolic Church that lit the fire inside. That's when my walk with Christ really began. I knew then that education was the way out of poverty, but my faith and trust in Jesus would be the one to propel me forward.

All these years I tucked the abuse away in a box in my mind, buried beneath the busyness, beneath the survival. All this time I was thinking it was okay, no one needs to know.

Looking back now, I realize that it was not okay. I was just surviving, not healing. I often wonder how different life would be if this awful situation was not part of my childhood. If there were available resources, if these scenarios were more openly talked about, if someone would have seen my pain. However, I don't carry bitterness. My parents were doing their best, working tirelessly just to feed the twelve of us and them. Even though love was there, so was pain, and survival.

Even with all that understanding, it wasn't until I was sixteen or seventeen that I began to realize what had happened. The shame, the fear, the heartbreak, the weight of it all surfaced. It was then that I contemplated telling someone, maybe my parents. Five siblings crammed into one room, dad always working, mom always doing house chores. The pain it would cause them, the ripple effect; it just felt too heavy to add another burden to their shoulders. So, I kept it in the memory box and carried it in silence. I told myself maybe it was not the right time yet, or maybe I was not to ever share about this.

I was just a child. The only one that knew besides the abusers was God. He knew my story, my heart, and the pain I did not want to cause my parents.

Later in my twenties I thought about sharing this with my mother, but again, the fear of breaking her heart stopped me. My father is still alive, but I would not want to cause him any pain.

Therefore, I carried it all alone. I could have turned to drugs, drinking or even anger, but didn't. God did not allow it. Many can question, why did this happen to an innocent child? Why does this happen to children? Why do bad things happen to good people? Well, at some point in my teenage years I asked God why, but He gave me peace.

I believe my mother's prayers helped me carry through all the circumstances. And instead of running away from God questioning, her prayers brought me closer to Him. I found peace by letting go, giving it to God, and surrendering my pain and knowing that He had a plan and purpose for this.

In many Mexican households, the common thing to do is to protect the family name, instead of the victim. I was the youngest of twelve, too many people, not enough conversations. No sit-down moments, to advise right from wrong. No "Mijita, I'm here for you, you can count on me." I never blamed my parents. I know they were doing their best.

The silence was loud and it shaped me into who I am today. Not just this but all my life struggles and adversities. But now? It's different, the absence taught me the importance of presence, the power of speaking up, the transformation that can be possible by truth. Now I'm having these open conversations, the sit-down moments with my own children. Bold, honest dialogue that should be present at every home. I'm breaking the cycle with my voice, with truth, and with God's promises of always being with me. Because healing is not just for me, but for generations to come.

The only person I ever told was my husband, before we married. At times, I've wondered if that was a mistake. But now, I'm sharing it with you. If you're reading this, you now know a piece of my childhood—my story. It needed to be told. Silence does not heal. The truth sets you free. And as sad or awful as it might be, it had to be spoken. I needed to speak up, to share it, so I could empower others to heal their own pain.

## Breaking the Cycle: Motherhood and Ganas

Later as an adult, as I experienced verbal, emotional and even physical abuse, I knew God was my answer. I gave it to Him. I opened up my heart and shared the pain and the abuse I was going through and cried out to Him and He answered. He took all the hurt, and it just disappeared after I was done with my cry. Just like that!

I have placed all my pain and worries in God's hands and I'm waiting on Him. I know we all have diverse challenges in life and we all deal differently with them. However, it has been my experience that Jesus has always been my refuge and my answer. I now walk in peace knowing that regardless of my difficult situations, God sees me. He knows what I'm going through and He would not let any of my tears be in vain. I trust God and I'm certain all will be okay. He comforts me, provides me with what I need, and things will fall in place at the right time because the Bible says that His timing is perfect. I know that even though my heart has been broken into one thousand pieces at times, God is still God and one day I will see why He allowed it.

I wish I could say that was the only pain I endured, but life kept throwing stones. Diagnoses. Mental abuse. Spiritual warfare. There were many times I cried in the shower just so my children would not hear me. At times I cried myself to sleep, whispering the name of Jesus into my pillow. But even in those moments—especially in those moments—I felt His presence. I never heard an audible voice, but I felt His whisper: "I'm right here. I know. I'm with you."

I know He has a purpose for my pain. And I choose to trust God and His plan.

Because God has been there through it all, I try to stay as close to Him as possible. The drowning moment taught me that I can go at any second. From my childhood experience, I learned that bad things happen even to the most vulnerable. The abuse as an adult taught me that I need to break the cycle. Through it all I have learned to trust in Jesus. He sees me, He knows my name, and He has a perfect plan for me.

Now I know not to take life for granted, to live with intention, to be thankful in every situation, to walk with purpose and to wait on Jesus.

My life experiences have taught me that I have a choice and I choose not to be bitter, but better. The pain and struggles have made me resilient, persistent. Life has thrown many stones and I choose to get up and stand again. For my children, for those that one day will read this story. I'm an overcomer, I'm stronger than I look, braver than I ever knew. I choose to be better. And just like me you can always count on Jesus!

It's okay to speak up. I've realized now that it's okay to use my voice, these lines to share my story. Silence and boxed up memories may have shaped my childhood but not my future.

God is only a cry, a prayer away.

God chose me, died for me. I'm part of His perfect plan. Jesus is the One that has kept me from crumbling, from breaking, and staying down. Trusting God is the reason I'm still standing – for my children.

Reflecting on the old school discipline growing up: la manguera *(water hose)*, la chancla *(sandal)*, fly swatter, the iron cord; these were temporary marks on my body, but not on my heart. This was part of the culture somehow normalized. But I chose better.

I chose to break the cycle of abuse, poverty, and silence by raising my children with love, patience and compassion, not fear, with guidance instead of pain.

Because life is precious and God is faithful, we need to stay close to Him.

And that truth has changed everything.

I began to see the attacks on my life not as evidence of abandonment, but as confirmation of my calling. The enemy fights hardest against those who carry the most purpose—so I knew then, I had to keep going. For my children. For the generations after me. For every woman who's ever felt unseen.

My turning point wasn't just at a given moment in my life. It has been a continuous turning it over to God, surrendering all, the decision to become better, the choice to rise every single time life or circumstances have pushed me down. Choosing God and choosing to be an example.

One of my favorite Bible verses is *"I can do all things through Christ who strengthens me."* (Philippians 4:13) When life was too much, when that person that I loved turned into my enemy, God was there holding me up. Helping me to get out of bed those mornings that I wanted to just give up. There were plenty of reasons and countless times that I could not do it anymore. I don't think I have the words to describe it. God just placed the ganas (desire/heart/drive) in me and He didn't let me give up. God gave me the ganas (purpose/grit/persistence) and I know He won't quit on me.

**Called to Rise: Purpose and Legacy**

I know now that life isn't meant to be about surviving, but about truly living with purpose and intention. I understand now that I was called to be the one who changes the pattern. Research shows that the lower the socioeconomic status, the higher the chances of abuse, hardship, and misfortune. That's why it's so important for us to rise above generational patterns, to refuse to become another statistic. We must choose better, speak up, and educate ourselves on the issues that affect our children. I pursued my education not just for myself, but for my children, my grandchildren, and the generations to come.

I know God has been tugging at my spirit. He's been calling, and today I chose to answer. *The harvest is plenty, but the laborers are few.* I chose to be one of the few. I want to be an example of His love to others. To those that would humble themselves and will surrender to Jesus.

I came to realize that my pain has a purpose. And by God's grace I will be the light for others still walking in darkness.

"Si Dios quiere" - "God willing"—was more than a phrase; it was ingrained in us to always put God first. Like every sentence's last name, it followed each phrase we spoke. When one of us forgot it, my parents made sure to remind us. These words were powerful seeds that were planted when I was young, and now they have grown and I'm reaping what my maternal grandparents planted. These seeds have flourished into the faith that God is powerful, and not even one leaf moves without His will, and that He has purpose and a perfect plan for each of us.

Even though I didn't fully understand the weight of that three-word phrase back then, I know now that it's powerful. I recall a prayer that mentioned that "God was with me, that He was aware of what was going on, that He knew my heart, and He was never going to leave me." This was a reassurance that Jesus had my back regardless of what came my way.

In the chaos and in the healing, His presence never wavered. Since I know what it is to have the minimum, be broken and in despair; I want to be there for others. I try my best to live and lead with empathy. I want to be the voice, the hug, the prayer, and the mentor that I needed when I was younger—breaking cycles from a place of understanding.

I'm now living on my abuelita's and mother's prayers. Walking through fire just gives you a different kind of inner flame. Every answered prayer is a reminder that God is faithful. What the enemy meant for evil, God turned it into good. I will keep on hoping, praying, and waiting on God's perfect timing.

Now I walk not only by faith but in peace. I'm not alone. I'll keep my life anchored in Jesus since He's the one that was there when no one else was. I have made a divine decision, to break the cycle, shatter the curse, and silence the patterns.

I refuse to repeat what broke me or walk the familiar road of bitterness and rebellion. I choose healing. I choose freedom.

**I choose God.**

For my heart.
For my children.
For every generation that follows, may they know peace because I chose war in the spirit.

It ends with me. And something new begins.

Freedom came the moment I decided to share my story. I hope others can see life after the trauma, after the chaos, and after the heartbreak. You don't have to be defined by what happened to you, and the enemy doesn't get the final say.

You need to let go and let God. Speak up, forgive. I have gone from surviving to thriving because of God's love. Now a mother, a doctoral graduate, a business owner, but most important the daughter of a King.

My mindset: you can do anything through Jesus, *si se puede, con ganas*. God's grace is woven into every thread of my life. God has handpicked me to go beyond my family and my circle. That's why the enemy has tried so hard to stop me, but Jesus has always been there.

My story is not just about survival, but of God's grace, His plan. The glow comes from God's goodness, the golden threads are His power. He's the reason I can rise again and again.

If I could be there with you, I would hold your hands, look into your eyes, and tell you this:

Jesus is there through it all. Jesus is right here. I cannot be there for you or every single person, but Jesus listens to your prayers. He is with you when you are all alone. He will hug you when you need a hug. You can cry out, yell, or just stay quiet. It's okay, He can hear your cry, the yells, or your silence. He is going to lift you up. Be the mother, father, friend you never had. He can supply every need and all you have to do is call on Jesus. He can make your heart whole again. Because he is the wonderful, powerful God. He is the answered prayer. One day, He will wipe away every tear and reward your faith with far more than you ever wished or prayed for.

Regardless of what has happened to you, let it go.
Choose to move forward.
Choose to rise.

Let Jesus work on your behalf—but do your part, too. Adopt a mindset that says, *I can be better. I will grow. I will go beyond, because I am God's daughter.*

I will overcome the very things that were meant to break me, through His grace and His love. With Jesus and *ganas*—the deep desire to become better—I will rise from the pit. His light will shine upon me, and my story will become my greatest testimony.

So don't give up, keep going *hermana*. I can't wait to see what God has in store in your future.

The Bible says, "I can do all things through Christ who strengthens me." And He did. He gave me the strength to keep going—to earn my degrees, to lead in both boardrooms and classrooms, to raise my children in faith.

He gave me strength to rise above the abuse that once tried to silence me, and the courage to share my story now. All because He has a plan and a purpose for it all.

This story is for anyone who has ever felt forgotten in their pain. For the survivor of abuse, the one facing impossible circumstances, or the one struggling through poverty—this is your reminder: **nothing** disqualifies you from being used by God. There are no excuses that can limit Him.

My journey is living proof that every hardship—every moment of physical, emotional, and sexual abuse, every diagnosis, every time I was told I had breast or thyroid cancer—was not wasted. Jesus was with me through it all.

My life declares that there is purpose in the pain, and that God can use anyone—anyone—to bring healing, hope, and transformation.

My prayer is that God showers you with peace, strengthens your faith, fills you with love, and embraces you with hope and a warm hug. Never doubt His promises; they will come to pass.

> *"Do not be anxious about anything, but in every situation, by prayer and petition, with thanksgiving, present your requests to God. And the peace of God, which transcends all understanding, will guard your heart and your minds in Christ Jesus."* (Philippians 4:6-7)

Jesus and Ganas!

### Dr. Esmeralda Adame

**Instagram:** @theleadershipdoctora

# Section Four

# The Crown

*"Blessed is the one who perseveres under trial, because, having stood the test, that person will receive the crown of life that the Lord has promised to those who love Him."*
—**James 1:12**

The journey always leads here. To grace. To legacy. To the crown.

The crown isn't just a symbol of victory; it's a promise kept. It's forgiveness given. It's wisdom shared. It's the joy of realizing that what once broke you is now the very thing that helps others heal.

In this section, you will meet women who turned their scars into seeds, who chose forgiveness when bitterness seemed easier, who carried the faith of generations and dared to hand it forward. Their voices are steady. Their hope is contagious. Their legacy is eternal.

The crown is not reserved for the perfect; it's for the faithful. And as you close this book, may you feel its weight upon your own head—not heavy, but radiant. A reminder that your story too is a victory unfolding, a legacy in the making, a crown waiting to be revealed.

# Chapter 17

# From Knowing About God to Knowing God

*by: Marie Salazar Garcia*

*"'For I know the plans I have for you,' declares the Lord, 'plans to prosper you and not to harm you, plans to give you hope and a future.'"*
— **Jeremiah 29:11 (NIV)**

### From Tradition to Transformation

I used to think that having a relationship with God meant following a list of rules—going to church, kneeling at the right time, saying the right prayers, doing all the things I was taught to do as a child. But I still felt something was missing, and then I was invited to accept Jesus as my personal Lord and savior. Everything changed for me from that point on.

I began to understand that God was after my heart and a relationship with God meant conversation, not confusion, and connection, not obligation. I could talk to Him in the car, in the kitchen, or in the middle of a hard moment, and He would meet me there. I discovered that His presence wasn't confined to a building or a Sunday service; it was alive and available in every part of my daily life.

What once felt heavy with obligation became light with love. Instead of striving to be perfect, I learned to surrender. Instead of routine, I learned to listen. Instead of guilt, I found grace. And through that grace, I discovered the joy of walking with a God who is not distant, but personal, faithful, and near.

As Jesus said in John 15:5, *"I am the vine; you are the branches. If you remain in me and I in you, you will bear much fruit; apart from me you can do nothing."* Now my relationship is about remaining in Him, and through Him, experiencing the life, freedom, and love I was always searching for.

**A Living, Ongoing Conversation**

Today, the heartbeat of my relationship with God is constant awareness. I talk to Him when I get home, when I feel uncertain about a situation, when someone says something that stirs up my emotions. Instead of reacting, I respond by whispering, *"Lord, I surrender this to You."* When I feel something, I don't want to carry, I simply say, *"Lord, take this feeling away."*

Over time, I've realized prayer is not just an event; it is the atmosphere of my life. It's like breathing; it flows naturally in and out of every moment. Sometimes it's a quiet thought, other times a grateful outburst of praise, and often a simple cry for help. In every form, God meets me with His peace.

My relationship with God is not about perfection; it's about presence. It's a rhythm of love, belief, and trust. It's a continual surrender that draws me closer to Him. I no longer see Him as distant or unreachable, but as a Father who delights in every conversation, no matter how small. That closeness never leaves me and has grown stronger each day, reminding me that life with God is not a checklist, but a living, ongoing dialogue that transforms me moment by moment. That simple act of turning my attention toward Him brings peace and clarity.

**Beginning Each Day with Him**

I also talk to God when I first wake up in the morning, before I even get ready for the day. As I go through my morning routine, while I'm dressing, and even as I'm packing what I need for the hours ahead, I invite Him into every detail. I ask Him to help me be the woman He created me to be, to guide my thoughts, and to lead me exactly where He needs me. Before I step out of my home, I remind myself that I don't walk out alone; His Spirit goes before me, making a way.

My connection to God is living and breathing, never distant or dormant. It's like a steady heartbeat pulsing through every part of my day, constant, life-giving, and grounding. Beginning each morning with Him doesn't just set the tone; it anchors my entire day in His presence, reminding me that I am never without His guidance, His love, and His strength.

As Psalm 143:8 declares: *"Let the morning bring me word of your unfailing love, for I have put my trust in you. Show me the way I should go, for to you I entrust my life."* This scripture has become my daily declaration. It is a reminder that each new day is an opportunity to walk in His love, trust His leading, and live in His purpose.

**Activating the Holy Spirit**

When I first accepted Jesus, I didn't fully understand what it meant to activate the Holy Spirit in my life. I knew of God, but I didn't truly know Him. I was aware of His presence in a distant way, but I hadn't yet tapped into the power He promised when He said, *"I am leaving, but I will leave you with the Holy Spirit."*

For a long time, I walked in faith but without fully accessing the gift of the Holy Spirit living within me. I didn't realize that the Holy Spirit is not only a presence, but also a power—a guide, a teacher, and a comforter. The moment I surrendered and invited Him to lead me daily, everything shifted. He became my strength when I felt weak, my calm in the middle of chaos, and the gentle whisper of assurance when doubt tried to creep in.

Activating the Holy Spirit opened my eyes to see beyond the natural and into the supernatural. He sharpened my discernment, deepened my prayers, and gave me wisdom I could never find on my own. He reminds me that I am never alone, because His power resides within me.

My relationship with God is now more than a belief, it is my salvation, my promise, and my legacy. It's not just for me; it's a covering I am establishing for my children, my grandchildren, and even my community. Through the Holy Spirit, I am empowered to leave behind a legacy of faith, strength, and vision that will ripple through generations.

**Rock Bottom to Restoration**

There was a time when I hit rock bottom. Spiritually, emotionally, mentally, I was completely emptied before I knew God as my personal savior. I walked into a church one day during my lunch hour, and I just sat there and cried. I didn't know where to go or what to do next. That's when I saw a Bible on the bench next to me. It wasn't an ordinary Bible; it was called a Speed Bible. The words in red were meant to give you the message faster. I opened it and landed in the book of Job. And in that moment after reading the pages, it felt like God Himself was speaking to me: after reading the pages, it felt like God Himself was speaking to me: *'You are being tested, but like Job, you will be restored.'"* That moment marked the beginning of my transformation and my desire to know God on a more personal level.

What brought me to that point at that time? I was navigating overwhelming responsibilities, trying to be strong for everyone around me while feeling empty inside. I was doing all the things I thought I was supposed to do, but I still felt disconnected. It was in that honest moment of surrender that God revealed His nearness to me. He wasn't waiting for me to fix myself, He was waiting for me to give Him everything. It was also during that time I **learned** Nehemiah 8:10 *"The joy of the Lord is my strength"*. From that day forward it was my goal to remain joyful in all seasons of my life.

**Freedom in Christ**

I had grown up with structure, with a mindset of do's and don'ts, and the constant pressure of never feeling like I was enough. I thought God was all about rules, measuring me by my mistakes and shortcomings. But what I discovered in my relationship with Him was something far greater—freedom. True freedom.

God doesn't ask us for perfection; He asks us for love. His Word reminds us of the greatest commandment, to love Him with all our heart, soul, and mind, and to love others as ourselves (Matthew 22:37–39). When I began to grasp this truth, my whole perspective shifted. Love became the lens through which I began to see my life and others.

When you understand the power of His love, you walk differently. You speak with more kindness. You forgive more freely. You extend grace more quickly, because you realize how much grace has been given to you. Love transforms rules into relationships, obligations into opportunities, and burdens into blessings.

I now walk in that freedom. I've learned to love people right where they are, without judgment, just as He loves me. It doesn't mean I've abandoned truth, it means I've embraced it in its purest form, through love. For it is love that sets us free, and it is love that reflects the very heart of God.

As Galatians 5:1 declares: *"It is for freedom that Christ has set us free. Stand firm, then, and do not let yourselves be burdened again by a yoke of slavery."* This is the freedom I now live in, not bound by rules, but released by grace, rooted in love, and empowered to walk in His truth.

**Audience of One**

I remember times when I felt judged for not fitting in, or misunderstood for walking out my faith in a way that felt more personal than traditional. Those moments were heavy, because I often wrestled with the tension of wanting to be accepted by people but sensing a deeper call to be set apart for God. But in His gentle way, God reminded me: *"You're not called to please people—you're called to pursue Me."*

The more I fixed my eyes on Him, the freer I became from the weight of other people's opinions. Their approval could no longer define my worth, because my identity was anchored in His truth, not their perception. I began to realize that people's opinions shift with the wind, but God's Word is unshakable. Pleasing people is exhausting, because the standard always changes, but pleasing God brings peace, direction, and joy that cannot be taken away.

When I shifted my eyes from the crowd to the cross, I discovered the beauty of living authentically, wholeheartedly, and unapologetically for Christ. I didn't have to perform to be loved; I was already chosen, already forgiven, already enough in Him. That truth became my freedom. The freedom to stand tall in my faith, the freedom to love without fear of rejection, and the freedom to walk in purpose with confidence.

Now, instead of striving to gain acceptance, I live to reflect His presence. Instead of seeking applause, I seek His will. And in doing so, I've found the abundant life He promised. It's one marked not by pressure or pretense, but by peace, joy, and the unwavering assurance that my life is secure in Him.

As Galatians 1:10 declares: *"Am I now trying to win the approval of human beings, or of God? Or am I trying to please people? If I were still trying to please people, I would not be a servant of Christ."* These words remind me that my calling is not to the crowd, but to Christ, and in Him, I already have all the approval I'll ever need.

**My Inheritance**

Growing up, I was surrounded by women of faith whose lives became living testimonies for me. One of my grandmothers kept a sacred altar in her home and prayed daily on her knees, showing me what it looked like to humble yourself before God with consistency and devotion. My other grandmother, though she was technically my aunt, was honored as a grandmother because she raised my father from the age of two. She carried a bold and outspoken faith.

She reminded us constantly that what mattered most was a true relationship with God. Though their practices and expressions of worship looked different, their message was the same: God must be the center of our lives.

Their consistency became the foundation of my own faith, something I didn't just inherit but eventually made personal. Over time, I took what they passed down, combined it with the unwavering faith of my mother, and allowed God to shape it uniquely in me. I realized that the greatest inheritance they gave me wasn't material, it was spiritual. It was the gift of reverence, the confidence to believe in miracles, and the assurance that God is faithful from generation to generation.

Their devotion taught me discipline; their prayers taught me perseverance; their testimonies taught me hope. I inherited their passion, their commitment, and their belief in miracles. And I believe, not simply because I was told to, but because I have witnessed too many miracles in my own journey not to believe. I've seen prayers answered, doors opened, hearts restored, and lives transformed. Each miracle has become another reminder that the same God who was faithful to my grandmothers and my mother is the same God who is faithful to me, and through me, to the next generation.

As Paul wrote in 2 Timothy 1:5, *"I am reminded of your sincere faith, which first lived in your grandmother Lois and in your mother Eunice and, I am persuaded, now lives in you also."* This scripture reflects my own story—a legacy of faith passed down through the women who came before me, and now alive in me, so it may continue to flow into the generations yet to come.

**Miracles in Everyday Life**

Many believe and expect miracles only in tragic moments, but I see miracles in everyday life. Someone once told me, "You talk about miracles like they happen all the time. I've never had one." But the truth is, you don't have to go through tragedy to see a miracle. Miracles are everywhere when you learn to recognize them. I saw a miracle even in the loss of both my parents, not in their passing, but in how God carried me through. Their deaths could have broken me forever. Instead, they became sacred pivots in my journey, drawing me closer to God while having the honor and obligation to continue my parent's legacy. Which is compassion (my mother) and passion (my father) along with the excitement of one day seeing them both again in our heavenly home.

I love the word enthusiasm and soon learned the meaning, which is a Greek word which means God within. That's the joy and energy I've carried into my relationship with Him and everyone I meet. I hope others feel it too, because this closeness with God isn't just for me. He wants it with all of us. Especially for the woman who didn't have a father or who feels like she doesn't know where she belongs. God is waiting to be your Redeemer. You don't have to know everything or wait until everything is right or perfect. You just ask. He will meet you right where you are at, He did for me. God can provide whatever you are lacking.

**God the Provider**

One of the greatest miracles of my life happened during a season of being a single mom to my three young children. I clung to Psalm 68:5, *"A father to the fatherless."* That verse became my anchor. I prayed bold prayers with the confidence of His promises; one of them was for a new home for my children. And God didn't just answer—He exceeded. I bought a beautiful home for a fraction of the cost. This was the testimony my children realized that God was our provider. Later, my son at the age of seven said boldly, "Now let's pray for a new car," and we received one seven months later through a direct selling company and since then it has been replaced with a new car every two years for the past thirty years. This too was another testimony to show my children how important it was to have a relationship with God and to always have faith that He would provide.

Through both of those testimonies, we came to understand the truth of Proverbs 18:21, which says that death and life are in the power of the tongue. We knew we needed to choose our words carefully. The first lesson I taught my children was never to say "if", but "when"—because God is faithful. They are now adult children and they don't say the word "if" and now my grandchildren have learned the same. Since then, there are several other words that have become consistent in our home.

Another example is instead of saying good we say great. Now my children and grandchildren know: God answers. Maybe not always how we expect, but always with something better. That is legacy.

**Generational Fruit**

I am so blessed and honored to now see how my adult children and grandchildren love the Lord and how they have developed their own personal relationship with Him. It is the living testimony of Proverbs 22:6: *"Train up a child in the way he should go, and when he is old he will not depart from it."* What once began as seeds of faith planted in their hearts has now blossomed into generational fruit.

I had the special privilege of pouring into my firstborn grandson from a young age; every New Year's, beginning when he was ten, I cared for him, and together we would sit down to create a vision board, guided by one of the leadership tools I created—my Purpose-Driven Life worksheet. Those moments became sacred traditions, where I watched his faith and vision grow right before my eyes. God's grace has been evident in his life in incredible ways. When he was crowned Prom King his senior year, I knew it wasn't just a title; it was God giving me a glimpse of the royal legacy He was establishing in our family line. And when my grandson was accepted into NYU, it felt like the launching pad for the global impact God has in store for him and for our family.

I have also witnessed God's faithfulness in my younger daughter, who became the first in our family to receive a PhD. The moment she walked across that graduation stage six months pregnant with her first daughter, our princess granddaughter, I knew in my spirit it was symbolic. She carried both knowledge and legacy into the next generation, showing that God's promises flow through both her accomplishments and her role as a mother.

Beyond my children and grandchildren, I see God's hand moving among my siblings, nieces, and nephews. Each of them carrying pieces of His purpose in their lives. It fills me with gratitude to see how one family's obedience can ripple into generations.

Now together my husband and I walk in His grace and purpose, praying for and cheering on our three adult children (and their spouses) and six grandchildren. To see them all thriving is nothing short of God's grace, favor, and promises made real. I am reminded daily that legacy is not built in one moment, but over a lifetime of faithfulness, prayer, and love, and that is the true inheritance I long to pass on.

As Deuteronomy 7:9 declares: *"Know therefore that the Lord your God is God; He is the faithful God, keeping His covenant of love to a thousand generations of those who love Him and keep His commandments."* This is the legacy I am witnessing—the blessing of God's covenant carried through my family, generation after generation.

## Woman of Vision

My journey shifted when I prayed to become a woman of vision. I no longer walk by sight but by faith, living with passion, boldness, and purpose.

## Daily Habits

- **Morning Alignment:** Begin with prayer, worship, and gratitude to set vision over distraction.
- **Journaling:** Record dreams, lessons, and prayers to see God's hand at work.
- **Evening Reflection:** Ask, *"Where did I see God today?"* to end in peace, not stress.

## Scriptures That Anchor Me

- *"Write the vision and make it plain."*—Habakkuk 2:2
- *"We walk by faith, not by sight."*—2 Corinthians 5:7
- *"Trust in the Lord…"*—Proverbs 3:5–6
- *"The joy of the Lord is my strength."*—Nehemiah 8:10

## Declarations I Speak

- I am a daughter of the King, crowned with confidence.
- I will thrive with vision and purpose.

- I trust God's timing and process.
- My voice carries weight to lift others.

These habits, scriptures, and affirmations sharpen my vision, teaching me not to react to life but to respond with clarity and faith.

**Esther's Courage, My Call**

When I read Esther's story, I felt like God was whispering directly to me: "You are chosen for such a time as this." What stood out wasn't just her courage before the king, but the quiet strength she carried in the waiting. She didn't rush ahead—she prayed, she fasted, she prepared, and then she stepped forward in obedience.

That mirrored my own journey. For so long, I lived in survival mode, reacting instead of leading, pushing instead of pausing. But like Esther, I realized my identity wasn't tied to my fear, my past, or even my title. My identity was in the vision God placed inside me. Esther's story made me feel seen as a woman who could rise above circumstance and step into purpose with *Godfidence*.

It showed me that God's plans unfold when we trust His timing, not our own. Our obedience matters. Even when afraid, saying "yes" to God changes everything. Our identity matters. Esther was a queen before she wore the crown, and I, too, could embrace my royalty as a daughter of the King.

This revelation is what inspired my mindset "Fix Your Crown and Turn Around." Because, just like Esther, every little girl and every woman needs to know: You don't have to stay in survival mode. You can rise with vision, confidence, and purpose with your own crown.

**Walking in Grace**

When a woman walks with God, it shows in her steps. She carries peace instead of fear, clarity instead of confusion, and joy that circumstances cannot steal. Her "yes" is firm, her "no" is clear, and her worth is anchored in Him. *"She is clothed with strength and dignity, and she laughs without fear of the future"* Proverbs 31:25. She rests securely and speaks boldly because she knows she does not walk alone. Even in the storm, she lifts her head, adjusts her crown, and moves forward being guided by His presence, and sustained by His love.

**The Legacy I Am Building Now**

Before I became a woman of vision, I was simply surviving, managing the day-to-day, responding to needs, and carrying burdens without ever looking at the bigger picture.

Now, with vision, I see legacy differently. I'm no longer just working for today, I'm building for generations.

**A Legacy of Voice**
I'm using my story, my platforms, and my pen to create resources like Fix Your Crown and Turn Around that will outlive me. My voice is no longer just for my circle; it's shaping how the next generation of women and girls see themselves.

**A Legacy of Leadership**
Through mentoring, coaching, and creating spaces like Vision Coaching, I'm leaving behind more than accomplishments; I'm leaving behind leaders. Women who will rise, take their place, and multiply impact long after I'm gone.

**A Legacy of Faith**
I'm anchoring my family and my community in the truth that we are daughters of the King. My children, my "personal executive board," will inherit more than businesses or properties. They'll inherit a spiritual foundation and a one-hundred-year plan rooted in vision and purpose.

**A Legacy of Impact**
I'm aligning my work with a greater mission: to build people, not just projects. To ensure that every door I walk through, I leave open for someone else.

What I couldn't have built before my vision was intentionality. Now every decision, every yes, every project is filtered through legacy. And that legacy is not about my name being remembered, it's about God's name being glorified in what I leave behind.

**An Invitation Home**

You are not forgotten. You are not broken. You are God's beloved daughter, and there is still a divine purpose for your life.

If you feel distant from God, weighed down by guilt, silence, or shame, remember this: He sees it all. He chooses you. He's not asking for your perfection. He wants your presence.

You don't have to be perfect to come to Him. Just start. Talk to Him like a friend and ask Him, "God, if You're real, show me. Speak to me. I want to know You for myself."

Let me pray for you: "Father, I lift up my sister reading this. You know her heart, her wounds, her desires, and her doubts. Meet her right where she is. Wrap her in peace. Stir something new in her, a hunger to know You deeply. Show her that she doesn't have to earn Your love, just receive it. Restore what was lost. Renew what has been broken. Make her a woman of vision. In Jesus' name, Amen."

**Daily Affirmation Statement**

I am a daughter of the King, created with purpose and crowned with confidence. I walk in vision, releasing fear and choosing faith, clarity and abundance. My voice carries power, my hands build legacy, and my heart reflects God's love. I am chosen for such a time as this, equipped with wisdom, strengthened by the Spirit, and anchored in hope. No weapon formed against me shall prosper, for I am renewed, redeemed, and released into destiny. Wherever I go, I shine as His daughter who has been called, anointed, and appointed.

**Invitation to know Jesus as your personal Savior.**

The **Prayer of Salvation** isn't a word-for-word prayer written in the Bible, but it comes from the truths found in scripture about receiving Jesus Christ as Lord and Savior.

Here are the main scriptures it's based on:

- Romans 10:9–10 – *"If you declare with your mouth, 'Jesus is Lord,' and believe in your heart that God raised him from the dead, you will be saved. For it is with your heart that you believe and are justified, and it is with your mouth that you profess your faith and are saved."*

- John 3:16 – *"For God so loved the world that He gave His one and only Son, that whoever believes in Him shall not perish but have eternal life."*

- Ephesians 2:8–9 – *"For it is by grace you have been saved, through faith—and this is not from yourselves, it is the gift of God—not by works, so that no one can boast."*

**A Prayer to Receive the Gift of Eternal Life**

"Heavenly Father, I come to You in the name of Jesus. I confess that I am a sinner, and I ask for Your forgiveness. I believe that Jesus Christ is Your Son, that He died on the cross for my sins, and that You raised Him from the dead. Today, I turn from my old ways and invite Jesus into my heart and life to be my Lord and Savior. Thank You for saving me, forgiving me, and giving me eternal life. In Jesus' name, Amen."

**Marie Salazar Garcia**

**Instagram:** @motivationalmarie

# Chapter 18

# The Woman Who Danced Beside Me

*by Maribel De La Fuente*

*"Trust in the Lord with all your heart and lean not on your own understanding; in all your ways submit to Him, and He will make your paths straight."*
— **Proverbs 3:5–6 (NIV)**

There are moments in life that feel like endings, when the thing you love most is taken from you, and you don't yet understand why. I was only ten years old when my world shifted, when grief, confusion, and anger began to stir in my spirit. I didn't have the words for it then. All I knew was that something sacred was being taken away from me.

What was being taken wasn't just dance—it was *me*.

My father had passed away, though I didn't know it at the time. The people around me kept it from me for two years. They didn't know how to tell a little girl that her daddy was gone, and maybe they thought they were protecting me. But when the truth finally came out, it didn't feel like protection. It felt like betrayal.

Grief arrived late, and it came in the form of anger. I had always been a bubbly, energetic, girly girl. I loved folklórico. I loved dancing. My dad introduced me to it. He picked me up, took me to rehearsals, and told everyone that his daughter could dance circles around anyone. Even after he and my mom stopped living together, he stayed close. I was deeply attached to him.

So when he was gone, and then my mom told me I could no longer dance, it felt like my entire world was unraveling. I couldn't understand. I only knew that I was devastated. I began to act out. Rebellious, angry, confused. The one thing that brought me joy was suddenly out of reach. I felt like a door had slammed shut on the one place where I could still breathe.

My reaction was anger. I didn't know how to process it any other way. All I knew was that something I loved was being taken, and I didn't understand why.

It was devastating. It felt like someone had reached inside and taken the biggest part of me. I had just lost my dad—and now, I was losing the one thing that helped me feel connected to him. Dance wasn't just something I enjoyed; it was my world. Being told I couldn't do it anymore felt like the light had gone out. My body felt heavy. My spirit felt crushed. I didn't know how to explain it back then, but it felt like everything that gave me joy was being stripped away, one piece at a time.

And then, God sent her.

**The Phone Call That Changed Everything**

It was a simple phone call, but it changed the trajectory of my life. Mrs. Canales called my mom and gently said, "You can't take away what makes your daughter happy." Her tone was comforting, like one mother speaking to another. She told her that just because she couldn't afford the lessons didn't mean I had to lose what I loved. She offered to help, to sponsor me.

That conversation opened a door to healing. She began to spend more time with me in the studio. She invested in me, not just financially, but emotionally, spiritually. At ten years old, I was chosen. Sponsored. Cared for.

It was exciting. It was an honor. But I didn't fully grasp the magnitude of what was happening until I got older. Looking back now, I see that was the moment everything changed. It wasn't just about keeping me in dance. It was about keeping me whole.

Being chosen at ten years old felt like someone had breathed life back into me. After feeling like the world had turned its back on me, first with the loss of my dad and then with the loss of dance, her "yes" was like a warm light piercing through all the darkness I had been carrying.

She didn't have to do it. She didn't owe me anything. But she saw something in me. She knew how much dancing meant to me, and she made a choice to invest, not just in my ability, but in my heart. That meant everything.

From that point on, I became eager to learn more. I showed up early. I practiced harder. I wanted to prove her right, to show that I was worth the time, the support, and the belief. As I poured myself into the dances she taught me, I began to realize that there was something inside me she had recognized long before I ever did. Her belief planted a seed. It told me: *You matter. You belong. You're worth pouring into.*

And that truth changed everything.

**The Girl Who Danced Through Grief**

Before my dad passed, all I ever dreamed of was dancing. I didn't know anything else. Dance was my world. It was his gift to me. He and Mrs. Canales had been close, and he was proud that I danced. Maybe that's why my mom had a hard time letting me continue. There was tension, jealousy, and pain, but it wasn't my fault.

When I found out he had passed—two years later—I didn't know how to act. I didn't know how to cry, or be angry, or grieve. But I carried a deep anger in my heart. At him. At my family. At the world. That anger became a constant companion.

My mom and siblings never told me he had died. When I finally learned the truth, it shattered my world. I was caught between emotions, too confused to grieve, too angry to cry, and too broken to understand.

Dance became more than movement. It became medicine. It was the only place I could feel free.

Dance was my therapy. On the days when the pain felt too heavy or the silence at home too loud, dance became my escape. It was like stepping into another world, one where I hadn't experienced loss, where I didn't feel abandoned or broken. When I danced, I felt free. Everything else disappeared. The grief, the anger, and the confusion all melted away the moment the music started. It gave me something to hold on to when everything else felt uncertain. Dance helped me breathe again. It helped me survive. And eventually, it helped me heal.

**Becoming Her Daughter**

As I got older, my bond with Mrs. Canales deepened. When I was sixteen, I moved in with her. She became everything to me. She was my second mom, my mentor, my teacher. She didn't just guide me in dance, she taught me how to live.

She was stricter than my own mom. She demanded discipline, hard work, respect. If I wanted a lead role or a solo, I had to earn it. I had to raise money for my costumes, for classes, for travel. We sold barbecue plates, candy, ads for recital books. I always led in sales, but that didn't mean I got to keep it all. She taught me to share my earnings with other girls who couldn't sell. That felt unfair at first, but she reminded me, we are a team. If you have more, you give more.

She taught me that success is nothing without humility.

I remember watching her give everything she had to our community, her time, her heart, her resources. She poured herself into building something beautiful, something meaningful, and yet the support she deserved was never fully returned from the community. It was heartbreaking to witness. It made me angry and confused. I couldn't understand how someone so devoted could be overlooked.

That's when she taught me one of the hardest but most powerful lessons of all. She told me, "You don't do it for the applause. You do it because it's who you are. You do it because it's your calling."

She helped me understand that no matter how hard you work, not everyone will appreciate you. Some people will ignore your efforts, or even try to tear them down. But that doesn't mean you stop. You keep going. You stay rooted in your purpose. You do it for yourself, and for the people who *do* see you. That shift in perspective brought me back to grace, and I've carried it with me ever since.

When I walked into a room with her, it felt like entering with royalty. Everyone noticed her. All eyes were on her. She was elegant, classy, radiant. I watched her and thought, "That's who I want to be."

She had little sayings that still echo in my mind. *"El que quiere celeste, que le cueste."* If you want something beautiful, it will cost you. She taught us not to worry about boys, to focus on our goals, to carry ourselves with pride. She always told us not to depend on anyone. Have your own car. Your own place. Your own money. Your own business.

She was my everything. I adored her. I still do. The way I looked at her then is the way my dogs look at me now, with complete admiration. I couldn't get enough of her presence. She made me feel seen, valued, and safe.

**Tough Love That Worked**

She didn't play favorites. If I missed practice, I was moved to the back. If I was late, I didn't perform. She held a standard, and she never lowered it, not even for me. And because of that, I learned what excellence looked like.

Practices were long, intense, and non-negotiable. Twice a week, sometimes three times a week, for hours. She brought in maestros from other cities to teach us new dances. If you missed a single class, you weren't in the front. You might not even perform at all. It was painful, but it built character.

And I did have haters. Other girls would question why I was always in front, why I got the best parts. They didn't know how hard I worked. They didn't know the story behind my spotlight. But she did. And that was enough.

I saw her make sacrifices most people never noticed. She gave up time with her own family, her husband, and her children because she believed so deeply in the work she was doing. Her students, her school, and her mission came first. She poured so much of herself into us that there wasn't always much left for those at home.

As a young woman watching her navigate that, it taught me something hard but real: sometimes even the people closest to you won't understand your calling. Sometimes, you'll walk alone. And that's when you have to decide—will you give up, or will you press forward?

She showed me that success often requires painful choices, and that you have to be willing to do what others won't in order to become who you're meant to be. Her sacrifice wasn't in vain. It shaped me into a woman who knows how to stay focused, even when support is missing. Because of her, I learned that purpose sometimes costs something—but the impact is worth it.

**Seeds That Still Bear Fruit**

Because of her, I learned to work hard, to ask boldly, and to lead with heart. I learned that the world may not always be fair, but I can still be kind. She taught me how to be a businesswoman, how to face rejection, and how to walk into any space with dignity.

She always told me, "Patience. After a thousand no's, there will be one yes that opens the biggest door of your life."

I still hear her voice when I want to give up.

She taught me how to be generous, to share my light, to lift up others. From my father I inherited entrepreneurship, but from her, I learned how to pair it with purpose and people.

One of the greatest lessons she taught me was to never hesitate when something big and meaningful comes your way. If it's good, if it's aligned, go after it—and don't overthink it. She used to say that if it doesn't scare you a little, it's probably not big enough. But if it *does* scare you, you're likely on the right track. That's where the growth is. That's where the breakthroughs are waiting.

I watched her live this out boldly. She opened doors for us to perform for dignitaries, elected officials, and leaders in places many of us never imagined we'd go. She never let fear stop her, even though she didn't speak a word of English. And yet, she accomplished far more than many who do.

That taught me that courage isn't about having all the right words, it's about showing up anyway. Because of her, I don't let fear dictate my choices. I pursue the opportunities that stretch me, knowing they're often the ones that will elevate me. She taught me to lead with boldness, walk with faith, and trust that if God placed it in my path, I'm meant to rise to it.

**The Legacy We Built**

Her belief in me lit a fire that still burns. Because she opened one door, I was able to walk through many. Through pageantry, through scholarships, through leadership roles. I earned two proclamations from two lifelong friends of hers—a state senator and a state representative. Back to back. Things that had never been done in our region.

She would look at me and say, *"Yo sabía que siempre lo ibas a hacer con mucho ánimo, aun sin muchos recursos. Aprendiste algo de mí."*

She would be proud. I know it.

She took folklórico to three different countries. She brought home the key to the city. She received the Medal of Honor from President Fox in Mexico City. She did all of that with elegance and grit. And somehow, she still had enough love left to pour into a hurting little girl.

Today, I am the proud owner of my own esthetician studio. It is a space where I pour into women the same way she once poured into me. The grace, excellence, and confidence she embodied now live on in how I serve others. Through every treatment and every conversation, I help women feel seen, celebrated, and radiant from the inside out. It's more than skincare, it's about helping them reclaim their light, walk boldly in their beauty, and glow with purpose, one woman at a time.

**God's Hand in It All**

God used her to save me. There is no other way to put it.

When my father died, and I felt alone, He sent someone who could hold my heart. She put me back where I belonged—on the dance floor, in my purpose, inside joy.

Most people pay thousands for the kind of mentorship and education she gave me. I got it through love. Through grace. Through sacrifice.

Everything she poured into me, I now pour into others. Whether through dance, leadership, or simple acts of kindness—her legacy lives on.

One moment that truly touched my heart was when a woman from Dallas—someone I had never met in person—reached out after following me on social media. She said, "I need *you* to give me a facial. I want to glow like *you* do." She didn't care that we were in different cities or that she had access to high-end spas and elite estheticians in her area. She wanted *me*—because she saw something deeper than skin. She saw the standard of excellence I carry, the same one that was modeled for me by Mrs. Canales.

That call reminded me that God will take everything we've been through, all the pain, the discipline, the lessons and use it to shine through us in ways we never imagined. What began as a little girl struggling to hold on to her passion has now become a woman who helps others rediscover their light. Because of her, I serve with heart. Because of God, that heart reaches further than I ever thought it could.

**To the Girl Who Feels Alone**

If you're reading this and feel unseen or unsupported, know this: God is already with you. Even in the silence, even in the waiting—He hasn't forgotten you. And in His perfect timing, He will send someone to help you rise. Don't give up. Don't stop dreaming. There is always that one person who will come into your life and change everything for the better. But even before they arrive, your Heavenly Father is already working behind the scenes, preparing the way. And when that moment comes, you'll know it was divinely orchestrated.

**Maribel De La Fuente**

**Instagram:** @lavishfaceandskinspa_

# Chapter 19
# Saved by Grace

*by Geraldine Valdez*

*"For our struggle is not against flesh and blood, but against the rulers, against the authorities, against the powers of this dark world and against the spiritual forces of evil in the heavenly realms. Therefore put on the full armor of God..."*
— **Ephesians 6:12–13 (NIV)**

**The Life I Built**

Have you ever wondered what your purpose in life is? Why did God create you?

Have you ever waited for the other shoe to drop? Like life was going too well not to?

That wasn't my mindset at all.

By February 2023, I was finally on my way to living the dream I had worked so hard to build. Business was booming, I was closing deal after deal in real estate. I was living in a beautiful luxury one-bedroom apartment in New York City, a major flex when you're in your early thirties. I felt proud. Settled. Like I was finally tasting the fruits of all the seeds I had planted. I wanted to share it with everyone I loved—friends, family, chosen sisters. I had no boundaries, just an open heart.

But God was about to show me something deeper.

Looking back, I realize now, I've always been a Soul Sherpa. A connector. People are often drawn to me in their darkest seasons and I've been the one to sit with them, love them through it, or connect them to the breakthrough they needed. But the hard part? Many of those same people would move on and forget me. They'd only call when they needed something. And I told myself, "It's okay. Your good deed is done." But it stung and as time went on I began to see it as normal.

**The Awakening**

And then life unraveled.

One night in February 2023, I had a nightmare in which I was in a pitch-black room and I could hear evil voices laughing, taunting me, claiming they would take my soul. At that moment I realized I was under a demonic attack. I would go on to spend the rest of the night screaming ' You can take everything I have, but you'll never take my soul.' "I'm blessed and covered by the blood of Jesus Christ, Yeshua." Finally, my screams would be heard by my cousin and she woke me up. I was distraught and confused, filled with questions. What had that nightmare meant? Was there something evil lurking that I couldn't see?

My friend Gaia (whom most times I truly believe is an angel on earth) blessed my home with holy water and performed a Reiki healing cleanse. Reiki healing is a Japanese technique for stress reduction and relaxation that promotes healing. t involves laying hands on the recipient to transfer unseen life-force energy, which is believed to enhance emotional and physical healing. Gaia prayed over me and when she was done she gave me water and told me to go to bed.

To this day, I am convinced my soul traveled to another realm or time. I couldn't tell you when I fell asleep or when I woke up. All I remember is laying my head on the pillow and I was immediately transported to a military type campsite; it looked like a warzone campsite. I was sitting in front of two beings (they looked human however their eyes were completely black and soulless). I was terrified. I couldn't speak and I knew they were relishing off my fears. At that moment it happened, someone put their right hand on my left. When I looked up it was my father, telling me to not be scared, reminding me that I wasn't alone. I felt a sense of peace and calmness I have never felt in my life.

The two communicated telepathically, telling me they would take everything from me. I very calmly responded " You can take it all from me, my career, my home, my material possessions but you'll never have my soul. I am covered by the blood of Jesus Christ, Yeshua, filled and protected by the Holy Spirit. No matter what you say or do, you'll never have it." I repeated it as a chant with sereneness. I've never felt such hatred from anyone. The two disappeared. My father proceeded to walk me through the campsite and next thing I knew I was in a bright, all white room.

The room was filled with many women (I've never met in my life) who came together. It was a celebration, hugging and laughing. The women were breaking bread together at a long table. Some loaves were sweet with honey, others were rich with cheese. I woke up with that image burning in my spirit. It felt holy, like a glimpse of something I didn't yet understand. I immediately researched the dream interpretation because my subconscious seemed to know it was a message I needed to decipher.

*This is what I found : The spiritual meaning of "breaking bread" during a white room gathering can be profound. It often symbolizes Christ's presence and sacrifice, as seen in the Last Supper where Jesus took bread and broke it, representing His body and blood. This practice serves as a reminder of His death and resurrection, fostering a sense of community and connection among believers. Dreams involving women breaking bread often symbolize a nurturing and comforting presence, representing a connection to spirituality and the divine feminine. The bread itself, in a spiritual context, can signify the Word of God, life, sustenance, and the divine presence.*

> *When a woman is seen breaking bread, it may indicate a spiritual blessing, guidance, or the sharing of wisdom and knowledge. The fact that there were different toppings—honey, cheese, etc.—speaks to the diversity of gifts, stories, and blessings each woman carries. Honey often symbolizes abundance, sweetness and God's favor, "a land flowing with milk and honey". (Source: www.hiddensignificance.com)*

This dream suggests I am either being called to create or nurture spaces where women come together to share their unique gifts, testimonies and wisdom nourishing one another spiritually and emotionally. It's a reminder that everyone brings something valuable to the table and in unity, there's healing, provision, and divine sweetness.

It's also God confirming my role as a soul sherpa, connector—bringing women together to feast not just on food, but on purpose, faith and fellowship.

So, what do I know now, that I didn't know then?

First, to my core I know it was the Lord himself showing up as my father holding my hand in that dream. He gave me the courage to face the demons and led me through the campsite to the women.

The message? In the darkest of times, he is there guiding you, protecting you. You only need to take several deep breaths and listen. Surrender. Give the Lord your fear. Remember, God, Yahweh made you in his image. Secondly, the breaking of the bread with women wasn't a dream but a revelation of what was to come. My saving grace, my community, The Latina Empire.

**When Grief Came Knocking**

Over the span of a year and a half, I would go on to lose several loved ones. March 27, 2023, I lost my younger cousin to mental illness after he committed suicide. Nine months to the day I would lose my cousin Zahrat.

Life as I knew would forever change.

I am the eldest granddaughter on both sides of my family. On my father's side, my cousin Zahrat was the eldest. Zahrat was the big brother I never had. Loyal. Protective. Fearless. Qualities I picked up. I don't think I ever told him, thank you. I knew no matter where I was in the world. If I called, he'd be there in an instant. Zahrat had survived fifteen unjust years in prison, rebuilt his life, and was preparing to start college. Zahrat saw the goodness and greatness in others before they could see it themselves. Our family didn't know that we were secretly planning to build an empire. A way to retire our parents and help the next generation reach the next level and leave a legacy. He had done more in two years than most accomplish in a lifetime. And then, he was taken from us. Now, all I have left are our text messages, full of plans he will never see come to fruition.

The day Zahrat died, a part of me died with him. December 27, 2023. It was my brother's birthday and as I passed his room I got a pain in my chest. My heart felt like someone had squeezed it. I had an awful feeling and asked my brother about his plans, telling him to be safe. Ten minutes later, I got the call that Zahrat had been ambushed.

I sat in front of the doctor and saw it in her eyes before she spoke "He didn't make it." Those words will forever haunt me. What do you mean?' but I was speechless. I just looked at her, trying to process. Three seconds. That's what I had. Three seconds to process and pick myself up.

The first time I felt Zahrat's presence was as I walked out the bathroom at the hospital. I watched as grief took over my family and suddenly I felt his energy, spirit however you choose to word it. It felt as though he was right behind me. I stood frozen and my empathic ability knew he was trying to communicate. It was like the message was delivered straight to my heart. Keep them safe. Whatever differences the family we may have had went out the window.

At first, I kept busy, handling his affairs so his parents could grieve in peace.

As the days passed, isolation began. Grief is a state of pain I don't wish on my worst enemy. The weeks that followed I would continue to feel his presence. I knew he wanted to speak and give messages. I am not strong enough to handle the supernatural and he knew. There's this place, right between sleep and wakefulness, where the lines blur and you feel connected to something bigger. It was in that space where we met. At first, he would visit me asking me to look after his younger brother. I'd be lying in bed and he would stand next to my bed and all of a sudden, I would be looking at my younger cousin sleeping on my couch.

After a few weeks, I couldn't feel his energy anymore. At that point my grief went from denial to a deep sadness and rage. I'd figured maybe he moved on, he was at peace. I hate to say it but the rage and anger I had was towards him. I had warned him of potential wolves dressed as sheep in his inner circle. Now, I had to live life without my best friend. He had left me to protect a family that was in shambles. The day we buried him, I must have drunk an entire bottle of vodka. All it did was give me a headache so I threw myself into prayer for him, for the family and for myself.

In March 2024, he visited me in the same state between sleep and waking. I forget the initial part of the conversation but before he walked to the door to leave he said "Cuz, say yes, when she asks you, say yes, ya heard." As he opened the door, my sister came in. I realized I was awake looking at my sister, I just tucked the message away in my heart.

Perla Tamez-Casanovas is a dear friend from Texas I met years ago through a mutual friend. She relocated to New York City and the following week of the encounter with Zahrat she asked me to have dinner.

The moment she asked me if I would consider being the leader of the New York chapter for The Latina Empire. Those words came back to me "Cuz, say yes, when she asks you, say yes, ya heard." I realized, this is what he wanted me to say yes too and I could not. I was broken, I didn't think I would be capable of helping anyone. I had every reason and intention to say no. However, my mouth and mind were not in sync because while "Yes" came out of my mouth my mind was screaming NO!

What I didn't know then that I know now?

This would be the beginning of my healing journey. I would once again be reminded of my purpose on earth and more importantly I would fully listen to my discernment.

At my first Manahood event, I saw it—the vision from my dream. Women breaking bread, not just with food, but with their hearts. Sharing wisdom. Tears. Laughter. Healing.

Leading up to the event I had hired an intern, Sabrina. Sabrina had graduated college and I had met her through a previous client of mine. She asked if her mother Jennifer could attend and I said of course. Toward the end we did an ice breaker in which the ladies were paired up to interview one another.

As it turns out Jennifer was leaving a bad situation at home and had decided to stay in the United States. Jennifer paired up with the one person who could actually help her. Perla. I felt something click. I knew in that instant that Sabrina had come into my life not to be my intern, but to connect with Perla. It was like my soul whispered; *this is why you're here. This is your purpose!*

And then I realized God was doing something far greater than what I could see. Two women who had met through this journey ended up helping one another heal, one through her pain and the other through her purpose. Months later, I watched as transformation unfolded before my eyes, and it hit me: I had simply been the bridge. That wasn't coincidence; it was divine alignment.

**The Shift**

And the more I reflected, the more I began to realize, God had been using me all along, even in my own seasons of brokenness. I was listening. I was observing. The veil had lifted, I was seeing signs I would have missed prior, seeing people and situations for what they really were. However, even on purpose, spiritual warfare doesn't stop.

Darkness doesn't always show up as a shadow. Sometimes, it hides in people you love. I've seen envy twist hearts. I've watched people turn to dark magic to harm others without a second thought. I witnessed someone try to destroy my cousin's life out of malice and jealousy. Zahrat suffered deeply because of someone like that.

Zahrat's death consumed me with rage. I wanted revenge. I could've taken matters into my own hands. But standing at his grave, I heard the Holy Spirit whisper, *"Remember Lucinda. Remember your grandfather."* Those two names reminded me of who I am, where I come from, and what I carry. Those whispers were a reminder of what had happened to individuals that had caused harm and pain to my family. God had taken care of it and at the moment I surrendered. I gave it to God. I laid down the desire to avenge and picked up the peace of letting Him handle it. Then came another kind of battle, the kind you fight quietly.

For so long, I had been the one always reaching out, checking in, holding space for everyone else. The one who always picked up the call or answered texts. I was the one people vented to, leaned on, called when their world fell apart. However, by winter of 2024, something in me shifted. I stopped chasing people. I stopped calling and texting first. I just stopped.

And silence followed.

Zahrat's death had unintentionally pushed me to start setting boundaries and finally choosing myself. Friends who I had once considered family, whom I had bent over backwards for were MIA when I needed them the most. However, I had friends who live throughout the country and internationally who were there for me. These beautiful souls kept me moving forward, they taught me there were no excuses.

If someone wanted to be there, they would.

In June 2024, while dealing with grief, my isolation was disrupted. It started virtually with our Latina Empire Clarity mastermind classes. They didn't know it, but those weekly sessions brought me back to life. It was my therapy.

The realization of how one-sided many of my friendships were, with many being borderline toxic, stood out. Many times, I would want to reach out but something held me back. During our Latina Empire Mastermind class when Perla made several statements that resonated with me. Perla said "You can't pour onto others from an empty cup." "You have to let go of anything or anyone that doesn't add value to your life." I didn't just hear it that time, I felt it. And it changed me.

One person didn't reach out until about seven months after I had gone completely silent. Asking "Did I do something wrong?" Another person spoke negatively about me. It was like, as soon as I stopped being the dependable one—the person they could count on whenever they needed something—that's when I became the villain in their story. And you know what? I'm okay with that.

Setting these boundaries, opened doors and opportunities for me that I would have otherwise missed by not putting myself first.

What I know now, that I didn't know then?

God had guided me to my tribe. A group of amazing beautiful souls, each battling their own traumas and heartaches but providing a judgement free space. Giving one other love, encouragement and most importantly holding one another accountable.

I am no longer afraid of the dark, for it is in the darkness I found my community, my *manas*. I remember thinking back about that revelation and wondering what it all meant. I found my answer. Learning to live in my purpose, filling my cup so that I could continue to pour onto others.

**The Body Keeps Score**

After recovering from Covid, I developed Gastritis (or so I thought). Due to the diagnosis I gained weight, suffered appetite loss, unbalanced hormones and my metabolism slowed down.

In August 2024, I had a terrible pain in my abdomen and I was rushed to the ER. Turns out I had gallbladder stones and needed emergency surgery. I was taken to the operation room and didn't get a chance to see my mom or sister Gerube which made me extremely nervous. While I lay on the operating table being strapped in, I saw the nurse's face smiling, and then I saw him. It was Zahrat. Dressed in white in the most beautiful white light I've ever seen. I went to say his name, and the next thing I knew, I was being woken up.

The surgery should have been a simple one-hour procedure. However, once it started they realized I had a stone the size of a large egg. The surgery would go on to take five hours. Afterwards, I dealt with complications due to my liver levels being extremely high. I spent eleven days at the hospital.

I called this the closing of that chapter in my life.

I witnessed God's presence and grace. I had received visits from a doctor in a white coat who gave me updates (or so I thought) because later I would find out no one had actually come in.

In one instance, a lovely doctor lady in white coat checked on me and said I should let the nurse know I'll be having a 102 fever. She gave me instructions to ask for a particular medication and to not let them give me anything else.

About two hours later, a nurse came to take my temperature and I relayed the message the doctor had given me. The nurse said no doctor had checked on me and my temperature was normal. By that evening I had a 102 fever and the nurse (nor myself) could explain how I knew I would be having a fever and what medication to take. This was one of many occurrences.

On the day I was discharged, I received a final visit from the same lady doctor in white. I told her to stop bringing her up because I was afraid everyone would think I'm crazy. She smiled and we spoke for a while. Before leaving she turned and said "Now you know why you struggled to open your company."

I was baffled. I never told her about my struggles to open my own company.

As I laid there I had an epiphany. I wasn't healthy and didn't know it. I wouldn't have been physically able to work or be responsible for the wellbeing of my employees. In the next few weeks that followed my surgery, I met (virtually) an amazing woman Francesca (with her own story) who owns her own hedge fund in New York. What had taken me three years to figure out she did in less than a month.

Mental vulnerability when you have surgery isn't something you don't realize exists. My sister Gerube (whom I adore) took care of me during my recovery process. The first time I used the bathroom 14 days post-surgery and couldn't clean myself I started to cry. She asked me what's wrong and I told her, I couldn't clean myself. Gerube said "That's not a problem. Turn around" and proceeded to grab a wipe. I called one of my manas from The Latina Empire and told her, "I think I've hit rock bottom."

Her response made me laugh through my tears: "Oh no, you didn't! You didn't crap the bed, did you?"

I said, "No! My sister had to wipe me!"

Without missing a beat, she said, "Girl, call me when you crap the bed and have to wait for someone to help you up and bathe you because you can't. That's when you've really hit rock bottom!"

I laughed. I hadn't laughed like that in months and I felt a sense of liberation. Understanding why I had that revelation those years ago. This community has lifted me, helped with my healing process and even career goals.

What do I know now that I didn't know then?

Patience and God's timing go hand in hand. God was saving me from storms I couldn't see. He wasn't just shielding my business. He was shielding me, because I wasn't ready to carry a battle that big. Not yet.

That experience solidified a deeper truth:

When God closes a door, it's not rejection, it's redirection. Sometimes His "NO" is saving you from a storm you can't see yet. He was protecting me, guiding me and just as he did for Perla, he had done for me because through Perla I was connected to Francesca.

Secondly, I finally adapted to what Perla had been preaching to us. I heard her but up until that point I hadn't really listened. Surround yourself with people who are smarter than you. Perla had been awarded a recognition a year prior and had mentioned my name in a room at an event I didn't even attend. God's small pebbles he had laid years prior would build the bridge I would need to cross.

Thirdly, I took a look in the mirror. Reminding myself of my own strength and purpose.

**What I Know Now**

Now, I carry the kind of wisdom I didn't even know I was praying for:

- Peace is my green light. If I have to force it, it's not for me.
- Saying no is a full sentence, and sometimes, the most powerful one.
- My calling isn't to fix everyone. It's to walk in obedience.
- I don't chase people anymore. I protect my space, my heart, my peace.
- My purpose is sacred and it starts with being aligned with God.
- Discernment is a gift, and I've learned to trust it.
- Not all connections are divine, some are distractions dressed as opportunity.

This story, my story, is where grief takes over and I fight my way to get back. Where life challenges are thrown and curses are broken. Ultimately is where my blessings begin.

I am no longer the woman who overextends, who waits for the other shoe to drop. I'm the woman who walks in discernment, who sees God's fingerprints in the delays, the redirections, and the whispers.

I've learned not to let the world change who I am at my core, a soul connector, soul sherpa. I've learned to really see people and situations for what they really are. I don't hold any animosity, grudges or resentment towards anyone. Sometimes you forgive for your own sake.

I'm still in the process. I don't have all the answers. But I do have a promise: that God wastes nothing. That every heartbreak, every silence, every yes and every no was bringing me here.

Looking back now, I realize God had been preparing me to face the biggest challenges of my life. These lessons would test my faith, my purpose in life and would lead me to a fork in the road.

I took the hardest path, the path of healing.

In a world obsessed with instant gratification, we often want quick fixes, easy answers, and overnight results. We're willing to grind for our careers, chase degrees, promotions, and success, but when it comes to our spiritual and mental well-being, we hesitate. We avoid the mirrors. We silence the still, small voice asking us to pause and look inward.

But healing doesn't come in with a snap of the finger, click of a button or on a weekend. It takes time, intention and deep inner work. I could no longer ignore the signs. The dreams I'd been having weren't just dreams anymore. The warnings from God weren't whispers—they were roars. God was speaking through everything—closed doors, misaligned relationships, the anxiety I kept pushing through, the way my body started reacting when my spirit was exhausted. I was being asked—*Will you keep running or will you finally stop and heal?*

That was the moment the lessons hit at full force. It wasn't gentle, I have battle wounds and scars imprinted in my soul but it was necessary. And I knew: if I wanted peace, purpose and alignment, I had to stop seeking the shortcuts.

As I write this, I find myself in tears but in good spirits; it's been a cathartic experience. The words seem to flow as if God's intention is for someone out there to read my story. To study. Learn. To know there is light at the end of the tunnel. I'm no longer afraid of the dark, for it was in the dark I shined the brightest. It was in my darkness, I found my faith, community and strength to lead myself out by the grace of God.

So, if I could. I'd hug the person reading this, I'd say:

You are not alone. You don't have to be everything to everyone. You don't have to chase what was never meant to stay. You don't have to explain why you're changing.

Just listen to God. Cancel the noise. He is speaking.

I didn't see it or know it then, but I see it now. His grace was with me the whole time.

And maybe you're there now, walking through something you don't understand. Wondering why it hurts. Wondering if it matters. Wondering if it will ever make sense.

Let me ask you:

Has there ever been a time where you didn't see God's grace then, but now you look back and realize He was covering you all along?

If so, you already know.

You're becoming. And you're not alone.

If not, hang in there! You have a purpose; you were put on earth for a reason!

Keep walking. Keep trusting and when in doubt, pray about it and trust your discernment.

Because you never know which "yes" will lead you back home to your purpose.

> *"No weapon that is formed against thee shall prosper; and every tongue that shall rise against thee in judgment thou shalt condemn. This is the heritage of the servants of the Lord, and their righteousness is of me, saith the Lord."* (Isaiah 54:17)

## Geraldine Valdez

**Instagram:** @geraldine_nyc

# Chapter 20

# Chains Broken: The Power of Forgiveness

*by Carmen Sauceda*

*"And they overcame him by the blood of the Lamb and by the word of their testimony; and they did not love their lives to the death."*
— **Revelation 12:11 (NKJV)**

### The Armor I Didn't Know I Was Building

I was just a little girl when I learned what fear felt like in the pit of my stomach. The sound of yelling in our home always came without warning, like a storm that rolled in fast, shaking the walls before anyone had a chance to brace for it. I would stand in the hallway, frozen, watching my mother take the blows of the man I thought was my father. My small hands would tremble at my sides, my heart pounding so loud I could hear it in my ears, and yet my feet felt nailed to the ground. Fear. Anger. Helplessness. They all lived inside me at once.

He worked from three in the afternoon until eleven at night. By the time he got home it was one or two in the morning, and that's when the dread would settle in me the deepest. I would lie awake in the dark, tears soaking my pillow, crying myself to sleep because I knew what was coming. I didn't always see it with my own eyes, but I heard it, the yelling, the blows, my mother's muffled cries. Those sounds became the background music of my childhood nights.

It broke something inside of me. I wanted to scream, to run in and push him away, but I was too small. I hated the frustration that rose up in me, knowing that I couldn't stop him. And so, at only nine years old, I made a vow. I clenched my tiny fists and whispered to myself, *I will never let a man treat me like this. Never.* That vow hardened something in me. It became my armor. I didn't know then that it would also become a prison.

Years later, when he died, I thought my nightmare was over. I sat in the pew at his funeral with my brothers, my chest still heavy with the confusion of love and fear mixed together. That man was gone, but the bruises on my mother's spirit remained. It wasn't until that day, when I overheard my mother and aunt whispering, that I discovered the truth; he wasn't even my real father. Shock ran through me like ice water. How could he not be my dad when he had raised me, treated me and my brothers with kindness, given us his name? He had always been good to us, except when it came to my mom.

The truth is, my mother was raised in chaos long before I ever came along. Her father, my grandfather, had stolen her away from his own wife. His mother was actually my mother's stepmother. My mom was handed over to be raised not by her real mother but by my grandfather's mother and two sisters. Violence wasn't something she learned from a stranger; it was something she breathed in like air. Abuse was the language of her childhood.

So, when she married, she entered into what she thought was safety, but what became another cycle of pain. She didn't know another way. And I, her daughter, absorbed every bruise, every scream, every moment of silence that followed a fight.

That vow I made at nine years old, to never be treated the way my mother was wrapped around my heart like barbed wire. It hardened me. It taught me that love was dangerous, that to be soft was to be destroyed. I decided that strength meant coldness, that survival meant never giving a man the power to hurt me. Later, when I became a wife myself, that vow followed me like a shadow. I was compassionate toward my children, but with men I was harsh, even cruel. I thought love was a game where whoever fell deepest would be the one to lose. And I swore to myself that it would never be me.

**Nightmares That Didn't End**

When I was eleven, I thought maybe, just maybe, life would get better. The man who used to beat my mom had died. I remember sitting quietly, thinking my nightmare had finally ended. But only six months later, another man walked into our lives. And with him came a darkness I wasn't ready for.

This one was worse. Violent, twisted, and predatory. He came not just to wound my mother, but to poison the innocence of her children. He carried a rage in his eyes that made my stomach turn cold. I was only a child, yet I felt the evil of his presence in the room.

One night, he pressed a gun to my head. I can still feel the cold steel against my skin, the sharp taste of fear filling my mouth. In those seconds, a thousand thoughts raced through me, but they were not the thoughts of a child, they were the thoughts of someone who had already carried far too much pain. My body trembled, but inside I felt something strange, almost like defiance. I said, *"If you're going to do it, then do it. End my misery. Put me out of this pain."*

Only weeks before that moment, I had thought of ending my own life. The abuse, the darkness, the silence from the very person who should have protected me, it all felt unbearable. I had stood in that place of decision at just fourteen years old, ready to give up. But in that moment, I heard a voice deep within me, clear and firm. The Holy Spirit whispered, *what will happen to your son? Who will take care of your brothers?*

That question pierced through the fog of despair. It stopped me from following through. I couldn't leave them. I couldn't abandon them the way I had been abandoned.

And now here I was, staring down the barrel of a gun, and instead of fear swallowing me whole, I almost welcomed it. *Go ahead,* I thought. *Do me a favor. Take me out of my misery.* It wasn't courage, it was exhaustion. I was tired of fighting, tired of surviving.

After he lowered the gun, silence filled the room. It wasn't the comforting kind of silence, it was the kind that presses down heavy on your chest. I felt numb. My adrenaline was still rushing, so it almost didn't matter. I didn't cry. I didn't scream. I just stood there hollow, so tired of everything. All I wanted was to find a way out, for me, for my brothers, for all of us.

In those moments, I didn't know God the way I do now. I would whisper desperate prayers into the dark: *If You exist, why are You letting this happen to me?* I didn't understand that His hand was there even then. Looking back now, I see it, how He kept the gun from firing, how He held me even in my numbness, how He was already writing a story of survival and redemption when all I saw was despair.

The abuse wasn't only violence, it was perversion. He would sneak into my room late at night, standing there in the shadows, touching himself while I lay frozen under the sheets. I would hold my breath, pretending to sleep, praying he wouldn't cross the line. He never fully did, but the torment of those moments carved deep scars into me. There were holes drilled in my closet walls so he could spy on me. He'd watch me through the window when I showered. And the worst part? My mother knew. She caught him once peeking in while I bathed, and she looked the other way. The betrayal of her silence cut deeper than his violence.

Looking back now, I see God's fingerprints even in that horror. That man could have taken so much more from me. He could have gone further. But the hand of God restrained him. The Lord never abandoned me, even when my house felt like a prison of fear. I didn't recognize it then, I only saw the shadows. But now I know it was His Spirit whispering to me at fourteen, keeping me alive for a future I couldn't see yet.

**Twelve and Carrying Life**

At twelve years old, when most little girls were still playing with dolls, I carried life inside of me. My body was too small, too young, too unprepared for what was happening. I was pregnant. My mother sent me away to an unwed mothers' home run by nuns. In a strange way, that place felt safer than home, because it meant I was far from the man who had tormented me.

The room I stayed in was plain: white walls, a narrow bed, and a silence that pressed down heavy at night. There were other girls there, each with her own story, though none of us had the words to share them out loud. No one had ever explained to me what was happening to my body. When I first had my period, I thought it was poop. My mother had never spoken to me about it, never prepared me for womanhood.

At the home they taught me things like how to crochet scarves and hats. I learned with clumsy fingers, but inside I held tightly to one clear decision: I would protect this baby with my life. He would never go through what I went through.

When the time came to give birth, I was in a small hospital room run by the Salvation Army. I was alone. No hand to hold, no voice to encourage me through the pain. When I first laid eyes on him, something in me shifted. He was so tiny, so fragile. His skin yellowed from jaundice, his body needing extra care before he could even come home with me. I stayed by his side, praying silently, watching every rise and fall of his chest.

I leaned close to him in those early days, whispering promises into his little ears, promises I meant with all my heart. *I will be strong for you. I will protect you. I will give my life for you. No one will ever separate us.* In my little girl's mind, I had already decided: I would never let my son or my brothers endure what I had endured.

That vow turned me into what some would later call a helicopter mom. I hovered. I overprotected. I checked doors, peeked through windows, listened for any sound out of place. My children would never know what it was like to live in fear under their own roof.

They would never have to beg for protection the way I had begged my mother. Even then, as a twelve-year-old child cradling another child, I was already both mother and warrior.

## Survival at Seventeen

By seventeen, my childhood was long gone. I dropped out of high school, not because I wanted to, but because survival demanded it. I was working, and so was my husband, my high school sweetheart. He was only eighteen himself, still more of a boy than a man, but he promised he would help me take care of my brothers. Together, with the little we earned, we bought a house.

It wasn't out of pride, or ambition, or even the excitement most people feel when they buy their first home. It was out of necessity. My brothers needed safety, and I was determined to give it to them.

I told my mother she could keep their VA checks, but in exchange, she would let me take full responsibility for raising them. In other words, we swapped the checks for my brothers. To me, it wasn't a bargain. It was freedom. It was the only way I could pull them out of the violence we had grown up in.

That house wasn't a home filled with childhood dreams. It was a fortress of survival. I didn't feel proud, or accomplished, or even grown. I only felt responsible. Every choice I made, every dollar I spent, was about them, not me.

**When Love Felt Like Betrayal**

Marriage came too early for me, just like everything else in my life. My high school sweetheart became my husband. For a season, I clung to the fragile hope that maybe, just maybe, we could build something steady together. He promised to help me with my brothers. He promised to help raise my son. And for a while, he did.

But promises are fragile things when they're built on broken foundations. He abandoned me when I was pregnant with my last baby. His absence was sharp, but his words cut deeper: *"Who's going to want you with all these kids?"* Those words planted lies in my heart that wrapped around my worth like weeds, choking out whatever confidence I had left.

At first, I judged him harshly, my chest burning with anger and bitterness at his selfishness. But slowly, without even realizing it, I became what I hated. I became him.

I see it clearly now. The moment I walked away from God, I became a player. I played with men's feelings, not knowing what real love was. My husband had been a womanizer, and in my own way, I mirrored him. Later in life, when I cheated on my second husband, the truth hit me like a tidal wave. God showed me that not only had I cheated on my husband, but I had also cheated on Him - my first love. My spiritual unfaithfulness had manifested in the physical. I didn't realize it until years later, after the divorce, but by then the damage was done.

Even though I had left God behind, I clung to a twisted sense of morality. I set boundaries: I wouldn't touch another woman's husband. I wouldn't cross that line. But within those limits, I let myself spiral. I was selfish. I was careless. I craved the attention of men, not because I wanted them, but because I needed proof that my ex-husband's words weren't true. I wanted someone to want me.

Men would fall in love with me, but I never let them past the front door of my real life. My children were sacred, untouchable. I never brought men around them. Inside my home, I tried to keep it pure and untarnished. But outside those walls, I lived a double life. I drank, never to the point of drunkenness, but enough to numb what I didn't want to feel. I toyed with men like pawns on a board, always keeping my heart at a safe distance. I had vowed that in love, the one who fell deepest would always be the one who lost. And I refused to let it be me.

Sex, for me, never felt like intimacy. Because of how it had first been introduced into my life—through shame, secrecy, and trauma—it was never about love. It was about survival. A transaction. A way to momentarily fill an emptiness that always came back. No matter how much I tried, that void was never satisfied.

**A Good Man, A Wounded Woman**

There was one man who didn't deserve what I gave him. A good man. A godly man. He treated me with the kind of love that scripture speaks about, the kind of love that covers a multitude of sins.

He cooked. He cleaned. He washed the clothes. He brought me roses. He treated me like a queen. He was gentle, steady, and faithful. And yet I couldn't receive his love. I was hardened, armored in ways he couldn't break through.

Instead of softening, I took control. I was the man in the relationship. I worked fourteen-hour days, seven days a week, running my business like a general. He kept regular hours, went to the gym, and rested. Resentment burned in me. I saw him as weak, even though all he wanted was to serve me and love me.

The imbalance consumed us. He nurtured while I fought. He wanted peace while I wanted control. He dreamed of being my husband in the truest sense, but I wouldn't let him lead me.

Eventually, I did the unthinkable. I cheated on him. Not because he failed me, but because I couldn't bear to be vulnerable. And when I did, I realized I had become the very thing I once despised.

He didn't deserve it. He was everything I thought I wanted in a God-fearing man. And yet, I didn't love him. I had married him for convenience, for the sake of my children, for the image of stability, for the role he could play. But once my youngest child was grown, I looked at him and felt nothing. The emptiness inside me had swallowed the love that could have been.

I asked him to leave.

Years later, I did apologize to him, though if I'm honest, it wasn't because I felt it deeply at the time. It was out of obedience to God. My heart was still hard, but I knew the Lord was asking me to humble myself. So, I said the words, even when I couldn't feel them. Looking back now, I see how much more he deserved, not just the apology, but the love and respect I never gave him.

**The Breaking Point**

My life had become a cycle of broken vows and hollow victories until one night, standing on a beach, I finally cried out to God. My boyfriend at the time loved fighting. Every day was a war of words, walls shaking from his anger. He was violent, and somewhere along the way, I had become violent too. I hated who I was with him, but I was terrified of being alone.

I walked barefoot along the sand, the waves licking at my ankles as tears streamed down my face. *"God, I cannot live this way anymore,"* I whispered into the night. *"If You give me the strength to leave this man, I promise I will serve You for the rest of my life."*

Weeks later, he was gone. God had heard me.

The first night after he left, I felt something I hadn't felt in years, peace. A deep relief settled into my body like an anchor. It was as if a storm had finally passed and I could breathe again. For so long, life with him had been like a rollercoaster, his emotions jerking me up and down until I thought I'd break. But now, silence, stillness, and peace.

Even my health shifted. I remember going to the doctor once during those years, my blood pressure through the roof. He looked me in the eye and said, *"The day you get rid of that man, your body will go back to normal."* Months later, I returned for a checkup. My blood pressure had leveled, my body calm again. The doctor smiled knowingly and said, *"You got rid of him, didn't you?"*

He was right.

And then my son, without knowing any of the details, without me ever speaking of the chaos, looked at me one day and said, *"Mom, you can't put a price on peace of mind."* His words pierced me. Out of the mouths of children, God speaks.

Even before I fully returned to Him, God was already using His voice to strengthen me. I remember venting to my best friend over and over about the same situations, the same fights. Finally, the Holy Spirit stopped me and said, *"Why do you keep calling her if you're not going to change anything? If you want to keep living that way, be quiet because that's your choice. But if you really want change, then do something about it."*

The Holy Spirit's bluntness and my son's wisdom collided in my soul like a ton of bricks. Something broke inside me. I knew I couldn't go back.

The void that had haunted me after every failed relationship finally began to close. For the first time, I asked God—not a man—to fill it. And He did.

**Restoration**

After he left, God didn't just quiet the storm—He began rebuilding the house from the studs. The first room He touched was the one labeled **mother**.

It started when my mom came to live with me. She was legally blind by then, stubborn as a cedar post, and still wired to worry, especially about my son Jim, her favorite. At first, she didn't want to stay with me. *She wanted to go live with my son, not with me.* She fought it, then finally agreed—suitcase in one hand, pride in the other.

Those early weeks were rough. She was diabetic, and I'd try to set boundaries around food—what she could eat, what she couldn't—and she'd bristle. We'd go a few rounds over tortillas, tamales, sodas, and I'd feel the old heat rising in my chest. One afternoon, in my frustration, I vented to Jim about her. He listened and then pierced me with a sentence so simple it disarmed me: *"What does it matter who's right or wrong? It's like arguing with a child. Why would you?"*

I went to my room and prayed the only honest prayer I had: *"Lord, I don't have the love I need for her. Give me Your heart. Take this heart of stone. Let me see her with Your eyes. Let me only hear what You want me to hear. Help me think like You think. Give me compassion...because I don't have it."*

God answered not all at once, but like soft rain that soaks the ground. He taught me to bathe her gently, to buy her clothes that made her feel pretty, to iron her blouses, wash her clothes. At night, I lay beside her in rehabilitation clinics and hospital rooms, watching Netflix on my phone while she drifted to sleep. Morning after morning, I rose to work; night after night, I returned to her side. The tasks became tender. Pride turned into care. *She was my mother, and I would take care of her.*

One day, we were driving—windows cracked, sun warm on our hands—when she broke the silence. "Carmen...can you forgive me?" Her voice was small, hesitant, like a child testing the water.

"For what, Mom?"

"For everything I did to you when you were a child...When I should have protected you, and I didn't."

Her face—oh, God—was lined with a sorrow I had never seen. Not defensive. Not deflecting. Just...repentant. I felt something holy move through the car, like the breath of God. Forgiveness rose up in me—not forced, not theoretical, but living. I forgave her. We both cried. Years of hardness softened under the weight of mercy.

And then I turned to her, with tears streaming down my own face, and said, *"Mom, will you forgive me, too? For the hatred I carried toward you all these years."* She didn't hesitate. She looked at me, nodded, and whispered, *"Yes."*

In that moment, forgiveness flowed both ways—her to me, and me to her. Something broke. Something lifted. The heaviness of generations shattered, replaced by a mercy neither of us could have manufactured on our own.

After that, we traveled together. She became my co-pilot, purse tucked against her, always ready before I was, eager to go anywhere with me. We found a rhythm. Laughter returned to our house. I chose to remember the good, because the good was finally louder than the past.

We didn't know Mom was going to die. It was supposed to be a routine surgery. Before that, when she broke her wrist, I slept beside her through rehab, learning the slow, sacred work of patience: helping her shower, dressing her carefully, smoothing lotion over skin that had carried me into this world. I ironed her slacks, paired her scarves, and felt pride rise in me—*this is my mother*. When she passed, a part of me went with her. The seat beside me in the car felt too light, my right hand reaching instinctively for someone who was no longer there. Still, I refused to reopen the vault of old memories that only stored pain. I wanted to remember her as God had restored her to me—repentant, tender, mine.

God gave me one more mercy before she went home. She lay in a hospital bed, two weeks of tests stretching into a fog of waiting. I was with her day and night. The Lord pressed Psalm 51 on my heart. *Read it to her. Have her repeat it.* So I did—line by line, prayer by prayer—until we reached: *"Wash me, and I shall be whiter than snow."* At those words, she began to weep. I saw repentance flood her face, the Spirit doing what only He can. We cried together. She gave herself to Jesus, asked for His forgiveness. Heaven felt very near. I didn't know then what I know now: God was letting me see her robes being washed. He knew I needed that peace.

**The Daughter Who Returned on Mother's Day**

I used to pray a secret prayer: *God, if nothing else, let me apologize to my daughter. Let me look her in the eyes and tell her why.* I had placed her for adoption at sixteen, not because I didn't love her, but because I refused to bring a daughter into the violence we were living in. I could endure hell; I wouldn't hand it to her.

Years later, God answered in a way only He could, through Ancestry.com. She found my granddaughter, Vanessa, because the blood match was high. Melanie reached out, thinking it was Vanessa; it turned out to be Vanessa's grandmother on her mother's side. Word traveled to Rachel, my son Jim's ex-wife. Rachel called Jim: *"There's a woman saying she's your sister."*

Jim said, *"No way."* I hadn't told my children. Shame is a silencer. But my youngest brother was in the car with Jim. *"It's true,"* he said softly. Jim—stunned—told Rachel to pass along his number. He and my brother spoke with Melanie. She said, *"I want to meet my mother."* The DNA confirmed she was a full sibling to my children; my high school sweetheart was her father.

When Melanie learned Jim was the oldest and that I had him at twelve, she asked the question that had lived in her bones: *"Why didn't she keep me at sixteen?"* My brother, steady and kind, told her the truth: *"She didn't want to bring you into what we were living through."*

They wanted to surprise me with her, to just bring her into the room one day and watch the reunion unfold. But they were afraid I would have a heart attack from the shock. *"Don't surprise her,"* they said. *"Not with something this big. Let's bring her in slowly."*

They planned how to tell me. My baby brother, who's always felt like a son, called me at work. *"Sit down,"* he said. I sat. *"Guess who's reached out to us? Your daughter. The one you placed for adoption."*

A sound tore out of me, half laugh, half cry. I shouted, and heads turned. All I could think was, *God, You heard me. You remembered my prayer.*

We met on Mother's Day. No coincidence—God writes with a poet's hand. We ran to each other, and that first hug felt like a door swinging open in a house I'd lived in my whole life but never entered. She looks like me—my face on a darker canvas. She told me her foster mother had made her feel "weird" and "different," but deep down she always knew she was mine. She brought a letter she'd written to me when she was eleven. I held the paper like a relic.

"I am so sorry," I told her. "I didn't want anyone to touch you or hurt you."

She said, "Mom, I understand. When I had my own children, I knew you did it to protect me. And God gave me a good family. I never had a problem like that."

Since then, we've folded each other into our lives as if no time had been lost. Being with her felt familiar, like she had always been here. Even her laugh, carried the same rhythm and tone as my youngest daughter's, their mannerisms mirroring one another, though they had never been around each other. The resemblance went beyond looks; it was in the way they moved, the way they lit up a room.

It made me think about the old debate of nature versus nurture. Some things you can't explain by environment or upbringing. She had been raised in an entirely different home, with different people, different customs, and yet so much of me lived in her. Blood has its own memory. There was something deeper at work, something God Himself had woven into her being that tied us together long before reunion.

I've met her husband, her children, even branches of the family tree I had never dared to climb. Now we call. We visit. We show up for each other. We belong.

And when I stand back and look at all my children, all of them educated, all of them professionals, all of them carrying themselves with dignity, I see the weight of God's faithfulness. I had no degree. I was a single mother more than once. But I raised them on the little I had: morals, values, and the truths I knew from God's Word. Somehow, God took those seeds and grew them into a forest. Even Melanie, another tree grafted in, is flourishing with the same roots of grace.

**Forgiving the Man I Planned to Kill**

I was about twenty-six when the Lord asked me to do what felt impossible. I had invited my stepfather, the man whose darkness had marked my childhood, to church. He came. During Bible study, I sensed God's unmistakable nudge: *Ask him to forgive you.*

*Me?* For what? For the hate. For the murder I'd already rehearsed in my mind. For the plots I'd laid like traps. God wasn't asking me to pretend his sins didn't happen; He was asking me to lay down the death I was carrying.

So, I stood—heart pounding—and said, in front of everyone, "I'm sorry for hating you so much that I planned your death."

I didn't feel fireworks. I didn't hear angels sing. But heaven heard obedience. Healing works like yeast: invisible, unstoppable, rising in secret. I can't tell you the day the chains fell; I only know I reached for them one morning and they were gone. God had cut them while I slept.

Why did God ask me to do it? Because hatred was poisoning every well in my life. My father's drinking, my stepfather's predation, and my husband's infidelity had taught me to hate men. That hate was shaping me, sharpening me into the very blade that had wounded me. Forgiveness wasn't about saying *it was okay*; it was about saying *I won't be owned by this anymore*. It was how God taught me to let go.

## Scriptures That Carried Me

Two chapters became my lifeline in the dark: Psalm 51 and Psalm 91.

Psalm 51 taught me what it meant to fall to my knees in true repentance. Not the surface kind, but the kind that breaks you open and allows God to wash what you could never cleanse on your own. Every time I read, *"Create in me a clean heart, O God, and renew a right spirit within me,"* I felt Him chiseling away the stone around my heart and replacing it with flesh.

Psalm 91 wrapped around me like armor when I had none. *"He who dwells in the secret place of the Most High shall abide under the shadow of the Almighty."* Those words were more than poetry; they were survival. They reminded me that I was not alone.

Those scriptures were not just verses on a page. They were breath in my lungs, light for my path, and the anchor that kept me from being swept away.

## To the Twelve-Year-Old Girl

**It's going to be okay.** God is with you, and if God is with you, no one can stand against you. The joy of the Lord will be your strength, even when you feel no joy at all. Hold on. You are in for a ride, but you are not alone on it. Keep your eyes on Jesus. Every man on earth can fail you; He won't. People make disastrous choices, but God's mercy is ocean-deep. He keeps pulling what we toss into the sea back to shore, cleaned and made useful. Through forgiveness, He will break the chains inside you, and what bound generations don't have to bind you. Free will can make a mess; forgiveness makes a future.

## God's Fingerprints on Every Page

Looking back, I can see the places where God's hand covered me even when I was running from Him:

- The lines not crossed by my stepfather that could have destroyed me; that was God's shield.

- The good, godly man He gave me, whom I didn't know how to love was proof that God tried to hand me a blessing before I had the wisdom to hold it.

- The man I thought was my father, who never turned his fists on me or my brothers, was mercy in a violent house.

- A mother who refused abortion when urged otherwise was God preserving a life He planned to redeem.

- An ex-boyfriend who was volatile and cruel, yet never laid a hand on me. Protection, even in danger.

- A pastor calling every Saturday, "just practicing," slipping sermons through the phone. That was God's voice in disguise, calling me home.

All along, I wanted to do it on my own. I carried power like a weapon: *I will never be weak again.* But the same power that raised Jesus from the dead didn't come to harden me; it came to heal me. Once I yielded, I saw it—God's fingerprints on every page. Lack of knowledge had driven my worst decisions; the knowledge of God began to rewrite them.

**The Word of My Testimony**

There is a scripture that names my victory and explains why I'm telling you all of this:

*"And they overcame him by the blood of the Lamb and by the word of their testimony; and they did not love their lives to the death."* (Revelation 12:11 NKJV)

The blood speaks of what Jesus did.
The testimony speaks of what He did **in me**.

This is my testimony: I was a frightened child who made a vow to never be hurt again and grew into a woman who hurt others instead. I was a mother who learned protection the hard way and a daughter who learned forgiveness the holy way. I was a planner of vengeance who chose mercy and a breaker of hearts who found my own. I was a runner who finally turned around and found God had been running toward me the whole time.

If He did it for me, He will do it for you. If He restored my mother, He can restore yours. If He brought my daughter home on Mother's Day, He can return what was lost in your story on the very day it cuts the deepest. If He turned my children into oaks of righteousness grown from the thin soil of a single mother with no diploma, He can make forests from your desert.

Forgiveness is not forgetting. It is the key God places in your hand so you can walk out of the cell, step into the light, and let Him lead you home. And home, I have learned, is not a safe house you buy at seventeen; it's a God who never leaves.

What doesn't kill you doesn't make you strong by itself.
God does when you walk with Him.

And now, by His grace, I do, and you can too.

**Carmen Sauceda**

**Instagram:** @itscarmensauceda

*"Therefore go and make disciples of all nations, baptizing them in the name of the Father and of the Son and of the Holy Spirit, and teaching them to obey everything I have commanded you. And surely I am with you always, to the very end of the age."*
— Matthew 28:19-20

# Epilogue

There is a moment, somewhere between heartbreak and healing, where you begin to realize the truth: God was never absent. His hand never left you. The silence you feared was not abandonment but invitation.

We often call it waiting—waiting for doors to open, waiting for prayers to be answered, waiting for miracles to unfold. But if we are honest, many times it is not us waiting on God, it is God waiting on us. Waiting on us to believe Him. Waiting on us to surrender what we have been clinging to. Waiting on us to trust that His ways are higher, His timing better, His love deeper than we ever imagined.

Surrender is the soil of miracles. When we let go of our will, we make room for God's. Too often, we cling tightly to our own plans when all the while He is longing to give us His plans that are *"exceedingly abundantly above all we could ask or imagine"* – Ephesians 3:20.

Our free will is our superpower. And belief is what supercharges it. Believing goes hand in hand with receiving. The good news is, God doesn't ask for perfect faith. He says if your belief is as small as a mustard seed, it can move mountains – Matthew 17:20. He takes our little and makes it much, because He is a good God.

And when He looks at you, He is not scanning for perfection. He is looking at your heart. That is where it begins. That is where everything changes.

So, I invite you, right here, right now, to open your heart to Jesus. Say it with all that you are: *"I believe You died for me. I believe You rose again. I believe You paid the penalty for my sins."* Try it. What do you have to lose? Only heaven to gain.

When you do, you will feel it: the awakening of your soul, the stirring of new life, the undeniable knowing that you are seen, forgiven, and loved beyond measure.

Because *God is willing, daughter* (*Diosito sí quiere, mija*). His promises have never wavered. Sometimes the miracle isn't waiting on His hand, it's waiting on your yes.

# Final Declaration Prayer

*"If you declare with your mouth, 'Jesus is Lord,' and believe in your heart that God raised him from the dead, you will be saved."*
— **Romans 10:9**

Lord Jesus,
I open my heart to You today.
I believe You died for me.
I believe You rose again.
I believe You paid the price for my sins.

I surrender my will and make room for Yours.
I believe You will do exceedingly abundantly above all I could ever ask or imagine.
I trust that even my mustard seed faith is enough for You to move mountains in my life.

Thank You for making much with my little.
Thank You for seeing my heart and calling me Your own.
From this day forward, I choose to walk in freedom,
I choose to walk in faith,
I choose to walk in You.

In Jesus' name, Amen.

*"Therefore, if anyone is in Christ, the new creation has come: The old has gone, the new is here!"*
— 2 Corinthians 5:17

# Acknowledgments

With a heart overflowing with gratitude, I want to pause and honor every single person who helped breathe life into this project. This book is not just words on paper; it is a labor of love, faith, and community, stitched together by the hands, prayers, and encouragement of many.

To the incredible contributors, thank you for your trust, bravery, honesty, and willingness to share pieces of your soul. Your stories carry the weight of truth, the beauty of healing, and the light of God's grace. Each of you has poured out something sacred, and together, we have created a book that will echo through generations.

To my family and friends, thank you for standing beside me in the late nights, the deadlines, and the moments of uncertainty. Your encouragement reminded me of my "why" and God's plans over my life.

To my M3 Mastermind *(m3mastermind_podcast)* sisters, thank you for your steadfast love and holy accountability, for always reflecting back to me who I am when I forget, and for never letting me settle for anything less than God's best. You've shown me what real sisterhood looks like. One that is rooted in truth, lifted by prayer, and wrapped in the kind of grace that calls a woman higher.

Above all, this project is dedicated to my Lord and Savior, Jesus Christ. I am simply His vessel, and He may do as He wishes with this work. Thank You, precious Lord, for the blessing of being used by You. May every page testify to Your glory and goodness.

And to you, dear reader, thank you for opening your heart, for journeying with us, and for allowing these words to meet you exactly where you are. My hope is that as you turn these pages, you begin to shed the layers this world has placed on you. That you step into your most authentic self, into the power God has given you that is inherently yours, and into the divine purpose only you can fulfill.

With deepest love and gratitude,

**Eliza Michelle Garza**

## About the Curator
## Eliza M. Garza

Eliza M. Garza is a best-selling children's book author, dynamic speaker, faith coach, and global leader with *The Latina Empire*. A gifted storyteller, she uses her voice to illuminate narratives that inspire faith, strengthen families, and foster a love of literacy.

Her acclaimed Spanglish titles, including *Raspas Con Mi Grandpa* and *Vendiendo Con Mi Grandpa*, celebrate culture while teaching timeless values of love, connection, and heritage. Through *Vendiendo Con Mi Grandpa*, she also spearheads a pioneering financial literacy program for children, equipping the next generation with entrepreneurial skills and practical money management tools.

Garza is the curator of the groundbreaking anthology *Si Diosito Quiere, Mija* (*God Willing, Daughter*) and the visionary behind the forthcoming podcast of the same name, designed to amplify the book and share powerful God stories that spark hope and transformation. She is also the founder of Mija Media House, a creative publishing house dedicated to helping authors bring their stories to life through purpose-driven storytelling, professional publishing guidance, and empowering author development.

As a faith coach, she walks alongside women to help them embrace their God-given identity, strip away the layers imposed by the world, and activate their unique calling. In her role with *The Latina Empire*, she uplifts and equips women globally, affirming them as vessels of influence, carriers of legacy, and builders of the future.

Her mission is clear and unwavering: to glorify God, empower the next generation, and ignite transformation.

*Invite Eliza to inspire your school, organization, or faith community through an **author visit, speaking engagement, or faith coaching experience**. Book now at elizamgarza.com*

# An Invitation to You

If this book has touched your heart, we invite you to take the next step and share *your* story with us. Testimonies have the power to heal, to inspire, and to remind others that they are not alone. Your voice matters, and we would be honored to hear it.

Follow the journey at @SiDiosito to connect, share your testimony, and discover more ways to stay inspired.

Continue the conversation with the authors! Follow their social media pages, encourage them, and let them know how their words impacted you.

**Your Story Matters**

We believe God is still writing stories through women like you. Here's how you can join us:

*Volume 2 – God Willing, Daughter / Si Diosito Quiere, Mija Anthology*
Apply to share your testimony in the next volume of *God Willing, Daughter* by emailing authorelizamgarza@gmail.com. You will receive a form to get started.

🎙 **Coming Soon**—*Si Diosito Quiere, Mija: The Podcast*
Powerful God stories from women who found faith, healing, and purpose through divine encounters.

Each episode features one of the incredible authors from the book. They share the parts of their journey you didn't get to read, the moments behind the pages, and the miracles that shaped their faith.

Scan to follow and be among the first to listen when the podcast launches. Together, we're building a community of faith, love, and transformation—one testimony at a time.

@SIDIOSITO

www.ingramcontent.com/pod-product-compliance
Lightning Source LLC
Chambersburg PA
CBHW072003150426
43194CB00008B/984